RICHARD EBERHART

The Progress
of an American Poet

RICHARD EBERHART

The Progress
of an American Poet

JOEL ROACHE

New York OXFORD UNIVERSITY PRESS 1971

···❧ For my wife, the best of us all ❧···

Acknowledgments

Virtually all the primary sources for this study are in the Richard Eberhart Collection in the Baker Library of Dartmouth College. They include manuscripts, diaries, and other materials, but the vast bulk of the Collection, and of the sources used here, is correspondence, especially carbon copies of Mr. Eberhart's letters over a period of more than half a century. These letters are filed chronologically and alphabetically, but I have decided not to distract the reader with notes referring to these files. Any scholar wishing to examine my specific use of these sources should see my dissertation, *Richard Eberhart: A Poet in America, 1904–1961* (University Microfilms: Ann Arbor, 1967), where documentation is complete. In the present study, the reader may assume that all quotations, unless otherwise indicated, are of Mr. Eberhart himself, usually in letters from the period under discussion, sometimes in diaries and similar records, and extremely rarely in conversation with myself. Clearly unintentional errors in spelling and punctuation, obvious slips of the pen, have been silently corrected, but the text is copied exactly otherwise; "sic" is used only when necessary to avoid misunderstanding. Notes are supplied only when the source is published and therefore likely to be available in any good research library.

My most grateful acknowledgment must be of the extraordinary co-operation and hospitality of Mr. and Mrs. Richard Eberhart, who opened not only Mr. Eberhart's files but their home to me and my family during the period of research; this study is in no sense, however, an "authorized" biography, and responsibility for any errors of fact or judgment rests solely with myself.

Professor Sculley Bradley of the University of Pennsylvania first suggested the study, and Professor Robert F. Lucid read it from its earliest stages, rendering invaluable assistance and guidance. Thanks are also due The Graduate School of Arts and Sciences, of the University of Pennsylvania, The Woodrow Wilson Foundation, The College of the Holy Cross, The University of Wisconsin, Mr. and Mrs. Frederic M. Minshall, and Mr. and Mrs. Joel H. Roache, Jr., for financial assistance; and Mr. and Mrs. Nathaniel Burleigh of Hanover, New Hampshire, for the use of their home during part of the period of research.

Various members of the staff of Baker Library of Dartmouth College were on innumerable occasions unusually co-operative and helpful. Thanks are also due Mrs. Frederic Minshall and Mrs. Becky Stickgold for editorial and clerical assistance. Those whose correspondence, book reviews, and other documents I have drawn upon, finally, are too numerous to name here. It is they, of course —many having graciously consented to quotation from letters between them and Mr. Eberhart—who made the publication of this book possible at all.

Contents

Introduction

The development of the career of Richard Eberhart reflects the history of poetry, perhaps of serious literature in general, in America in the twentieth century. Eberhart's whole generation of poets has moved, on the whole, from a position of rebellion and alienation to one of recognition and subsidization by society. This country now provides, primarily through its universities, both a market for books of poetry and relatively congenial employment for the makers of poetry. Even the singers of the so-called beat generation, as well as others engaged in making their dissent as visible as possible, manage to be published and heard, frequently commanding large fees for personal appearances and even receiving royalties from the large audiences gathered by universities and colleges. An attempt to speak realistically of "alienated poets" or of a "poetry of alienation" in America in the 1960's is to involve oneself in a massive complex of non sequiturs. Similarly, one can hardly speak of Richard Eberhart today as alienated from the society at large. As Professor of English and poet in residence at Dartmouth College he lives comfortably in his two-story frame colonial house overlooking the Connecticut River, where he holds seminars, entertains visiting literati, and generally enjoys the fruits of his labor and of American enterprise, as do hundreds of poets throughout the country.

There is sufficient demand for his work that he has published five books since his *Collected Poems,* in 1961. *Collected Verse Plays* was printed by the University of North Carolina Press in 1962, followed two years later by *The Quarry,* from the Oxford University Press in New York and Chatto and Windus in London, which have published his books since 1937. Only a year after the appearance of *The Quarry,* New Directions published *Selected Poems: 1930–1965,* which was awarded the Pulitzer Prize in 1966, followed by *Thirty One Sonnets* from the Eakins Press, and finally *Shifts of Being,* which appeared in the spring of 1968. The Pulitzer Prize is only the most recent example of his society's recognition of his gift. He has also won the Guarantor's Prize and the Harriet Monroe Memorial Prize from *Poetry,* the Harriet Monroe Memorial Award from the University of Chicago, the Shelley Memorial Prize from the Poetry Society of America, and a grant from the National Institute of Arts and Letters. His most important award, however, was the Bollingen Prize, which he shared with John Hall Wheelock in 1962. In recent years his recognition has taken very official forms, beginning with his appointment as Consultant in Poetry at the Library of Congress in 1959. He served in this position until 1961, and in 1963 he was appointed by the Library as Honorary Consultant in American Letters, 1963–1966, and reappointed for 1966–1969. He is also a member of the Advisory Committee of the John F. Kennedy Center, formerly the National Cultural Center. All of these honors, along with his position at Dartmouth, help to define his status as an Established Poet, and the last chapter of the present study concentrates on his activities in this position.

This book, however, concerns itself not with Eberhart's being an Established Poet, but primarily with his becoming one, for the integration of artistic and social roles implied by that term was not easily achieved. He did not receive his first academic appointment until he was forty-eight. Before that he had been a sailor, a slaughterhouse laborer, a tutor, a teacher of adolescent boys, a soldier (of sorts), and an executive in a polish company. Whatever the degree of his success in any of these fields, he was never, until 1952, hired or paid a living wage because he was a poet; his art, his pursuit of vision, was individual and separate from his professional life, unrecognized and unremunerated by society.

Eberhart was born into the upper middle class of the American Midwest and passed his childhood and adolescence in an environment that was extremely comfortable, conventional, and complacent, with every promise of fulfilling whatever ambition he chose to pursue. In 1922, the death of his mother and the collapse of his father's fortune wrenched him violently out of this virtually idyllic life, and these were probably the most crucial events of his life. He clung to his inherited values long enough to take a bachelor's degree at a conventionally good Eastern college and returned to take a job "as a Dartmouth graduate" in the basement of Marshall Field and Company in Chicago. But pursuing different, perhaps higher goals, he left and sailed on tramp steamers around the world and entered Cambridge University where, living on the remains of an inheritance from his mother, he encountered a way of life that always remained a model for him, a life of socially recognized learning and art, a life he was not to know again for twenty years.

For the idea of a university position without a Ph.D. was virtually unthinkable; his published book of poetry and his Cambridge degree were valueless for a stable and viable place in American society. After drifting from job to job, to Europe again and back, he borrowed money to enter graduate school at Harvard, where for a year he pursued courses and grades, footnotes and obsolete conjugations, in hopes of the coveted Ph.D. But the day of the Fellowship was far on the other side of the Great Depression and World War II; he could foresee only years of debt, and he needed very much the stability of a steady income and a place in society.

So he compromised and accepted a post as teacher in a very reputable New England preparatory school. Here he was at least able to pay his debts, and his summers were free for travel and writing. The work hardly engaged his highest capabilities, however, and when the exigencies of the Depression forced the school to let him go, he realized suddenly how little progress he had made. Despite six years' experience, a Cambridge M.A., and two published books, the doors of the universities were still closed to him, and living from his work as a poet was completely out of the question.

His poetry from this period, read with an awareness of the vicissitudes of his life, points up the importance of the crises of 1922, for despite the various fluctuations of his fortunes, his poetry consistently returns to themes related to that sudden initiation into adult reality. The poem "Maze," for instance, though written during his relatively contented months at Cambridge, is structured on the idea of sudden disillusionment:

> I have a tree in my arm,
> There are two hounds in my feet,
> The earth can do me no harm
> And the lake of my eyes is sweet.
>
> But a fire has burnt the tree down,
> I have no blood for the hounds.
> Why has the will made me a crown
> For a human mind that has bounds?
>
> Who made the tree? Who made fire?
> The hounds have gone back to the master.
> The earth has killed my desire
> That leaped up faster and faster.
>
> It is man did it, man,
> Who imagined imagination,
> And he did what man can,
> He uncreated creation.
>
> There is no tree in my arm,
> I have no hounds in my feet,
> The earth can soothe me and harm,
> And the lake of my eyes is a cheat.

The dominant theme of "Maze" is also the central idea of "If I Could Only Live at the Pitch That Is Near Madness," which was written when he was at St. Mark's School and "was a struggling poet and had . . . no status:"

> If I could only live at the pitch that is near madness
> When everything is as it was in my childhood
> Violent, vivid, and of infinite possibility:
> That the sun and the moon broke over my head.
>
> Then I cast time out of the trees and fields,
> Then I stood immaculate in the Ego;
> Then I eyed the world with all delight,
> Reality was the perfection of my sight.
>
> And time has big handles on the hands,
> Fields and trees a way of being themselves.
> I saw battalions of the race of mankind
> Standing stolid, demanding a moral answer.
>
> I gave the moral answer and I died
> And into a realm of complexity came
> Where nothing is possible but necessity
> And the truth wailing there like a red babe.

Throughout these years he seems to have been haunted by the contrast between that world "of infinite possibility" and the "red babe" of reality. The effort to reconcile them led him to concern himself with the most coercive reality of all: death. Some of his many poems on this theme involve simply recognition of the reality of death, and are often subdued in tone, as is "I Walked Over the Grave of Henry James":

> I walked over the grave of Henry James
> But recently, and one eye kept the dry stone.
> The other leaned on boys at games away,
> My soul was balanced in my body cold.
>
> I am one of those prodigals of hell
> Whom ten years have seen cram with battle;

> Returns to what he canted from, grants it good,
> As asthma makes itself a new resolution.
>
> I crushed a knob of earth between my fingers,
> This is a very ordinary experience.
> A name may be glorious but death is death,
> I thought, and took a street-car back to Harvard Square.

It is interesting that here the awareness of death, of the inevitable dissolution of the body into "a knob of earth," helps the poet to be reconciled with life, with the world of street-cars and Harvard Square.

The reconciliation in most of these poems, however, is with death, as in the very early "Cover Me Over":

> Cover me over, clover;
> Cover me over, grass.
> The mellow day is over
> And there is night to pass.
>
> Green arms about my head,
> Green fingers on my hands,
> Earth has no quieter bed
> In all her quiet lands.

This idea of death simply as rest is developed in a somewhat later lyric into the theme, implicit in the double-entendre in the last line, of death as a fusion with all life:

> I saw on the slant hill a putrid lamb,
> Propped with daisies. The sleep looked deep,
> The face nudged in the green pillow
> But the guts were out for the crows to eat.
>
> Where's the lamb? whose tender plaint
> Said all for the mute breezes.
> Say he's in the wind somewhere,
> Say, there's a lamb in the daisies.

In "The Groundhog" the idea of life-in-death is much more
highly elaborated than in "For a Lamb," and the emphasis on mind
adds another dimension:

In June, amid the golden fields,
I saw a groundhog lying dead.
Dead lay he; my senses shook,
And mind outshot our naked frailty.
There lowly in the vigorous summer
His form began its senseless change,
And made my senses waver dim
Seeing nature ferocious in him.
Inspecting close his maggots' might
And seething cauldron of his being,
Half with loathing, half with a strange love,
I poked him with an angry stick.
The fever arose, became a flame
And Vigour circumscribed the skies,
Immense energy in the sun,
And through my frame a sunless trembling.
My stick had done nor good nor harm.
Then stood I silent in the day
Watching the object as before;
And kept my reverence for knowledge
Trying for control, to be still,
To quell the passion of the blood;
Until I had bent down on my knees
Praying for joy in the sight of decay.
And so I left; and I returned
In Autumn strict of eye, to see
The sap gone out of the groundhog,
But the bony sodden hulk remained.
But the year had lost its meaning,
And in intellectual chains
I lost both love and loathing,
Mured up in the wall of wisdom.
Another summer took the fields again

Massive and burning, full of life,
But when I chanced upon the spot
There was only a little hair left,
And bones bleaching in the sunlight
Beautiful as architecture;
I watched them like a geometer,
And cut a walking stick from a birch.
It has been three years, now.
There is no sign of the groundhog.
I stood there in the whirling summer,
My hand capped a withered heart,
And thought of China and of Greece,
Of Alexander in his tent;
Of Montaigne in his tower,
Of Saint Theresa in her wild lament.

It is important to notice that the center of significance in "The Groundhog" is the intellect; it is the mind that controls the emotions expressed. It first conceives of death, then of life-in-death. Then through reflection it creates the "wall of wisdom" that can "quell the passion of the blood" and allow the poet sufficient tranquility to realize a vision of time and humanity controlled by the same forces that work in the decaying groundhog.

In "The Groundhog," however, as in many of Eberhart's poems, the mind takes its materials from very concrete, earthly reality, and the unified vision reached by the poem would seem to be "the mind's harmony" mentioned in "The Goal of Intellectual Man":

The goal of intellectual man
Striving to do what he can
To bring down out of uncreated light
Illumination to our night

Is not possession of the fire
Annihilation of his own desire
To the source a secret soaring
And all his self outpouring

Nor is it an imageless place
Wherein there is no human face
Nor laws, nor hierarchies, nor dooms
And only the cold weight of the tomb

But it is human love, love
Concrete, specific, in a natural move
Gathering goodness, it is free
In the blood as in the mind's harmony,

It is love discoverable here
Difficult, dangerous, pure, clear,
The truth of the positive hour
Composing all of human power.

This poem operates on a different level from "The Groundhog;" it is, in a sense, *about* "The Groundhog," for it is about what the poet attempts to do to bring "Illumination to our night."

The conception here of earthly reality as "night," darkness, chaos, is representative of his vision of life before World War II. Most of the poems written during this period are characterized by a sense of inevitable conflict between the world and the spirit, and most of these poems attempt to reconcile these opposites, never quite to the poet's final satisfaction:

And I have eased reality and fiction
Into a kind of intellectual fruition
Strength in solitude, life in death,
Compassion by suffering, love in strife,
And ever and still the weight of mystery
Arrows a way between my words and me.

The sense of conflict that pervades these poems is of course a function of Eberhart's sense of his own life. We have seen him write of it as "cram with battle" in "I Walked Over the Grave of Henry James," and much of his correspondence uses the same martial terminology. These feelings were especially intense immediately after he left St. Mark's. He had heretofore attempted to keep himself relatively free for his art, but the months of despair in looking for a new position made him realize his isolation. The rigors of relative freedom made him long for the comforts of not only economic but emotional security. So he took another teaching job, closer to Boston, and married.

Then within a year he was thrown, along with the rest of America, into the actual battle of World War II. His correspondence during the war shows a certain enthusiasm for his work as a gunnery instructor in the Navy, as if "doing his bit," despite its remoteness from the things that were vitally important to him as an individual, provided him with a sense of engagement that never attended his labors either as poet or as teacher. With this period of contentment in his marriage and his work, a new direction in his poetry becomes apparent. His obsession with the opposition between the human spirit and the inhuman world seems to give place to the conviction that that spirit, however imperfect, has a place in that world, however mysterious. Both the imperfection of the one and the mystery of the other are constant in his work, but an important change of emphasis is nevertheless notable.

In "Dam Neck, Virginia," for instance, the last line of the first stanza can be stated tranquilly, almost flatly:

> Anti-aircraft from a certain distance
> On a steely blue night say a mile away
> Flowers on the air absolutely dream-like
> The vision has no relation to the reality.

It was in confronting the lack of apparent relation between vision and reality that he "died" in "If I Could Only Live at the Pitch That Is Near Madness," but now he can speak of it as "beautiful":

> As this sight and show is gentle and false,
> The truth of guns is fierce that aims at death.
> Of war in the animal sinews let us speak not,
> But of the beautiful disrelation of the spiritual.

It should be emphasized that the poet calls here not for a spirit that is "disrelated," but for disrelation itself. In the often anthologized "The Fury of Aerial Bombardment," which was written during the same period, he finds all the disrelation he could want precisely in "war in the animal sinews":

> You would think the fury of aerial bombardment
> Would rouse God to relent; the infinite spaces
> Are still silent. He looks on shock-pried faces.
> History, even, does not know what is meant.
>
> You would feel that after so many centuries
> God would give man to repent; yet he can kill
> As Cain could, but with multitudinous will,
> No farther advanced than in his ancient furies.
>
> Was man made stupid to see his own stupidity?
> Is God by definition indifferent, beyond us all?
> Is the eternal truth man's fighting soul
> Wherein the Beast ravens in its own avidity?
>
> Of Van Wettering I speak, and Averill,
> Names on a list, whose faces I do not recall
> But they are gone to early death, who late in school
> Distinguished the belt feed lever from the belt holding pawl.

The sudden shift in the last stanza, besides being pivotal in the structure of the poem, stresses his relatively new concern with the world outside himself. The anger, and the abstraction, of the first three stanzas is typical of his earlier work, but in the midst of war he is compelled to remind us that all the theorizing about good and evil, God and man, comes down finally to the death of individual boys, faceless, their only identity a place on a list.

"Dam Neck, Virginia" and "The Fury of Aerial Bombardment" mark the transition from the early to the mature Eberhart. It is a change from diatribes against disrelation to metaphors for mystery, metaphors produced by a more active sympathy with the objects of perception, resulting more frequently in poems which depend for their effect less on the poet and more on themselves. His most important work in the 'thirties, such as "The Groundhog" and "If I Could Only Live at the Pitch That Is Near Madness," however much they are based in concrete reality, are fundamentally examinations of his own mind; his isolation had forced him to look inward. In the 'forties, however, his eye clearly turns to the outer world and its problems.

This change is even more apparent in "The Horse Chestnut Tree":

> Boys in sporadic but tenacious droves
> Come with sticks, as certainly as Autumn,
> To assault the great horse chestnut tree.
>
> There is a law governs their lawlessness.
> Desire is in them for a shining amulet
> And the best are those that are highest up.
>
> They will not pick them easily from the ground.
> With shrill arms they fling to the higher branches,
> To hurry the work of nature for their pleasure.
>
> I have seen them trooping down the street
> Their pockets stuffed with chestnuts shucked, unshucked.
> It is only evening that keeps them from their wish.
>
> Sometimes I run out in a kind of rage
> To chase the boys away: I catch an arm,
> Maybe, and laugh to think of being the lawgiver.
>
> I was once such a young sprout myself
> And fingered in my pocket the prize and trophy.
> But still I moralize upon the day
>
> And see that we, outlaws on God's property,
> Fling out imagination beyond the skies,
> Wishing a tangible good from the unknown.
>
> And likewise death will drive us from the scene
> With the great flowering world unbroken yet,
> Which we held in idea, a little handful.

In this poem, events in the material world are seen as analogous to those of the world of the human spirit, and a system of analogies provides the piece with an interesting structure. The poet as poet is analogous to the boys, both seeking an "amulet," a charm to preserve life; the poet as narrator, however, is parallelled with death, which "will drive us from the scene" as poet drives off the boys. If "a law governs" the boys, furthermore, then the poet is presumably also under compulsion, and if the poet is "lawgiver," then death, in the other half of the analogy, provides the law that requires the poet to "Fling imagination beyond the skies." Death, then, precisely because it insists on driving us from the scene, emerges as the mother of beauty. The perennially blooming tree, finally, corresponds to "the great flowering world," "the unknown," from which we wish "a tangible good."

We find in "The Horse Chestnut Tree," then, that the world no longer opposes the spirit but functions as a source of symbols for it, natural facts representing, in an almost Emersonian way, moral facts. A similar principle operates in another poem from the same period, "On a Squirrel Crossing the Road in Autumn, in New England":

> It is what he does not know,
> Crossing the road under the elm trees,
> About the mechanism of my car,
> About the Commonwealth of Massachusetts,
> About Mozart, India, Arcturus,
> That wins my praise. I engage
> At once in whirling squirrel-praise.
> He obeys the orders of nature
> Without knowing them.
> It is what he does not know
> That makes him beautiful.
> Such a knot of little purposeful nature!
>
> I who can see him as he cannot see himself
> Repose in the ignorance that is his blessing.

> It is what man does not know of God
> Composes the visible poem of the world.
> . . . Just missed him!

Here the squirrel is seen as standing in relation to Man and his ways as Man stands in relation to God and his, and the poem speculates at the same time, in the last line, that God's treatment of Man may be just as fortuitous as man's of the squirrel.

It soon becomes clear in these later poems that Eberhart is now less inclined to generalize upward toward God or "the spirit" than outward to find value in the existential human condition. In "Cousin Florence," for example, the ancient "life is short, art is long" dictum is virtually reversed:

> There it is, a block of leaping marble
> Given to me by an ancestor.
> The hands that passed it held down ninety years.
> She got it in the love-time of Swinburne.
>
> This woman with her stalwart mien,
> More like a Roman than a Greek,
> Fumbled among old bags of rubble
> For something indomitable that she could seek.
>
> She saw the light of ancient days around her,
> Calling in the hip-cracked hospital.
> She chose at last. Then the clear light
> Of reason stood up strong and tall.
>
> With a pure, commanding grace
> She handed me a piece of the Parthenon,
> Saying, this I broke with my own hands,
> And gave me the imagination of the Greeks.
>
> I thought the spirit of this woman
> The tallest that I had ever seen,
> Stronger than the marble that I have
> Who was herself imagination's dream
>
> By the moment of such sacrament,

A pure force transmitting love,
Endurance, steadfastness, her calm,
Her Roman heart, to mine, of dream.

I would rather keep her noble acts,
The blood of her powerful character, a mind
As good as any of her time, than search
My upward years for such a stone that leaps.

The stone relic is given its due. It "leaps;" it is "indomitable;" it carries "the clear light/Of reason" and "the imagination of the Greeks." But the poet nevertheless prefers the dying human personality to the immortal stone artifact. The latter is less important as symbol than as the substance of a "sacrament" enacted between human beings. The emphasis, furthermore, is not simply added by the last stanza; it is fundamental to the treatment of the material. That Cousin Florence broke the fragment with her own hands "in the love-time of Swinburne" is as impressive a fact as the survival of the Parthenon itself for so many centuries. The sense of her power and dignity is reinforced by the fact that she as a human being could do what time had not been able to do: consciously select, break, and preserve a piece of the monument to make it, at a given moment, the symbol of "A pure force transmitting love."

The same stress on the human particular is clear in "Half-Bent Man" and "Clam Diggers and Diggers of Sea Worms." In both poems the poet is observing individuals at work. In one they are

Four men universal
In bent attitude of work

. . .

The clam diggers,
The diggers of sea worms. . . .

and in the other:

a half-blind, burly, old
Man, half bent to earth

Who on the Princeton campus
Spears stray papers with a nail-
Ended stick. . . .

In both poems the men and their work are described in the vivid,
compelling detail characteristic of the later Eberhart. In both poems
they are made images of the human condition. The clam diggers
become "Man making a living," and as for the half-bent man at
Princeton,

it is his own, dark burdens
In his bent, half-seeing, weary attitude
I claim as man's and mine,
And O blind-man, rag-picker,
Paper-picker, cleanser of domains,
I shall not betray your meaning
As time bends us to the earth
And we pick what gems and scraps
There are from magnificence.

This tendency toward the existential application of specific experience and away from pretentious abstraction reaches its logical
conclusion in verse dramas such as *The Visionary Farms,* character sketches such as "Ruby Dagget," and monologues such as "A
Maine Roustabout," all based, like much of Eberhart's later work,
on specific, actual people and experience.

Of course, any attempt to place a life's work into a pattern of
development such as has been outlined here is subject to many
qualifications and caveats. In the first place, the problem is complicated by the fact that Eberhart's poems have not been published in
the order of their composition. "Indian Pipe," for instance, published in *Undercliff* in 1953, was written when the poet was a
teenager, and the poem which follows it in *Collected Poems,* "Go
to the Shine That's on a Tree," first appeared in *The New Yorker*
in the 'thirties. Another example, also from *Undercliff,* "Fragment
of New York, 1929," was written when Eberhart was working in

a New York slaughterhouse, in 1929, within a few weeks of "The Soul Longs to Return Whence It Came," which was published in *Song and Idea* in 1940 (1942 in the United States).

More importantly, poets rarely write only one or two kinds of poem for each "period" so carefully "discovered" by the critic or literary historian. We have already seen that there is as much anger in "The Fury of Aerial Bombardment" as in "If I Could Only Live . . . "; and "When Golden Flies Upon My Carcass Come" and "Now Is the World Made of Chiming Balls," both written in the 'thirties, are as concrete as the poems quoted above as examples of the "mature" period. So the present essay does not attempt to account for every poem, but only to point out the general direction of his most representative work, a direction continued in his most recent book, *Shifts of Being*. The third poem in this book, "The Birth of the Spirit," makes it clear that he has again learned to live at the pitch near madness, when everything is as it was in his childhood:

> Some desperation of the sense
> Has made me mad again.
> In that madness I am well
> And have the strength of ten.
>
> My vision springs alive, replete
> With life I am dreaming of
> In spite of the nature of man,
> A world of wholeness and of love.

And the change in attitude from his early work is evident in a comparison of the imagery of "If I Could Only Live . . . " with that of the last stanza of "The Birth of the Spirit":

> Blessed be madness and power
> For they so force the earth
> That spirit is a red flower,
> The pure red flower of birth.

The red flower of the spirit dominates the red babe of reality throughout *Shifts of Being,* as much in the relatively "objective" (one of Eberhart's favorite words for his later work) poems, such as "Marrakech," "Lions Copulating," and "Santa Claus in Oaxaca," as in the more obviously meditative ones like "The Standards," "Whenever I See Beauty I See Death," and "The Birth of the Spirit." This is not to say that he has grown complacent or become less aware of the naturalistic world. His awareness of natural hostility to individual identity is clear in such a poem as "On Returning to a Lake in Spring," which begins with an exuberant Whitmanesque stroll among the frogs along the shore

> walking in triumph
> As a king of the frogs, glad to be among them,
> As they touched my legs as I moved along.

But the end of the poem documents vividly the other side of the vital coin:

> I returned to the picnic on the hill exulting.
> In our party a young woman moving in her youth
> Seemed to jump at the glory of the springtime;
> Nevertheless she did not speak of the spring peepers.
> A month later, in a southern bog, she slit her throat.

There remains throughout the book, however, a sense of tranquility that can only come "of wholeness and of love." As he puts in "The Standards":

> Time is the tone all fates foretell,
> The birth cry and the funeral bell,
> My will can wish and my psyche tell
> Only that mystery surpasses well.

The direction that seems to reach fulfillment in these poems began, as we have seen, during the war and developed afterwards when Eberhart, living in Cambridge, Massachusetts, was able to have a little of the life he had wanted ever since he left Cambridge, England. His participation in the cultural life around Harvard, however, was still separate from his primary role in society, and it was not until 1952, when he was invited to be a visiting professor at the University of Washington, that his identity as litterateur became his profession. From Washington he went to the University of Connecticut, then to Wheaton College, then to Princeton, and finally to his present enviable position.

The present study finds its justification, then, in two assumptions. The first was mentioned briefly at the beginning of this introduction: the career of Richard Eberhart parallels the development of the place of poetry in American society, and therefore study of that career should tell us something, directly or indirectly, about that society. Secondly, the organizing hypothesis of this book is that the relationship between the changes in his work and the development of his career is not accidental. Beginning from these assumptions, the present study concentrates on the discoverable facts of the poet's life as he moved from a position outside of his social environment to first compromise, then capitulation, and finally acceptance. This final acceptance, moreover, goes both ways: his acceptance of and integration into society could not become complete until he was himself accepted, as poet, by it. As we examine his successive confrontations with reality, furthermore, we shall also see that the literary life has its own peculiar realities: the very concrete processes whereby poems are published and marketed, and their reception by critics and the public, as well as the poet's functions and activities as a public figure and a member of an educational institution. It should be emphasized, finally, that the idea of a poet's progress toward integration with his society is not intended as a rigid mould to force data into preconceived categories, but as a flexible framework, a convenient way of selecting and organizing the facts of a poet's life, in the hope that, as Eberhart has said, "There may be some merit in dispassionate perceptions set in order."

RICHARD EBERHART

The Progress
of an American Poet

CHAPTER ONE
1904–1922

Richard Eberhart's early life was passed in a family that typified the ideals of its place and time, the product of one man's hard-won realization of the American Dream. For Alpha LaRue Eberhart (1867–1937), an exemplar of the virtues of hard work and self-reliance held sacred by his generation, earned a virtually unsurpassed status in his community. The son of a Methodist minister in Albion, Iowa, he went to work as a farm hand at fourteen. A year later he went to Chicago and saved enough money to open his own store for men's furnishings, at twenty-one. He soon sold out that business, however, and went on the road as a glove salesman. When the panic of 1890 forced him out of that job, he returned to Chicago where, after a short time, he held a political position at about $30 a week. In Chicago he met George H. Swift, whose parents had long been friends of his parents. Swift persuaded Eberhart to get out of politics and found a place for him in the Swift organization, at about half the salary he had been earning. He advanced rapidly, however, and was in charge of the Car Route Department in South St. Paul, Minnesota, when he left to join the young Hormel company in Austin, Minnesota.

During his years with Hormel, between 1900 and 1922, A. L. Eberhart reached the pinnacle of his career as a self-made man. He held several positions, finally reaching that of vice-president, but his most important work in the early years was in the training of sales-men and the development of new markets, helping the company to grow and expand to the leading position it held when he left it in 1922. By buying Hormel stock and investing funds borrowed against it, especially in land, he was able to accumulate a fortune second only to that of the Hormels themselves in Austin and to build, in 1916, a more than comfortable home on forty acres in Aus-tin known as Burr Oaks, at a cost of $50,000.

By the time Richard Eberhart was born, on April 5, 1904, he, his brother Dryden (b. 1902) and his sister Elizabeth (b. 1910) could be provided with all the best that the American Middle West could af-ford, and especially so after they moved into Burr Oaks. The wood and stucco house had eighteen large rooms, and a gymnasium in the basement which, while less than the standard size, could be used for basketball or easily converted into a ballroom for dances and banquets. It was built at the end of a long driveway lined with peonies and at the beginning of another driveway bordered in iris to the apple orchard, where every spring the local high school girls danced around a Maypole steadied by the young Richard at an annual picnic given by Mrs. Eberhart. On the other side of the apple orchard was the "Mad House," an exact replica of a rest house at the Grand Canyon. Family and community picnics were often held there, and the boys' Scout troop used it for meetings. Besides Burr Oaks, they had a farm, known as Whispering Pines, on the outskirts of Austin, where they regularly went for picnics and hikes. They could also afford fishing and hunting trips to the north woods, along with such luxuries as their own birch bark canoe.

But of course Eberhart's childhood was not, any more than any-one's, spent exclusively in the bosom of his family; he ranged around the town and countryside pursuing juvenile adventure with the spirit of Tom Sawyer, if not the freedom of Huckleberry Finn. Years later, from the turmoil of World War II, Eberhart recalled those times in a letter to Judge Catherwood, the father of his best boyhood friend, Roger:

> Long after the cause of my naughtiness has been forgotten, I remember vividly being "kicked off the Catherwoods' front porch" by Mrs. Catherwood when I was small, and running helter-skelter away: I have quite forgotten my offense, but no doubt it was horrendous. I also remember how much Roger, Dryden, and I took precautions lest you yourself, striding home in your great height and dignity, should find out our secret hiding place in your old barn; we used to get in some far corner through Alice-in-Wonderland tactics, through constructed tunnels of hay, and in the farthest place we had our secret rendezvous. I also cannot remember what we did in there, but I expect that it was smoking cigarettes, and that it was a very dangerous practice indeed in that old barn: the whole thing might have gone up in smoke, and us with it, along with all our childish dreams of the future.

Later the boys frequently went for hikes up the Cedar River to a place identified in Eberhart's diary as "the shack." One of these trips, in 1917, was particularly adventurous, and the events emerged later in the poem, "The Transfer." There were six boys along, including his brother Dryden and Roger Catherwood, and great ice cakes were floating in the river. The boys cut young trees to use as oars and tried to ride the ice floes down the river:

> The first "ships" went out of sight around a far bend. My cake could not be steered from midstream to the shore by use of the pole; the water was too cold and the current too strong to make it safe to swim. The final danger of the masses of churning ice just before the dam was seen. It was a stroke of luck and fate to pass under an overhanging limb of a great tree before the possibility of imminent destruction. I remember jumping up just at the right moment and catching the limb under my arms and seeing the "ship" of ice move on a few hundred feet to total destruction. After further adventures of fording a stream

in breast-high water and climbing a rugged hill we found a farm house. A farm lady gave the shivering, soaked boys a hot communal bath in a great round wooden tub and put us to bed under an enormous feather quilt.

And a diary entry from 1919 captures the spirit of their childhood:

I went down to Rog's . . . and read him my new poem "The Hidden Coda." We got to talking and I said we ought to bury a treasure. He took me at my word and we presented the case to the Judge. Rog got off, changed clothes and loaded up with burying material and we came to our house. . . . I put on my old clothes and football shoes and loaded up too. . . .

It was dark, chill and damp when we forsook the melodious strains of "I'm forever blowing bubbles" to delve into the mysterious night with our secret. We were ladened with tin box, ax, spade, dark lantern, flash light and pockets full of miscellanea. . . . We crossed the bridge of logs by which to get to our shack at 9:30 and plunged thru the dripping foliage up river on the other side. We jumped the creek from the back of [illegible word], that is I did as Rog fell half way in.

Then they followed the fence line to their burial site and buried the treasure including an owl's beak and an arrowhead.

Then I wrote, as best I could, in the rain, a note stating time, date, et cetera and affirming that we would not dig up the treasure for five years, and Rog and I solemnly and officially signed the document. We hurriedly proceeded to . . . put the soil over it . . . the treasure buried—ah—and not a soul to know.

A boy's life in Austin, however, was destined for institutionalization. Eberhart's sister remembers her brothers as Boy Scouts, but Richard was apparently no longer a Scout when he began keeping a diary, in January 1918. Running throughout his diary, are frequent brief comments involving "our Club," which had been recently organized and for which he was writing a constitution based on that of his brother's club, the Duodecim Literary Society. These plans never came to fruition, or if they did they did not involve Eberhart; for in December 1918 he was taken into Duodecim itself, and from then until his graduation in 1921 he kept a record of its activities. The entry dealing with his own entrance into the society indicates the centrality of the club to his life at this period.

Dec. 5, '18: Downheartedly I started for another day of study. Half-way down the first block a voice hailed me and I turned around to see Edward Usem running to me, a broad smile covering his face. "Congratulations," he yelled, and clasping my hand tightly, announced, "You're a member of Duodecim!!" O I was so surprised I didn't know what to do. He told me all about it. . . . Across from Ken Lewis' house, Rog, my best friend, put his Duo pin on me (the emblem which I was to wear steadily for three years, and pledge loyalty to for life). . . . At school I shook hands with all the members. Oh! Boy! "ain't it gran' and glorious feelin'!"

Dec. 11, 1918: I went to my first Duo meeting—at Jensen's. The secretary read the constitution and I was asked to sign it. A queer sensation came over me as I took the pen, but I wrote my name, or rather scribbled it, because I was so excited I couldn't write straight.

Throughout high school he never lost his pride in his membership in the "crooked circle" of the "Twelve good men and true" to which the club's constitution limited it.

Although primarily a social organization, Duodecim (and its rival, the Knights of the Round Table) had sincere intellectual ambitions. The boys held thirty-odd meetings a year, and after business was finished (such as membership, plans for social functions, or resolutions of condolence to the families of deceased luminaries such as Theodore Roosevelt and William Dean Howells), they would deliver short papers on such topics as "The Ku Klux Klan," "Clemenceau, Tiger of France," "Paderewski: Pianist and Patriot,"

"Attack on Mt. Everest," "Poems by Robert Burns," and "New Water Passage in Belgium," and it was expected that these topics would be carefully prepared. Then followed a session of parliamentary drill, with the boys taking turns as chairman and secretary. Finally, if there was no visiting alumnus or leading citizen to provide uplifting remarks, one of the members would deliver a "critic's report" on the proceedings.

The mother of the boy holding the meeting was expected to provide a "feed" (Mrs. Eberhart provided six of these during one year when both her sons were of the Twelve), and after the meal, the boys would retire to their automobiles or to some appropriate recreation area (such as the gym or billiard room at Burr Oaks) or perhaps join in "hot discussions on cliffdwellers and evolution." Of course not all the meetings ran perfectly smoothly. One which was left out of "Duo Days" was preserved in Eberhart's personal diary:

> Wednesday - Feb. 23, 1921—. . . . Went to meeting. . . . First time at Hanson's. Erick and Moze late. Rotten order. Twice during the meeting I [as president] ripped into them for the foolishness they acted. Had banquet topics. Then a big "Mrs. Hanson" feed after which Bockett got hard with me, knocked the chip off and I took him down and, o boy, on a full stomach, planted his shoulders on the rug. I paid for it tho, with a possible black eye tomorrow, and a bang that nearly knocked my nose-wound open again. Left shortly after. This was the memorable meeting when Dupe, Parl. drill Chair, with four on their feet for the floor, and Bockett yelling, "Mr. Chairman," glowered down at Bockett and said, "Villa."

The club held, of course, dances and parties and an annual banquet, but their social life is reflected best by this account of a Duo picnic in May of 1920.

> Sat. May 15: An ideal day for the picnic. . . . Dryd driving, and loaded with cameras and eats we got Mary Jane Hubbard, Leona and Mutt with a XII [the club emblem] pillow, the victor [Victrola], went to Bud's to meet the rest of the gang,

but they hadn't assembled so, with Duo pennants on all sides, we set sail westward, arrived at "Whispering Pines" and took pictures. Fooled around till the other cars came—tore around the place trying to find amusement and at the further pine clump had a ball game. Dryd . . . when falling, caught a log on his collar bone. It swelled so Dryd and Mutt went to town to see a doctor and get the ice cream. While gone, we were delightfully entertained by Miss Lewis on the Uke—some player. The car returned and we made ready for the Big Eats. After the procedure it was bumming around till dark when we started a huge fire. Darkness, marshmallows, songs, ghost stories, et cetera. By the weird light of the cars amid the pines, to the tune of the "Vic," Rog, Ed, and Moze tripped the light fantastic on the pine needles. At length the gang dispersed. We rode in town . . . having beforehand arranged to meet Bud and finish the ice cream. . . . Met Bud at the little park at Kenwood-Lansing point, ate rather crammed ice cream in the darkness. Then who should come in his car but Rog with all his gang—minus Jeannette and the chaps. Re-united. Ate more. Bang—up slides Otto, and there we had the whole crowd again. A merry meeting. Someone suggested Lansing. We're off! Speed?—we finally led in, Rog attempting to open up but couldn't pass. . . . Otto maintenant est arrive. After this third reunion we sped for home. Some picnic. Dryd left me at Leona's. She narrated: bum time at KRT picnic—scandal i.e. near beer—Sam, Danser and Knox stude (comparatively) spoiling party: that she couldn't see any difference in the societies at the beginning of year but she realized by now that "it seems as tho' they (KRTs) are just the left-overs."

Whatever the accuracy of "Leona's" account of the Knights of the Round Table, Eberhart's inclusion of it indicates the intense sense of competition that gave the clubs their chief role within the school, for they measured themselves by the achievements of their members. Careful track was kept of how many members of each club were in the student government, the debate society, and the athletic teams. They would nominate each other for offices, try to "split the vote" of opposing factions, and work together for the election of their own candidates. Eberhart even recounts how, when he went out for basketball, the three KRTs on the team hogged the ball to keep him, a Duo, from distinguishing himself, and the Duos could be equally devious. The rivalry finally reached the point where Eberhart's friend Roger Catherwood felt it necessary to admonish the boys, in the Duodecim annual for 1922, against putting the prestige of the club ahead of the good of the school.

Eberhart himself, encouraged of course by his family, made a considerable contribution to the stature of Duodecim, although he was only a competent student who kept his grades up as much by hard work as by native ability. His diary records his frequently staying after school for help in algebra and Latin, and occasional admonitions to himself to bring up his marks. Only English seems to have come easily to him, but his grades were generally respectable, being consistently low only in Latin. His chief contribution to Duodecim's prestige, however, was in extra-curricular activities. His teachers' remarks in his memory book consistently compliment his enthusiasm and ambition, and his sister's statement that he "ran the school practically," while perhaps exaggerated, is supported by the list of his activities and offices. Besides playing saxophone in the school orchestra and singing in the chorus, he was active in the student government and excelled in debating and athletics. He was president of his junior class and in his senior year was president of Duodecim and the Debating League, captain of the football team, and Editor-in-Chief of the annual. As a member of the Board of Control (the student government) he voted against a special award for the best all-around athlete on the grounds that it was dangerous to encourage individual recognition in a small school where teamwork was so important. But the measure passed and Eberhart, convinced that the chief sponsor of the award expected to win it himself, resolved to beat him out of it, and did.

Eberhart's status as a kind of archetypal "boy most likely to succeed" is the strongest evidence if his enthusiastic acceptance of the values of his community, his tendency to smoke in barn lofts notwithstanding. He also went to Sunday School regularly and apparently willingly, at least until he was about fifteen, at the Congregational church attended by his family, and he is often found in his diary and in "Duo Days" selling tickets and otherwise supporting various civic activities. His identity with his community is nowhere more evident, however, than in his patriotic enthusiasm during World War I. He regularly copied headlines about the war into his diary and finally, in March 1918, began a separate "War Diary," which he kept faithfully along with his regular one. Both diaries are replete with references to helping America to victory, and he was proud of his mother's work with the Red Cross, primarily sewing bandages. He himself earned a place in the history of *Mower County in the Great War* by joining the Austin Boys' Band. He once gave a speech in the high school assembly "about waste, and Gov't thrift and War Savings stamps," and that he practiced what he preached is clear from this entry on January 18, 1918:

> Today I bought $3.00 worth of thrift stamps. I now have $15.00. In 1923 they will be worth $19.00. Hurrah for the U. S. We'll lick the Kaiser because everytime we lick a stamp we help to lick the Kaiser. Lets *stamp* him out.

His "Americanism" is also clear from this entry on February 24, 1918, when he

> started the book Ma brought us, "Holding the Line" by Sergeant Harold Baldwin who was one of Canada's contingent to France. (He is a survivor of the Battle of Ypres). At 7:30 the bells began to ring and the band began to play. Why? For the same reason that the author of our new book went into the war whole and sound and came out with only one leg and badly shot up—for democracy, non-kaiserism and freedom of the seas. Our patriotic people were welcoming Mower County's quota of loyal boys who are going to Camp Dodge tomorrow to a dinner and a good time (there [are] 90 Austin draft[ee]s alone). They are going to "get in the fight" and we cannot be too partial with our patriotism shown to them.

That he was not immune to the kind of hysteria that grips any nation at war is clear from his ready acceptance of any measure put forth as helpful to the cause, from price controls to daylight-saving time, and the tendency of the newspaper headlines to see spies everywhere was bound to be reflected by a thirteen-year-old diarist:

> There is a U. S. Secret Service man in town who is clearing up all the Pro-Germans (3 cheers—if we can't get our hands on the Kaiser's person, we lock up all his tool[s]).

One section of his diary, finally, is dedicated "to anyone who wants to take the time to read it. . . . ," but the dedication was then amended: ". . . this means everyone who is not a *pro-german* or in any way favors Germany's Damn Hellish Kaiserism!!! America First." That Austin also had the conventional awareness of the horrors of war is apparent in one of Eberhart's poems from this period, "The Shell Vase," which was published in the Austinian of 1921, the year he graduated, as the "Best Serious Poem" of the year. Its clichés reflect the shallowness of a boy's response to a distant war:

> It is so slender, shapely now—
>   The vase that holds those graceful flowers,
> But something does, alas somehow,
>   Withdraw its magic beauty powers.
>
> I feel each flower really knows
>   It was not meant to be a vase.
> A war-time grimness boldly shows
>   Beneath its pretty chiselled face.
>
> I know those flowers all must feel
>   The drenching chill of no-mans-land;
> For is it not a sad appeal,
>   The languid way in which they stand?
>
> They still must feel the murky night,
>   The stealth, the gore of blood and death—

For, tell me, what else could affright
   The balmy fragrance from their breath?

They're dying now, the shell-vase more
   Is called to play its bloody part.
The acid taint of bitter war
   Has crushed them—crushed them to its heart.

This is only one of many poems Eberhart wrote during his adolescence. He remembers Tennyson as the chief literary influence in his early life, and a volume of Tennyson's poems inscribed by Mrs. Eberhart shortly before her death in 1922 survives. Tennyson does not appear in his diary, however, although many other writers do. Several entries deal with Mrs. Eberhart's telling or reading stories to the children before going to bed; Eberhart's sister Elizabeth remembers hearing these stories every night, especially from a collection called *Stories to Tell to Children, Little Women,* the Oz books, *Robinson Crusoe,* and *Alice in Wonderland.* Eberhart himself was older, of course, and his diary includes different titles. He also read a good deal himself, especially when school was not in session. This entry from the Christmas vacation of 1917–18 is typical: "Read 'The Return of Tarzan' by Edgar Rice Burroughs, after supper. . . . Also Ma read us, 'Mark Tidd, Editor,' out of the American Boy." He also read "about Thomas Beckett," during this vacation, and other titles mentioned include *Penrod, Ivanhoe,* and *The Last of the Mohicans.*

Some of this reading shows up in two short stories written in his teens, which are preserved in his personal library. One is a tale of love and the discovery of a universal antidote and is not any worse, or any better, than the popular romances of the late nineteenth century. The other is a little more interesting, a kind of Romeo and Juliet story of love, war, and death among the Chippewas and Cheyennes of primeval Minnesota. It is, to be sure, a juvenile piece, but it is plotted with sufficient care to make it adequate for a motion picture or television show, and more importantly it sometimes points, if in a primitive way, toward the descriptive power that characterizes much of his mature poetry:

> Before daybreak. The storm had passed and everything was bright and clear. To the east the great sun was just breaking over the horizon, and it glowed through a clump of trees on the right and the woods on the left. The horizon was a dark purple and the faint rays of the sun could be seen penetrating the moist air to blend into a soft veil-like mist on the ground. The sun was half out now and the dark purple had turned a deep azure on the clear sky. The sun's rays were more brilliant and the soft veil-like softness of the mist had merged into a sturdier, more radiant sparkling on the dew.
>
> A time elapsed as White Eagle rode on until the sun was above the horizon and shown [sic] forth with a golden glow which turned the deep azure to a dainty light blue and seemed to set everything afire with its deep color and warmth. Everything had lost its indistinctness and was fresh, clear, and bright. The day had come.

References to poetry are less frequent in the diary, and they are usually connected with school work, as is this one, from February 19, 1918:

> After supper I studied the two poems I have to give in expression week after next Monday. They are "The Duel" by Eugene Field and "I got to go to school" by Nixon Waterman.

To the best of Eberhart's memory, however, his chief motivation to write poetry came from within the family, from Mrs. Eberhart's brother, Henry Polk Lowenstein, a prolific writer of magazine verse. A slender, paperback volume of "Uncle Polk's" work, dedicated to the American Legion, is preserved in the Eberhart Collection. Most of the poems in this volume are on military or patriotic themes, under such titles as "How to Win the War," "If God Be With the Kaiser," "My Buddie on the Marne," "Our President," "Pershing's Sword," and three different titles referring to Flanders Fields. Other themes are also represented, as in "Labor Day":

The right to labor is Divine,
　　And given its own reward,
Its pay is more than gold refined,
　　Its joy is of the Lord.

To earn thy bread by sweat of face,
　　Ordained of God himself,
Is sweeter far and more of grace,
　　Than piles of paltry pelf.

. . . .

And now again on Labor Day,
　　We pledge our strength to work,
And never cease to laugh and play,
　　And ne'er our duty shirk.

We stand as ONE, erect and strong,
　　With hammer in our hand,
To help the weary world along,
　　And bless our happy land.

"The Rainbow and the Rose" seems more likely to have moved the young Eberhart:

I sometimes doubt there is a God,
　　When well I know that all who live must die,
　　　And then at last my eye-lids close;
　　But when I see the rainbow in the sky,
　　　And behold the blossom of the rose,
'Tis then I know there is a God.

"No and Yes" is addressed to young maidens:

If Old Temptation comes along
　　To lure you to his show
With his deceit and artful song,
　　Say no, say NO, say *NO!*

If old Dame Fashion passes by
　　To take you to her show,

> With waist down low and skirt up high,
> Say no, say NO, say *NO!*
>
> . . . .
>
> And when you're in your cottage home
> And both your love confess,
> If little strangers want to come,
> Say yes, say YES, say *YES!*
>
> And when St. Peter bids you in
> His holy hand to press,
> To wash away your guilty sin,
> Say yes, say YES, say *YES!*

Eberhart's own early verse is not so replete with moral uplift as his uncle's, but usually concentrates on a single image. "The Shell Vase," and "Indian Pipe," are good examples. Both are preserved in a little notebook, entitled "Twigs," in the Eberhart Collection. This one, "A Statue," is in the same collection:

> Life-like in molds of hoary stone
> Each warrior's ready for the fray,
> Uncovered weapons carved of bone [stone?]
> Do flash and glitter their array.
>
> Gay decked with battle axe and sword
> And mounted on their chargers fast
> The ancient mercenaries' word
> Bids fair to fight until the last.

Another poem, on the effects of the harvest moon, is more typical in its use of images he saw outdoors. The title is "Gold Dust," and this is the first stanza:

> What makes the dew
>   A-spark with molten, golden gleams?
> What makes the true
>   And silver tinkle in the streams?
> What makes the grass

A glamor of yellow and gold, at noon?
And the frosted mass
All twisted with a fringe of moon?

None of these poems gives Eberhart any claim to the status of prodigy, but they are interesting in that they show the beginnings of both the sharp eye for concrete images and the tendency to moralize upon them that are prominent in his later verse.

II

From all the extant evidence, then, the image of Eberhart's early life emerges as a kind of American idyll, directed and watched over by his parents, who have apparently been accurately drawn in *The Visionary Farms*. The elder Eberharts provided their children not only with means but with much of their motivation, in the form of encouragement and help. A very brief passage from "Duo Days," part of an account of the preparations for the annual banquet of 1920, will indicate to some extent the interest the Eberharts took in their sons' affairs:

> Feb. 25: O Fate—What next! At noon mother said they brought in three puny, small, blue turkeys. Dad saved the day— called Mpls. and had a man locate three good ones and bring them down. . . . Yet more!—Mother found out that we can't get any red and white flowers here—so we ordered all the decorations from the cities.

It is difficult to assess precisely, however, the parents' role in the home from surviving contemporary records. A teen-age boy does not reflect in his diary on his mother and father; they are a presence taken more or less for granted. This is especially true of Eberhart's father, who appears in the diary only infrequently, playing billiards or telling jokes with the boys, and often in the act of appearing he disappears, leaving on business for Minneapolis or Chicago or even New York. Eberhart's sister remembers her father as always "on the go," but she also remembers his playing the piano and singing with the family after supper, and that he "was always for the great (or good) life and used to have barrels of fresh oysters and clams shipped in packed in ice." She also recalls him being around more than in the period of Eberhart's diary:

> My father used to involve himself completely with each activity we had—also my mother—and we loved it. When the boys went on overnight Boy Scout trips Father would get some other father to drive out to where they had hiked to— and at the campfire he'd present the group with a whole stalk of bananas or a huge box of marshmallows for them to toast, stay a while and leave.

Probably the very energy and drive that kept him away from home, either at the office or on business trips, were the source of Mr. Eberhart's most important function in the family, at least for the boys: that of a living example of the faithful pursuit of the ideals of the community, and of the success that resulted.

Mrs. Eberhart's personality was apparently exactly opposite to that of her husband. "She and my father were in love," Elizabeth recalls, "but he sometimes overpowered her with his eternal and great energy and enthusiasm." She seems to have been a very gentle person, and the Eberhart children remember her as "spiritual," with a deep sympathy with other people and their problems. In any event, it is clear that she did most of the "work" of parenthood: the listening to declamatory rehearsals, the transportation to ball practice, the supervision of Duo "feeds." Her less tangible contributions are evident in the one long diary entry involving her before her final illness. It is an account of what was apparently Richard's one "serious" failure in high school. Because it shows so much the influence of his parents, it is quoted here at some length. It involves the state high school declamatory competition. The diary tells of the trip to the district contest in Hayfield and of the other contestants from other high schools throughout the area. Then Eberhart began his "oration," entitled "The Turk Must Go":

I had gotten ⅔ thru and was absolutely going fine when I came to the anti-climax—". . . a living reproach to our common humanity. . ."—on "humanity" I felt an absolute veil drawn over my brain—my thought just faded away and stopped. I moved a step. The seconds began ticking off. It didn't come and it took me fully a half minute, head bowed, perfectly still otherwise and trying as hard as I ever tried to think, to concentrate, to realize that I was lost. Then my first impulse was to turn—to run and bury myself. But I would be no coward. It's queer what thoughts flash thru one's mind in such a predicament. There were all that Austin gang expecting me to win and there I was—with no control over my mind. It was so still as I stood there, that you could easily have heard a pin drop. . . . Once outside, the wave of regret swept over me. Foolishly I wondered if I could only have another chance, and then the thought that the biggest thing of its nature I had attempted—and with [the] school behind me—I had failed. I was defeated. . . . When the orations were over, it took courage to walk in the other room and face the audience with a disgrace. But I tried to bear defeat as I often wished I could. . . .

One cannot help speculating that the moral stamina in evidence here is an inheritance from his father, and certainly what follows shows his mother and her faith as sources of consolation:

We brought the folks to the house for a root beer or grape juice. They left. I thank God for the most wonderful Mother. In my room she and I, I asked her saying "There is a Divine power that shapes our ways" and she believed this, and let me understand that she believed God meant for me just what was given me. I told her how last night I had prayed and asked Christ to give me strength and faith to put it over—the biggest thing yet. I had just read from Matthew "Ask, and it shall be given you, seek, and you shall find."—and tonight—it might seem God had heard me not. But then my dear Mother, when I asked her about praying, said there was only once, when she was a young girl that, praying fervently, she was lifted into a radiance that seemed not of material things. And when she came to, the surroundings seemed "sordid, commonplace." And Mother said, "Ever since that I have been so positive in my faith that I can think of no other thing" as being the way of God. And so it was God's wish, that for my own good, I was given to face a humiliating defeat. Mother said she tried to pray for me before I came on the stage, as she does before I enter any conflict, but she said there was an impenetrable something that made her unable to attain the spirit of prayer, and that something held back from me the paragraph beginning "Lord Salisbury" and put the school out of the state championship race.

Eberhart's sister also remembers this episode and recalls that her mother, who knew the speech by heart from listening to Richard's rehearsals, said later that had she been a swearing woman she would have said, "Oh Lord!" and her son would have gone right on from there. It is in such roles that she appears, like her husband, only now and then in the young Eberhart's diary, until 1921, when he could no longer take her presence for granted.

For in the year following Richard's graduation from high school, both parents were struck down by misfortune. In the summer of 1921, it was discovered that one R. J. Thompson, a trusted lieutenant of the Hormel management, had embezzled over a million and a half dollars in an eight-year period. Taking advantage of the complete trust placed in him by Eberhart and Hormel, he had developed an elaborate system of kiting checks and balancing books that was foolproof, until he forgot one little item and it was discovered by Hormel's son. Then the sky caved in, not only on Thompson but on the Hormel company. Confidence in the corporation was shaken severely, and the stock plummeted, with the result that A. L. Eberhart lost almost $209,000 (on paper) practically overnight.

Since most of his other assets were in land and could not be liquidated, these events put the family in relatively serious straits, and A. L. was able to stay solvent only through personal loans against the land from various friends, most notably George H. Swift, his old friend and former employer. But the heaviest blow did not fall until January of 1922, when because of a misunderstanding with the Hor-

mels, A. L. resigned from the company, whereupon the Hormels
took advantage of a by-law of the corporation to call in his stock in
the company at its current depressed value. A. L. took a loss of almost $134,000, and the money he did realize from the sale was al-
most immediately eaten up by debts outstanding. But he remained
solvent, and when he took a job in Omaha that year, his only remaining creditor, as nearly as can be made out from available documents, was Swift, whom he finally repaid with interest some years
later.

Although some belt-tightening was in order, all financial troubles
were overshadowed by a more serious, human tragedy; for at precisely the time when A. L. was so frantically trying to cover his
notes, his wife fell mortally ill with cancer of the lung. From the
summer of 1921 until her death on June 22, 1922, she was unable to
run the household. As a result, Richard did not follow his brother
to the University of Minnesota that fall, but remained at Burr Oaks
to help the nurses and neighbors take care of his mother.

During that last winter he read to his mother a good deal, and although he sometimes read *Post* stories, it was more often the Bible,
something called "God's Law of Adjustment," and a great deal of
Christian Science literature. The family apparently put considerable,
although not exclusive, reliance on Christian Science, and Mrs. Hormel visited frequently to read and meditate. That it was some comfort to the son, if not to the mother, is evident from part of the
entry for November 19, 1921, in his diary:

> Read Science and Health for a long time. Don't know when
> I have felt such absolute peace of mind as afterwards when
> the minutes drifted by as I strummed uke to myself. There
> must have been a long time when my mind was at perfect rest
> and peace after reading that. It was a beautiful sensation. . . .

But his mother was less impressed. On November 22, she told her
son:

> I think Science would be all right if you took it when well and
> strong. Then if you were sick you could fall back on it. But

when you have this pain all the time, it's pretty hard. As I heard Mrs. Hormel read on and on, who has hardly ever been sick, I wondered if she could read with the same faith if she was down. I don't think she could. But then, maybe it's only a weakness of faith in me. . . . the Scientists' prayers are not the only ones that are answered.

That Christian Science was given a chance at this time perhaps indicates the nature of the religious faith in the Eberhart household. While it was far from any strident fundamentalism, it was a simple, strong, traditional devotion that was very much part of their daily lives, or at least of the daily life of young Richard and his mother during her last year.

Much of this life survives in the diary kept between November 8 and December 19, 1921. It is a particularly engaging account, written with the unself-conscious candor of a seventeen-year-old. There is no apparent effort at "literary" effect, but moments of considerable emotion are woven into a fabric of straightforward, factual narrative in such a way as to approach an unconsciously aesthetic effect. It must be remembered that the daily routine, for the young diarist at least, was organized entirely around the care of a beloved woman almost totally invalided and in virtually constant pain that could be controlled only by repeated medication, primarily in the form of codeine tablets and morphine injections. The nurse was apparently not full-time; A. L. was struggling to save his fortune; Dryden was away at college; Elizabeth was only eleven; so the primary responsibility of running the household fell on the seventeen-year-old Richard. The following passage gives a clear sense of the rhythm of their existence, and of the diary:

Sunday Nov. 27—1921: Mother had a very poor night—about three hours sleep—wearing pain in shoulder. She looks bright, however. A wet snow fall this morning. After breakfast (8:30) Mother went to sleep and slept until 11:45. One fine nap. Dad and Eliz tramped at Whispering Pines while I froze ice cream and shoveled snow, etc. At noon pain started up and after nurse left in P. M. I stayed with Mother, giving doses of pills every ½ hr. until about 5 but it let up only a little. She took a little apple and when I asked if I could have some of it Mother said "Anything I have is yours without asking, my dear."

Uncle Polk came at 4:40 and she with us was mighty glad to see him. He visited with her off and on the rest of the day. Ev. V. brought us some venison and Dad and I cooked some for Mother's supper. Eliz was over at Terry's. When she came back we both visited with Mother, one on each side of her day bed with an arm over her body and I said "We all want a monopoly on Mother" she answered as she caressed us each with a hand "And I want a monopoly on my kiddies."

Jennie brought her wonderful handwork and Mother saw her a bit. Mrs. C. up just as Polk came and Mrs. S. later. Dr. about 6 and after he had gone she said "Well, that's rather discouraging that the X-ray is not even sure to give relief."

. . . the procession marched in to say goodnight. I read her a little poem I had picked up.

This passage gives a clear idea of the degree to which the family managed to maintain the normal pace of its life. The rest of the entry plus the beginning of the next day shows the horror that perpetually hung over them.

Later at 10 P.M. I went in and she was nervously crying—the pain had come on again. "Just as I was so sleepy." She didn't want to cry. I tried hard to soothe her—finally talked of Dryd. "Yes" she said "I thought quite a bit of him last night . . . The telegram that father signed my name to didn't sound like me at all, did it?" And she smiled in the darkness. . . . She became a little more calm. O! God, if I am any comfort to her, I am thankful. I had 40 min. before called Mrs. H. but the nurse gave her a hypo at 10:20.

Yester P.M. when we had that religious talk remember she said "I never look at a dead person but what I realize how much our bodies are just clay. Our real selves are soul." And when E. came in, "Here she comes, my little rosy cheeks."

Mon. Nov. 28—1921: This has been Mother's hardest and worst day. The Dr. came at 2 A.M. when she had a nervous chill and gave her another hypo. She only slept three hours. This A.M. she is almost too weak to whisper, and the pain still on. Doped on different pills. At 10:30 while I was with her she vomited, taking a lot of strength but giving relief.

These conditions continued, substantially, until her death, although there were some cheerful periods, usually when the whole family was together. They were of course under extraordinary tension, constantly trying to cheer one another up, and they occasionally talked seriously about her death (without ever admitting its imminence) and about the likelihood of success in various methods of treatment, and there are several places where the diary breaks off with the frustrated remark that the words and feelings that passed at a particular time simply cannot be written.

In early December, a small X-ray machine was brought in to Burr Oaks, but it soon proved insufficient and after consultation Mrs. Eberhart went to Chicago for a last-ditch effort with a new and very powerful machine. She seemed to improve but soon got worse after her return. When Eberhart typed this diary in 1939, he added the following coda, which effectively ends the story of that year:

Here the Ms. ends. I cannot recall why I did not keep it up after Mother's return from Chicago [he did, but in a different form]. The treatments probably added a few months to her life; but the pain increased with time. Since cancer was never mentioned among any of us, I have usually thought that she did not know the nature of her illness. But even in reading this old Ms. it would seem as if so intelligent a person must have known, to herself at least. I remember filling her room, the north guest room, with pussy willows in the early spring of 1922. In early June we took her down stairs for the last time. I remember when she gave father back his wedding ring. She talked with each of us children personally in turn. On the night of June 22, 1922, the twenty-fourth anniversary of her marriage, I remember lying on the other bed next to hers in the north room: at about 9:30 P.M. in the luminous stillness some strange exaltation of spirit caused me to write a poem to her. I helped her take a sip of water from a glass tube in a water glass. Then the nurse had told me to run for the Doctor. I remember careening through the streets in the big heavy Cadillac limousine at 70 miles an hour, down the hill and over the bridge to LaFayette Park, where Chataqua was in session, and called for the Doctor. When I returned all was silence. I remember the last kiss.

It is very likely that the "exaltation" that produced the last poem he wrote during his mother's life was a sense of relief at the approaching release from months of tension. He had watched her agony for almost a year. For at least seven months of that time, he had known that there was no hope. So there is small wonder that, in the poem, the death seemed "timely":

Thou'rt not unkind, o timely death,
   Who comes to still our mother's pain.
She lives, tho gone her human breath,
   In God's eternal love again.
. . . .
Sleep. Peace. How you have prayed for these!
   For all your sufferings intense
Reward is thine now from disease
   And thou art gone—we know not whence.

The confession of ignorance that ends this piece is supported by much that is in the little personal essays to himself that replaced the diary after his mother returned from Chicago. But although he was beginning to ask questions, he still could "not conceive of faith under her terrible circumstances being unrepaid, nor a beautiful life without complete reward. . . . There must be some first cause for life." Within a few weeks, the boys joined their father in Omaha and worked for the rest of the summer in a packing house, and the shattering of the poet's unusually integrated, extraordinarily *whole* early life was complete.

It is difficult to assess accurately the effects of this violent initiation into reality, but it is possible to make some general observations. It could be argued that the family's business reverses constituted a refutation of the individualistic ideal that had served the father so well, and indeed the poet came later to view the events in this light. But in 1922, it never occurred to him to reflect on the catastrophes crashing about him. There is virtually no evidence in the diaries quoted above that he realized the magnitude of his father's losses, and as late as the end of February 1922 he could write,

> Man, if he possess strength of character, is master of his own destiny to a great degree. . . . a man's integrity, ambition and his hard work, time and thought, when diligently applied, will allow him to realize an ideal he has set.

His belief in individual achievement, reflected most emphatically by his successes in high school, had paradoxically become more institutionalized than his religious faith. What had been for the father an immediate, practical necessity, was for the sons a socially recognized and rewarded virtue, with only a long-range relationship to reality. The young poet found his identity, therefore, primarily in his role as a member of the community and its various groups: his club, his school and its activities, and above all his family, which supported and encouraged his other roles. In short, everything he did or believed, his very conception of himself as a person, was unequivocally sanctioned by his entire environment, giving him the sense of belonging that created the unqualified wholeness of his life. When he left this life, and when his family was broken by the death of his mother and the change of his father's operations, this wholeness was destroyed; but his belief in its validity, in its reality, was not, and he was to spend many years in trying to re-create it.

CHAPTER TWO
1922–1927

In the fall of 1922, more or less automatically, Eberhart followed his brother to the University of Minnesota, where he pursued the standard freshman curriculum, including English, French, History, Physics, Chemistry, and Physical Education. Very few details of his year at Minnesota survive, but he seems, by virtue of a kind of momentum, a habit acquired in high school, to have taken an active part in campus life. He joined his brother's fraternity, Alpha Delta Phi, and served as a reporter on the fraternity newspaper. He also served on the Freshman Commission and in the spring ran track, winning a medal for doing the hundred-yard dash in ten seconds flat.

Little is known of his intellectual life at Minnesota, but it was here that he had what he later called his "first literary 'aesthetic' experience," Joseph Warren Beach's "queer and quiring voice" reciting "La Belle Dame Sans Merci." Years later he could "still remember the strange and powerful thrill" in the voice and in the poem. There is no way of knowing how frequent or infrequent such experiences were, but in any event he soon became dissatisfied and within a few months had decided to look for something better.

Dartmouth College at that time had begun recruiting top men from the West and Midwest, and though he had virtually "never heard of Harvard," he had somewhere acquired a vision of Ivy

League schools as sort of Socratic academies, where one would inevitably absorb near-perfect wisdom almost by osmosis. This ideal vision, this conviction of the superiority of Dartmouth to anything he had ever known, produced an unwonted diffidence, so that when he transferred to Dartmouth in the fall of 1923, he did not attempt to take the leading role that had come naturally in high school and, to a lesser extent, at Minnesota. Instead he began to explore the intellectual and literary life of the campus while concentrating, especially in his first year, on his studies.

Perhaps because he had done poorly in Latin in high school, he decided to fulfill Dartmouth's ancient language requirement with Greek, and did still worse. In five semesters he earned two C's, two D's, and an E. In the natural sciences he did little better, with D's in chemistry and Botany, but a redeeming A in Zoology. In the social sciences he was an average student, while in philosophy and literature he received almost straight A's. Like most students, he did well in proportion to the interest the subject held for him. To say that he did well in philosophy and literature, furthermore, is to say more than it seems to, for these two disciplines, as taught at Dartmouth, were closely related. There are many class notebooks and papers that he wrote at this time, preserved in his personal library, which reflect this cross-disciplinary emphasis. Ideas are stressed more than form, and the study of Wordsworth and Coleridge, for example, is not merely prefaced with the usual perfunctory nod at Rousseau and perhaps Kant but is part of a broad study of European Romanticism. It is probably no accident, therefore, that the courses he considered most rewarding were W. K. Stewart's in comparative literature.

This crossing of academic lines, tending to de-crystallize categories and weaken any tendencies to be rigidly doctrinaire, made Dartmouth important in Eberhart's intellectual life. There were required courses designed specifically to pry open young minds, "endeavoring," in the words of a student publication, "to break down prejudices that are common to most Americans to show the value of reason in examining the problems of life." And large doses of Schopenhauer and Nietzsche were administered in Eberhart's words, as a "favorite method of adolescent eye-opening. . . ." But at least as important to this process were the exchanges of viewpoints that could be enjoyed in the coffee shop, fraternity house, and dormitory. The effect of such exchanges is recorded in a paper, otherwise not outstanding, that Eberhart wrote early in his Dartmouth career, entitled "The Man with the Green Glasses." At the end of the paper he confesses that it is about himself.

To cite a specific case, consider the liquor question at Dartmouth. Jocko had been raised in such an environment that, upon his arrival here, disgust was the natural reaction he experienced upon witnessing college drinking parties. He abhorred the practice; his point of view was strict and narrow. He judged the activities of his friends from the limited view of personal prejudice—he wore Green Glasses. But he has cast away those double harbingers of vanity. He now appreciates the fact that most college drinkers have been raised in a metropolitan and social environment that tolerates—even accepts without reserve—the use of intoxicants. That which to him appeared immoral and a sign of inferiority was to them mere convention. Their points of view were different. . . .
    Another time Jocko found himself in the midst of a group of college boys enjoying one of the heated—and oft times irrelevant—arguments common to the fraternity house. The subject was religion and centered around the question of going to church. Jocko's convictions were dogmatic. He believed that regular attendance at church was a vital factor in being a Christian, and that being a Christian was a positive necessity for immortality. Fortunately he held his tongue. The others each gave reasons for not going to church at all, for attending church as an aesthetic pleasure, and for going to church to study the sermon scientifically. It slowly dawned on Jocko that his brothers' ideas were good ones. He came to realize that the agnostics, pantheists, and atheists were different from himself only because their viewpoints were different.

This kind of wide-open-mindedness has of course its attendant evils. By giving "the other fellow" a blank check to think what he wants to, one tends to abrogate his responsibility for critical thinking. That Eberhart fell victim to this excess, to some extent at least, is apparent in another paper, entitled "Whatsoever a Man Had Rather Were True, He More Readily Believes." Here he takes the position that perception and reason are functions of the "ego," and that with man's limitations of vision, it is necessary to provide himself with delusions in order to get any satisfaction out of existence:

> I am content to grasp at shadows, wondering what is behind them that can make them so delicate and strong. If one knew what the wheels were and their precise diameters, what a little tin god one would be and how stupid the whole disarming affair! . . . . I feel after life everywhere. I love it when I touch it. I would rather ask it no questions about being good— or bad.

From this time forward Eberhart has been the convinced relativist, refusing to be "dogmatic," "absolutistic." But this sort of open-ended liberalism has also led to looseness of thought, a lack of conceptual precision that has, as we shall see, been the target of a good deal of criticism of his poetry.

There can be no doubt that Dartmouth under President Hopkins tried to foster a certain degree of "liberalism," but a question remains as to whether Dartmouth liberalism provided a creative atmosphere, one where a potential artist could live and thrive. Robert Frost had left the college years earlier because

> school and college have been conducted with the almost express purpose of keeping [the potential poet] busy with something else till the danger of his ever creating anything is past.

The editors of *The Tower,* a very good undergraduate literary magazine, published an article entitled "Dartmouth Versus Art":

> There are still tendencies in Dartmouth to repress rather than express the individuality of any one student. An education largely standardized is given to every student. The majority of

his courses are directly compulsory, or are compromizes to fill out a not impossibly inconvenient schedule card. No provision is made for the man of exceptional interests. The artist is always an exceptional man. Dartmouth, which makes no provision for the exceptional man automatically discourages his interest in the college. . . . Either he leaves, or his individuality is subject to a pernicious weakening process.

Elsewhere, and in a different tone, the editors apologize to the girls coming to Hanover for the Winter Carnival:

Against the imposing list easily prepared by Harvard, Yale, or Vassar, we have only Richard Hovey and Ben Ames Williams. . . . [But] your wittiest word is not entirely lost here even though it would later appear in a novel if saved for New Haven.

Of course, the fact that there was sufficient interest in the problem for these remarks to be published suggests that things were not quite as bad as they were pictured. Though a glance at the catalogues for 1923–26 suggests that *The Tower's* description of the curriculum is substantially accurate, it is doubtful that course requirements were any more confining than at any other college. And just a few months later, the editors of the same publication praised the decline of the "rah-rah spirit" at the college and the increase of student participation and influence on faculty and administration policy.

There was a good deal of activity in the arts, and it was encouraged. An organization which did a great deal in this regard was "The Arts," to which Eberhart belonged. This group met regularly for conversation and to plan "cultural" functions, especially visits by luminaries in various fields. In Eberhart's senior year, members of "The Arts" were responsible for the campus visits of Carl Sandburg, Stephen Leacock, and Richard Le Gallienne. Eberhart still recalls Sherwood Anderson's visit. He and another student met Anderson at the train and were immediately worried about his condition. He seemed either very ill or else drunk. But the audience was waiting, so they took him in and introduced him, whereupon he produced a manuscript and began reading from it. Everything went well through the first three pages, but then at the end of the third page Anderson's fingers slipped and the page just fluttered in the air and settled back down before him. He read it again, and he turned it again, and he missed again. So he read it again, and again. Finally the boys escorted him off the stage and back to the Hanover Inn, to the great embarrassment of the organizers of the visit.

Of course few of "The Arts'" events were so unfortunate. When Edna St. Vincent Millay (who, he said in 1924, "supplies all I need in poetry") died in 1950, Eberhart wrote Conrad Aiken of her visit to Dartmouth:

> Goodbye, Edna Millay. When I was an undergraduate at Dartmouth I sat spellbound in a large hall, like many of my contemporaries more taken by the mysterious "female" quality you radiated than by the words now long since forgotten. You were the mysterious, the unknown feminine. That flush of the cheeks, that scarlet dress. I recall that when you swished out of the hall about 50 of us followed after, positively drooling. Your short husband followed along far behind, discreet with briefcase.

Presumably out of a more intellectual interest, "The Arts" also contacted Richard Le Gallienne for a campus visit. There ensued a considerable correspondence and Le Gallienne, expressing the conviction that Dartmouth was making great strides in preserving respect for art and beauty, contributed several poems to *The Tower,* one of which was "inspired," according to Le Gallienne, by a letter from Eberhart, and contains the phrase "Prince Eberhart" in the refrain.

The Tower itself is probably the best representative of the literary and intellectual atmosphere at Dartmouth in Eberhart's undergraduate years. Founded in 1924 as an alternative to the college newspaper and as a complement to *The Bema,* a campus magazine already in operation, its columns discussed trenchantly both the larger and the smaller issues affecting campus life. Though perhaps primarily an exercise in undergraduate polemics, its editorial columns, under the leadership of Alexander Laing and J. D. Altizer, approached everything from fraternity rushing to educational philosophy with unusual intelligence and sophistication, while it also provided an outlet for competent undergraduate verse and fiction.

Eberhart contributed poetry and book reviews to both magazines, and was on the editorial board of *The Tower* in his senior year. The pages of *The Bema* and especially *The Tower,* therefore, provide the first substantial body of his poetry, and he was first anthologized in *The Arts Anthology: Dartmouth Verse, 1925.* It was in Robert Frost's introduction to this little volume that he received his first notice from a full-fledged member of the literary world. Frost likened poetry to a water-spout, suggesting that a young poet is "a cloud of all the other poets he ever read," which

> reaches down toward the water from above and then the water reaches up toward the cloud from below and finally cloud and water join together to roll as one pillar between heaven and earth.

He then cited Eberhart's "The Village Daily" as one of the poems in the anthology that "at least get up the salt water."

> Worn linotype machines are clicking fast
> And there's a pungent smell of printer's ink
> About this ancient shop; and plates of zinc
> And dingy placards on the wall long cast.
> Below, the presses grind the paper past
> And feel quick cool metallic slaps and drink
> The stone smooth inks that on bare papers clink
> With spank, spank, spank, and heavier clouts at last.
>
> The daily village paper goes to press
> While all the people lie asleep in bed.
> The mechanism trains a flinty eye

On what the world forever has to stress
And every night it sets in rigid lead
Those who are born, who marry, and who die.

The consciousness of death that ends this sonnet is the dominant note in the undergraduate poems, a note which was to remain central in his poetry. The structure of "The Village Daily," however, with its sudden, ironic thrust at the end, is a less typical approach than that in "The Inevitable," where the point is stated immediately in the first three lines, before a gradual accumulation of supporting images.

His is a strange dumbness
And his lips are silent.
Yet it is spring. The world
Moves forward with a thrill. Trees, the
Singing grass; rivers, the fresh eyed flowers
Burst forth in a great throb of growth.
He lies there—his firm breath is gone.
He does not hear the still mystic
Life that shimmers
In the air.
For him
The vibrant twilight passes and a
Heavy garment's flung away. . . . [sic]

Of course the difference of technique in these two poems is, in part at least, a function of a difference in idea. The last line of "The Village Daily" points at the futility at the end of all the frantic activity in the rest of the sonnet, whereas "The Inevitable" finds consolation in death as rest amidst life that is as inevitable as death itself. This theme is repeated in "Nirvana," which later was published in *Burr Oaks* and is reprinted in *Collected Poems* as "Cover Me Over," and is present in many other poems, most notably the much anthologized "The Groundhog."

The sense of consolation in the beauty and vitality of nature often takes on a conventionally religious tone, as in "Impressions":

Rain and odor of grass,
Bloodroots and stars at night.
Water clearing its throat
Over stones.
Dirty urchins wondering about
Rainbows—
And you say there is no God?

An early poem in *The Bema,* "Ultimate," furthermore, suggests that man can achieve a kind of salvation by such celebration of nature's beauty:

The last man watched the carnival of death
And saw the pale rose fade, then darkness close,
And stars and sun go hissing down the sky.
And with the tired beats of his aching heart
He strangely raised his thin starved voice apart
And sang how beauty could not ever die
That lived one hour within the frailest rose,
    Or trailed upon the faintest wind's ambrosial breath.

But the saving power of the celebrant is clearly subordinate to and dependent upon the beauty and viability of the celebrated, both in "Ultimate" and especially in the better poem, "Sculptor":

I chisel flowers acutely for a keen fixed frieze.
And I shall weight my heart's red insufficiency
With boughs of palest green and marble thorns so white
That flesh is pierced. And eagerly I'll carve a bright
Unnecessary desolated Christ and three
Slim faithful withered angels fluttered by a
    breeze.

I'll hang the stone entablature across my heart's
Insistent cry. But a summer's rich fulfillment brings
Grain-lusciousness to earth: I thought, like idle snow
Swirled heedlessly, the years were planted long ago.

But when I walk through the fields the frailest grass
    spear sings;
The fixed frieze shatters with a thousand flame-sweet
    darts.

  Many of these undergraduate poems are, as might be expected, singularly unimpressive, characterized by the kind of facile emotion and hackneyed language that is evident in "Recognition," which came out of a visit to Fontainebleau in 1925:

Because Millet stood here
This common field of grain
Beneath the summer sun
Gleams brighter;
In the distance stands a tower,
A peaceful common tower,
In russet dressed.

I only knew the scene
Was beautiful
And France was likewise
Summer-beautiful
When first I passed.

Millet once heard the Angelus
Across the waving grain.
I only saw
A peaceful common tower
In russet dressed.

If the presence of Wordsworth is almost oppressive here, Shakespeare and Homer are only slightly better digested in "Circe":

Her quiet limbs in sleep no lovelier were
Nor whiter than the lavish blossom's wax
Of apples riotously sprawling; flax
In summer glistens slippery dry to stir
More plaintively, more redolent of myrrh,

Than when her slightest guileful turn attacks
Her captive lord to make his heart relax:
Odysseus, steadfast goodly voyager.

Aeaean goddess, Circe, sorceress,
Your snow-bold limbs and wand-spun magic art
Are not enchanting like black rain upon
Defenseless trees, or midnight's bleak caress
When all is sung, your futile wings depart
Down Pyriphlegethon to Acheron.

Throughout these poems, however, one catches occasionally a glitter
of expression, a freshness of metaphor. His "heart's red insufficiency," "the presses that grind the paper past," "Water clearing its
throat/ Over stones" and others promise talent, and point toward
the felicity of phrase that marks his later work. If his imagery is frequently trite, vague, or hardly existent, he can nevertheless show a
sharply incisive eye, as in "M. D.":

The way the moon shines through the trees
And cuts each branch against the light
Reminds me of the network veins
Within a dead man's withered arm,
Yet half dissected by a knife.

Somewhat less fully realized is the simile that ends "Moosilauke
Phantasy":

And ridges everlasting, firm,
And distant pointed peaks below,
Project their prominences
Out of the dense clouds
Like the half bodies of porpoises
Visible over the sea
Riding.

The major image in "Searcher" is less complex, but in its explicit fusion of the concrete with the abstract it is more characteristic of his
poetry as a whole:

Too many hands have labored
And too many mathematicians
Have scrawled their scratch pads
Full of fine lines
To fix an incandescent eye blazing
Out of the skyscraper's head.
The great eye strains and blinks
Searching the sky
For an answer.

Clearly, "the great eye" represents the kind of activity in which those who labored and scrawled to create it ought to engage. Technology has produced a symbol for wisdom.

One poem written during these years that was not published points most clearly toward the later work and contains, in the last line, the only direct autobiographical reference in any of the undergraduate pieces:

By unrest stung, yet beating on the wind,
Keep to your wild caprice above the sea,
O querulous gulls. You still may somehow find
An atmosphere that is less chained, and free.
   Cut the bright air with your wings
   And make mosaic of the sky
   And scoop the blue wave when it clings
   To deeper blue; then scatter high
   Across the sky the swells locked fast
   In broad-backed ocean's hand.
   Then mix your white with these; at last
   May form a pattern that will stand.
I know the quick unrest upon your wings,
The subtle knot built into sky and sea,
And fretfully strive no less for airier things:
I too have known the stealth of chancery.

The imagery of sea and sky, the spirit's struggle for freedom from the "subtle knot" with matter, appear again and again in the later work. The similarity of this poem to the much later "Seals, Terns, Time" is especially striking.

If these poems were the only available records for Eberhart's college years, they would be sufficient to indicate the steady broadening of the horizons of his world. The diary of the trip to Europe that his father gave him and his brother in the summer before his senior year provides further evidence, at least on a shallow level. The high school paragon, the stern Duo president enforcing order in Meeting, is found with friends on ship shouting

> for whiskeys until our rendition of "Old King Coal" [sic] was superb. . . . We lock stepped all over the boat, thru the main dining rooms and salons singing "Hail, Hail, the Gang's All Here." We put the little barkeep on our shoulders and carried him around the *zimmer* and on first deck after giving yells duly for the Captain, the Purser, and the *Andania,* we yelled for "the whole damned crew" and "the Atlantic Ocean."

They went on to take the standard tour of the standard places: Paris, the Loire, Marseilles, then south in the sooty Italian train to get lost in Venice and be duly overwhelmed by the timeless grandeur of the Colosseum in Rome. Then they went back up through Switzerland, Germany, Belgium, the Netherlands, and "typical wet English rain" in time to see *Julius Caesar* in Stratford-on-Avon's Shakespeare Memorial Theatre in August before sailing for home.

By the time he was graduated from Dartmouth in June of 1926, therefore, and came to live with his father and sister in Chicago, his vision of the world, both intellectual and geographical, had so expanded that dissatisfaction with the well-ordered routines of Midwestern life was almost inevitable. He had already, as early as June of 1925, considered graduate study, and poetry had become primary in his ideas about his future. But mostly out of a sense of obligation to his father, he came home and went to work in Marshall Field's. While his existence was anything but satisfactory to him, both the tone and substance of his account of his months of service to American enterprise show that he was far from miserable:

I started out in the basement of Field's selling hats to men and boys, learning a crazy lesson or two about people in the way they don a lid. Then I entered the advertising bureau and pounded out succinct and potent short adds for everything from umbrellas to Kotex. What with a little catacomb in which to dwell, with a typewriter and plenty of time for lunch, I fared well. Then came the ascension of Richard; I was lifted bodily and symbolically to the eighth floor where I helped write the high hat ads about Louis XV furniture and Persian rugs opened with the sand of Egypt . . . trickling out of them along with a few odd Oriental scorpions. This sort of thing so stimulated the people that they came in and lolled all over the furniture and bought nothing. So, in due time, after combatting the spirit of laissez faire in advertising with bombs of metaphor and shrapnel shells of simile in a cataclysmic war on the inertia of customers, I was descended to walk in humility among the little shopgirls of the basement. So I am again in basement advertizing, full of noise and sound and fury signifying enough a week to keep the traditional wolf from the door but not enough to wear a derby. . . . I have written more verse (pray, better!) than at any similar length of time before.

"Working has," he wrote to another friend, "contrary to the usual theory, stimulated me a considerable bit to the necessity of expression, the necessity of combat with the physical world to rise above it in verse." Although "yet undecided about a 'life work,'" he knew that he was "charged with great desire to objectify inner experiences and round these inner realities into smooth-flowing verse."

He made during these months several connections that provided support to these literary aspirations. Among these Harriet Monroe, "spinsterly goddess of all young versifiers," was probably the most important. "Miss Monroe," he wrote,

has just invited me to poet's rendezvous to meet Ford Madox Ford. Tonight I am attending a little dinner, after which four of us will read George Moore—a young man and his cameo-like wife, and a venerable old man [Alexander Greene], owner of a remarkable bookshop. The latter knew Rupert Brooke, has letters from him, as well as from Shaw, Wells, Barrie, Moore, Synge, Stephens and many more—he is a delightful person. . . . So this life in Chicago is bearable if not too intelligent . . . I still find time for solitude and excursions into my soul for the purpose of getting brain children there.

It is possible that much of his contentment, such as it was, during these months can be attributed to the fact that he was planning to leave. By the end of July 1926 he and his brother had already decided to work their way around the world, and Eberhart had been accepted by Cambridge University. Life was not intolerable in Chicago, "but I must be a wanderer to find the heart of reality. . . . Thus I go with great rejoicing to find outlet for energies in ideas and movements, rather than in static things."

After failing to win a post-graduate fellowship from Dartmouth, he arranged to get some of his mother's $5000 legacy, which he had lent to his father, planning to use it primarily for expenses at Cambridge. However pleasant and productive his months in Chicago had been, he was certain that that life represented inevitable intellectual and spiritual stasis. So on April 8, 1927, although his brother, "overcome by the slow wine of logic," had decided not to go, he left for San Francisco.

I left behind me the infernal machine called a time-clock, whereby man becomes automatic and non-individual. And I left behind me the rush and crowd of business, and ceriselipped shop girls with meager lives and many loves, the arrogant and stupid floorwalkers pacing their domains of flamboyant counters, and the circle of intelligent men who direct the destinies of big business. I remember one flabby floorman with mild eyes, who had stood on one spot in the basement of a store for twenty years! He must have answered millions of questions in that time. He walked back and forth all day long, twenty feet being the limits of his world, registering no longer any surprise or pleasure in life, nor any pain, but answering in sentences that had long become stereotypes, the stupid questions of the people. I swore to all the ancient gods that man must not become like that dull fellow, that man must make life through change, always new, and that the happiness bought at the expense of the same limited actions, repeated year after year, is not worth the security received as sure reward. Man must over-come the inertia that holds him down.

CHAPTER THREE
1927–1929

Eberhart went by train to St. Louis and from there by bus to Los Angeles, getting his first glimpse of the great plains, the Painted Desert, and the western mountains, helping to push the bus out of the mud and talking through the window with illicit hitchhikers clinging to the luggage rack. He got to know a "real cowboy," who illuminated the mysteries of his profession as they went together to Los Angeles and by electric train to San Pedro, where they took steerage passage on the S. S. *Humboldt* for San Francisco. He had the satisfaction of taking "the full sunshine on a hatch top" while his "neighbors were in their pews with new regalia for Easter," [1] and got enough sunburn for his trouble to spend his first week in San Francisco in bed at the apartment of Kenneth Daigneau, a former Austin friend turned actor.

"Job-hunting in San Francisco was a series of white lies and pleas to hard-faced employment agents" and

> lying on the Embarcadero watching the men and studying their faces, some drunken, some utterly hard, some coarse with hard years, some still fresh and firm, but all a little heavy with work and time.

He had letters of introduction to various influential shipping people, but they were slow in taking effect, and he had time to walk the docks, watching the ships like some latter-day Columbus. He also had time for parties and excursions with Daigneau, and to visit the giant redwoods, "perhaps the oldest living things on earth," which made him think "man's struggle . . . like the turbulence of maggots on stale meat" in comparison.

After three weeks he was finally hired as a deck boy on the *West Faralon,* sailing for Manila via Shanghai on May 25th. He was immediately set to work, along with the other deck boy, sweeping decks and polishing brass. When sailing time came, he was charged with the responsibility of removing the rat guards. Even this simple chore was so new to him that the first one fell unceremoniously into the sea. But he soon became a competent hand, and sailed westward with an enviable exuberance of spirit and freshness of eye. There were other young men like him aboard, and some of their talk must have sounded like an evening at "The Arts," but he was primarily a receiver of sensations, recording details on paper or in memory:

> Strange metamorphoses take place on board a ship. A rope loses caste and becomes a line. . . . The clock gives over its hours for bells and all maps become charts. . . . While overhauling a "pulley" to lubricate it with graphite I spoke of the "wheels," which occasioned a broad smile from the Finnish Bos'n. "Dem not wheels, dem greaves," he said, and likewise impressed upon me the importance of calling a pulley a "block." . . . The carpenter becomes "Chips." For a man to be reduced to "Chips," and especially our fat and jolly carpenter whose stomach so centers his being that he walks like a marionette, his arms and legs moving as if pulled by strings, is as if he were suffering in a new reincarnation the sins of some former mediocrity.

He also studied the characters of the crew, from "Toothless Jimmy," at once the most malicious man and the best sailor aboard, to "Slim" (Charles Paul), who wrote short stories, carried a large library in his sea bag, and was "always trying to catch the truth, sometimes spiritual, sometimes disgustingly physical, of life." He readily became close with Paul, the only man of the crew with whom he corresponded after the voyage.

The *West Faralon* was shorthanded, and the deck boys took on the duties of seamen.

Standing lookout on the foc's'le peak, it was thrilling to answer the pilot house bells every half hour by ringing the foc's'le bell and to shout into the night, presumably so the Mate could hear, "The lights are burning bright, sir." A green light shines from the starboard side of the ship and a red light from port and these must be reported as "burning bright" every half hour by the man on lookout.

Soon he was given the responsibility of the helm, watching the compass at first and later lining up a mast with a star, ignoring the prosaic needle.

And there, on my right, were the Big Dipper and the North Star. And on the left the constellation of Scorpio, poised in the sky, moving to and fro like a giant kite. Before me paced the Third Mate back and forth on the bridge, silent, slender, eagle-eyed, and I was glad from the depths of me to be steering straight for Shanghai over the broad Pacific in the moonlight.

Of course not all his duties were so gladdening. Most were predictably dull, and a few were downright dangerous. The stowing of the anchor chains, for example, required both strength and poise to avoid destruction. He and another man stood on a narrow platform around the wall of the chain locker and guided the lumbering, twisting, potentially crushing twelve-inch links into place as they dropped steadily from a steam winch through a little hole over their heads into the darkness of the locker. A careless instant would bring crushed fingers in the infolding links, and if one of them fell, the chain would be on him before the winch could be stopped.

Stripped to the waist and streaming with perspiration, it was like working against some awful impending doom that could

not be forestalled. It was as if the finality of death was upon us
and we were making the frantic struggles of trapped beasts
to escape it. It was a horrible and fantastic job.

But the fears, thrills, and boredoms of duty were forgotten in the
tumbling cataracts of experience that came with arrival in exotic
Oriental ports. In the mouth of the Yangtze swarms of Chinese
came aboard to unload and to keep watch and trade words with the
ship's own watchman, who "had more fun teaching those friendly
yellow men to count up to ten than in reading a dialogue of Plato."
His first shore leave was in Shanghai, and he threw himself into the
rush of activity in what was then a bustling outpost of British impe-
rialism, policed by majestic, bearded Sikhs. He walked, rickshawed,
and tram-carred all over the city, visiting attractions designed for
tourists and also those ideal for sailors on leave, observing in detail
the heterogenous hubbub of the people and tasting the strange food
and drinks, losing himself in the variegated ambiance of the city,
then rushing back to stand watch in the harbor and wait for his
more boisterous shipmates to arrive, occasionally under their own
power.

He was guilty of a little contempt for most of the crew, not out of
any midwestern puritanism but simply because they did not seem to
have much fun. In Manila, for instance:

> The sailors, being paid off, went through the various stages
> of their usual drunkenness, had a gang fight in a dance hall,
> were threatened by many natives with bolo knives, fought
> among themselves and tore up the upholstery of the car in
> which they came to the dock. Tom was wild-eyed again and so
> was Evans, the airman-wiper. As if to crown the evening's
> folly with a magnificent gesture, Evans crashed into the galley
> of the ship and seized a butcher knife which had just been
> sharpened. His idea was to drive it into the wood bulkhead (or
> sidewall) of the galley in a feat of grandiose energy. Being
> drunk, his right hand slipped from the handle down the blade,
> and he cut the last two fingers clear through to the bone. Re-

sult: possible amputation, pain, many stitches, hand perhaps crippled for life. The crew has strange ways of gaining souvenirs of their voyage.

For many of the crew, such were standard events for every liberty, and sometimes in between, so that later Eberhart wrote to Dartmouth's President Hopkins,

> It always took acting to mingle with the sailors as one of them, and I did not always succeed, nor could I always enter unreservedly into their limited appreciations. But there was a sincerity and fellowship among these men, the very dregs of society from all standard conventional values, that had human worth and was good to know.

He nevertheless describes a Filipino Americanophile whom he met on the trip by saying that "to her the 'States' was something ultimate and unattainable, like the Blue Flower to Novalis, Nirvana to the Buddhists, and reason to all sailors." Having reason, if only a twenty-three-year-old, Dartmouth kind of reason, he was moderate in his pleasures and emerged without scars and without disease.

Out of Manila the *West Faralon* coasted about the Philippines, stopping at various small ports, and the metropolitan attractions of Shanghai and Manila faded before the beauties of the Asian landscape.

> From Siain we sailed to Tabaco, seventy miles away. Behind it rises the majestic volcano, Mayon, to a height of 8,970 feet. Trees and grass struggle a third way up the perfectly symmetrical cone, but from there to the crater no life grows in the deep crevices of loose lava and ash. The crater itself is small but distinct at the top. The mountain commands the land in all directions and the intense morning sunlight on it produces a startling and unreal effect. At night the black mass is outlined against the very bluest sky and is lovely under the stars.

He did not spend all his time gazing at Mt. Mayon, however. He had a few beers with his shipmates and, after narrowly missing one of their characteristic brawls, survived to observe the mysteries of cock-fighting.

> Two birds were killed outright as I watched. I bet fifty centavos each time, won once, and lost four pesos. One had a deep three-inch gash across its side which its owner sucked dry of blood by way of first aid.

On the other side of the volcano he watched the hordes of laborers loading copra and was introduced to a beautiful snake by its impressario, who tried to wind it around the sailor's neck, but his "occidental dubiety intervened."

Back in Manila, he had to leave the *West Faralon,* which was going back to America, and find another ship. He tried several, including one or two that would have reached England exactly in time for the opening of term at Cambridge, but they had full crews, and although one amiable captain suggested that he stow away, he decided to seek some more conventional alternative. Finally, a friend in Manila who was shipping copra on a German freighter named the *Etha Rickmers* managed to have him taken on as a passenger; but once at sea, he found himself put to work in the engine room, and about three days out of Cebu, he was told by the second mate, a burly, iron-jawed man with a grudge (left over from World War I) against Americans, that he was to work ten hours a day. He protested to the captain, who agreed and spoke to the mate. That worthy was outraged and told Eberhart that he would work ten hours or leave the ship at the next port.

> My blood was up. I felt the hot blood tingle on my cheeks, rush to my eyes. To hell with him. I'd be damned if I'd work ten hours. Shanghaied. I told him I was getting no pay, was supposed to be a passenger, didn't like the engine room, it was too hot, and that I refused flatly to work ten hours a day.
>
> It was a glorious climax. We shouted at each other for five minutes. All the people around came into sight. . . . It was a dramatic moment. The Second thought I was an experienced

engineer, that I was being paid. When the captain told him I didn't like the engine room he was wild because I had slighted his authority as captain of the engine room. I knew too little of the ancient feud between the captain of the engine room and the captain of the ship, a potent fact on the sea. . . .

He raved on and I followed him volley for volley. He couldn't understand me because I talked too fast and in English, and I couldn't understand him because he lapsed into guttural German all the time. But I kept restating my case, refused absolutely to work ten hours a day, and looked him in the eye. How high passions carry you out of yourself, give you a super-human power! I felt as if I could face the whole German army at that moment. I would jump overboard before I would give in.

He finally said, "All right, you come my watch, four to eight."

I said "all right." We both glowered and retreated.

When he showed up for the next watch, he was put to work painting the ceiling of the engine room, at a temperature of 120°F. For four hours he labored away, thinking of Michaelangelo, while sweat ran off his forehead into his eyes, soaked his clothes, and formed little pools at his feet, or dropped off him and salted the paint. But he refused to quit or complain. Finally his body began to rebel, just as his teutonic Nemesis came over, motioned him down and grunted, "ventilator." After a few moments' relief under the fan, he went back to work, remaining on that job for three weeks and finally earning the respect of the captain of the engine room. When he finished the task, he was given the somewhat less strenuous responsibility of keeping the machinery oiled, which he did the rest of the way to Port Said.

Their last port in the Far East was Sabang, a little island off the top of Sumatra.

It had one street, in a long curve along the sea, totally arbored with some filmy kind of trees, the most graceful trees I had seen. The shops were crowded and open. Chinese women with bound feet came slowly along, with parasols. Deepeyed, swarthy Egyptian young men with faces chiselled out of bronze, in long skirts, ambled by. Turks with fezzes and native brown-skin men and women. Back from the sea a tall hill towered, palm-covered. . . . I bought luscious bananas at the market. The town was so still, so utterly peaceful, you would think it set in some Utopian isle in a greener earth. There was no architecture; there were indeed the melancholy lotus-eaters; nature did everything for them, and the perfect palm trees were nature's cathedral, far more subtly perfect than any architecture of man.

From Sabang they steered for twenty days across the Indian Ocean and up into the Red Sea, which justified its name with one vermilion sunset. At Port Said he began to worry about getting to Cambridge on time. It was already October, and the *Etha Rickmers* clearly was not going to get him there. He finally decided to jump ship and buy passage for the rest of the trip.

. . . I picked up my old work shoes, dashed out on deck and with a feverish gesture flung them into the Suez Canal. They had climbed 5000 steel steps in the ship (by accurate arithmetic), they had climbed the soil of China, climbed mountains in Luzon, been soaked many times with the sweat of my body in the engine room heat of 120°: they knew the oil and grit of a steel floor and the rough ashes of a fireroom. They were cut down slipper-wise for coolness. They were torn at their outer sides in great gashes by steel rails, were ripped at their soles, lop-sided at their heels, and withal were weary of life and had served their time. I heaved them with a gesture of utter finality into the sea!

He caught the S. S. *Rajputana* for London and "came down with a fever the minute [he] saw the ship's doctor," thus missing most of the trip to England, but he arrived safely.

There was no mail at the American Express. And I sat alone in a dismal section of a coach going through the dank fog to

Cambridge. A loneliness was in my heart. . . . But there was gladness, too, because I had done, if hectically, what I set out to do, and Cambridge was the goal, the fulfillment of desire.

II

He arrived in Cambridge on October 14th, a week late for the term, and plunged immediately into the life of the town and of the university. The first thing he noticed was the multiplicity of rules coexisting with a maximum of freedom. "There are a thousand rules here," he wrote Dryden, "and all are left unnoticed, except for the barest formalities." Among these formalities, of course, was the wearing of academic robes, and he enjoyed the image of himself "going about on a bicycle [his] academic black robes flying in the fog." The one limit to his freedom was the regular curfew and although his college, St. John's, was liberal in this regard, he did occasionally have to scale the walls after hours.

For his first three terms he lived outside the college, at 12 Canterbury Street, and was delighted with this mildly ascetic part of his life. "My digs are very small," he reported to a sweetheart of Dartmouth days,

> on the outskirts of town. And there are no electric lights, telephones, or running water in my rooms. One mounts the stairs candle in hand to the chill welcome of an icy bed, even as Newton, and Milton, and Spenser, and Wordsworth did!

There in his "digs" he lunched alone "on milk, bread and jam," but as required by the rules, he took supper in the "medieval atmosphere" of the college Hall, where as a first year man he was required to sit near the door,

> surrounded by many oil paintings of the great of former centuries, and served by a small army of meticulously dressed servers, resplendent in broad expanses of white shirt front . . . all looking like country gentlemen.

Of course, he was not required to stay in the vicinity. Everyone in Cambridge had a bicycle. Indeed, he could never quite become reconciled to women riding bicycles, and men proceeding in the cold damp, with a muffler tightened about their necks, but otherwise uncovered in the chill—as if to keep their metaphysics warm.

There was a kind of socialism in the Cambridge bicycle economy; the undergraduates stole them so regularly that it had become the custom, when one found his bike missing, to simply take the next one handy. On one or another of these bicycles he took frequent trips into the countryside. Within two weeks of his arrival he rode the sixteen miles to Ely to visit the cathedral there, and he often went out of town to study under a hedge or atop a haycock, especially in his favorite retreat, the Gog Magog hills, where he went to read whenever the weather would let him.

In the community, or within easy reach of it in London, he spent a great deal of time in non-academic cultural activities: debates, plays, concerts. These became so commonplace that in his letters from the later months at the university he only mentions them in passing, but early in his Cambridge career, fresh from the relative cultural poverty of the sea, he describes them at great length. Perhaps the most exciting of these was his week with George Bernard Shaw and his works. He was to attend tea with his tutor one afternoon and had accepted an invitation to supper and the theater that evening, but Andrew Foster, a fellow Johnian whom he had known at Dartmouth, told him that Shaw and Chesterton were to debate in London that evening, with Belloc in the chair. They rushed frantically about to secure permission to be absent from Hall and from tutorial, and Eberhart made phone calls rudely but understandably breaking his dates in order to take advantage of this "opportunity of a lifetime." Then they rushed to the station and caught a train arriving in London two minutes before the hour of the debate, and they were without tickets:

> Andy suggested the back door. We went down a side street, wiggled in, and stood in the hall way. Before one of the doors leading into the orchestra were about ten people. We craned

our necks above these. There was G. K. Chesterton, just like his cartoons, sitting in a chair at the speaker's table. It was thrilling just to see him, looking like a Walrus and as corpulent as Falstaff. Where was Shaw? We looked into the other side of the window, through a slit of light between two men's heads, and there was the immortal man! I shall not forget that first sight of Shaw. He is very tall, as slender as a youth, with the long white beard, and his intense slender hands were making decisive gestures. We were both happy just to see him, but could hear no word. His famous wit was at work: every now and then the whole audience would burst into laughter. There was an energy, a dynamic force about the man clearly felt in just seeing him in the act of speaking.

Finally they managed, for a half crown, to get into the back row of standees, where it was possible to hear at least some of the proceedings.

It was a profound experience to hear the debate. Belloc said little, and was old looking, with iron gray hair and a stern face. Chesterton spoke in his unique paradoxes, the subject of the debate being on State Socialism. He made clever allusions to Shaw. And when Shaw arose, an elderly man but with the very fire of youth, you could have heard a pin drop. He combatted Chesterton's arguments, had the audience in an uproar at some keen jab at the man, then as quickly had them pondering a subtle point about political theory and actual practice, challenging his opponent with direct questions. The master mind at work! I was amazed at the economy of the man, the litheness of his figure at his age, and his noble head, with its fierce eyes and quick expressions, was good to look upon. . . . We took a taxi straight to the depot and were rolling toward Cambridge. . . . And we got to our digs just at midnight, the deadline! And the whole escapade cost nearly four dollars and is one of the landmarks in my experience. To have heard Shaw and Chesterton, and seen Belloc, all in one night, is indeed glorious.

All this was on a Friday night, and the following week he was able to see four of Shaw's plays in Cambridge.

As in most university towns, cultural activities and social life were frequently indistinguishable. This was especially true of his many visits to the Scroop Terrace home of Mrs. Granville Gordon, where he frequently went for tea or supper, music, and talk. It was for him Cambridge's leading salon, where he heard the best music and conversation of his Cambridge years and met many of his more interesting classmates, including the young C. P. Snow. Of course there was a good deal of still less formal social activity, such as the frequent and almost interminable arguments with fellow students and bridge "one night or less per week." Probably because he was carrying on an epistolary love affair at the time, there is not much in his letters about women at Cambridge, but there is enough to show that he did not go out with them very often. He missed the delicacy and elegance that he remembered in American girls, as well as the quiet, natural energy of the Orient.

> The women of Cambridge are abominable. They are buxom with pink complexions, gunny-sack garments, and awkward motions. And inasmuch as they are Brains the human values are largely lost sight of. I sometimes wonder how the race continues at all and believe it must be through medieval incantations to the god of fertility.

He gained perspective outside of Cambridge, however, and found that there were English girls worth looking at, and even in Cambridge he met Kathleen Raine, whom he remembered over three decades later as "a marvel to behold, all peaches and cream and misty hale look, a look never produced on this continent."

Perhaps the chief advantage of Cambridge was its nearness to London and the Continent, a fact Eberhart took advantage of almost every vacation, for there was a rule forbidding students to stay in town during vacations. His two most important vacations, in spring 1928 when he began the long poem that became his first book, and spring, 1929 when he finally met the object of his affections-by-letter, are discussed below. During the Christmas vacation of 1927 he packed up his books and went to London for several days; then Paris, Rouen, Chartres, then Paris and London again, living as cheaply as possible and reading for his examinations whenever he was not admiring scenery or museums or cathedrals. He took a similar trip the next Christmas, going as far as Majorca.

His finest vacation, however, was in the summer of 1928, when he covered much of both France and Ireland. He tried to get a job for the summer, and even considered signing on for another voyage, this time to Rangoon, but decided against it, settling instead for a position as tutor on an estate in Nottingham for one month, at two pounds ten shillings a week, plus food and lodging. Early in the summer he tramped all over the face of France, sleeping in cheap hotels or in hayfields, pleading with peasants for the latter privilege in deliberately broken French. After his tenure as tutor in August, he went to Ireland where, armed with an introduction from his Chicago friend, Alexander Greene, he met Stephens, Yeats, Gogarty (who called him a "genius and a poet"), and AE who later accepted a poem for publication in *The Irish Statesman*.[2] He wrote a full-column review of *A Bravery of Earth* in the last number of *The Irish Statesman* saying that Eberhart "may become important to American literature."

Amidst all this cultural, social, and ambulatory activity, it is sometimes hard to believe that he studied at all. "Cambridge life is so pleasant," he wrote shortly after his first Christmas vacation, "that it becomes a kind of sly game to put in consecutive hours of work." In another letter, he went so far as to say that Cambridge was "destructive in some respects, being so overbalanced by the social niceties that one must be either a practical go-getter or a rabid genius to get in any solid work at all." He nevertheless approved the English system; just a few weeks after the letters just quoted, he wrote the president of Dartmouth:

> The system of letting an undergraduate do his own work with only weekly supervision is indeed an enlightened custom, mak-

ing, I think, for more original and honest thinking by each
man.

And he occasionally found himself so immersed in his studies that
he was moved to remark, "This monkish existence is not whole."

Indeed, he spent many monkish hours, especially in his first year,
for he was admitted, without entrance exams, to take a three-year
degree after only two years' work. The system of examinations at
the end of each year applied almost as much pressure as the American system of multiple exams, for there was virtually no limit on
what might be asked, and his supervisor incessantly talked about
them with a "furious intensity . . . in awe as if death were an hour
away." For a while he maintained a dignified aloofness, writing to
an old fraternity brother,

> I derive immense pleasure from my studies, but the demoniac
> energy necessary to win a first in the Tripos is somewhat want-
> ing with my present values. . . . And at my age the value of
> slaving for mere marks is abhorrent, a means to an end, when
> I want the end itself.

Apparently, however, his supervisor's "furious intensity" began to
affect him. By the first week of March 1928 his tune was somewhat
changed:

> I have read all winter with pleasure, but apparently the Trip is
> an exercise in synthesis, and already I grow shaky, and burrow
> hectically into middle English to find out Langland's attitude
> toward the Friars, as if this had something vital to do with
> my relation to the universe.

and by April, with exams still more than a month away: "term and
exams hang over me like suffocation."

He managed to survive the anxiety, however, and the Tripos.
"The four days were strenuous indeed, filled with three hour papers
in the august Senate House on everybody from Chaucer to Hardy."

His handwriting was so poor that Richards and others read his examinations twice, a humane benefit he thought he would not have received in America. Although he did not win a first, he did not do badly; he earned the next division down, a "Second Class, Division I," which his tutor called "a very creditable performance;" and I. A. Richards sent his congratulations, informing him that there were only about a half a dozen Firsts, and those by men with two years and experience on Tripos exams. Once the dust had settled over the exams, his tutor wrote him to find out what his topic was to be for the D Litt. thesis. He had no illusions about his ability as a scholar, however, and it was with satisfaction that he wrote Richards a Trinity scholar's remark: "Of course your poems pulled you up."

The second year took him into world literature. He had to learn at least enough Italian and Old French to bluff, and by February he was already nearly exhausted:

> Last year I came within an inch of a First on Two years' work in one; this year, doing a single year's work, I could not, I think, kame [sic] a First with all effort (Firsts are for technical scholars), so the marks don't matter much. . . . How I shall manage the Italian I don't know; to date I am a complete failure in it.

But he kept at it, and somehow won another Two, One.

At least as important as the subjects studied and the exams taken were the personalities with which he came in contact. Hugh Sykes Davies seemed "the most brilliant of the very young students," and Eberhart has recorded elsewhere his acquaintance with William Empson.[3] He took most advantage, of course, of the teachers who were available to him. One of his earliest enthusiasms at Cambridge was Quiller-Couch, at this time "a very old man, with great jowls and a firm lip, pipe in hand." It was perhaps the least formal class at the university. "The chairs promptly filled . . . and the overflow sat informally on the floor," without robes.

> The hour went like a minute! And you can bank that every Wednesday night I shall be absorbing wisdom from a most

venerable, aged, and humorous man, considering the Q course one of the real privileges in Cambridge.

At a much later and more crowded lecture, he

> gazed over the black gowns to the great skull of Gilbert Murray. He talked about Euripides, he read from his own translations, he interspersed with quiet humor, and the dignity of the man, his deep eyes and age, the strong jaw and towering forehead, made me almost believe it was a Greek standing there, speaking about life and death in soft tones of awe.

More important than these were the dons with whom he had close personal contact. Martin Charlesworth was his tutor, and his supervisors were W. P. Barrett in his first year and F. R. Leavis his second. F. L. Lucas helped to criticize some of his poems. He especially liked the "benign and funny don [Mansfield] Forbes." Of Leavis he said,

> He, like Forbes, is a kind of intellectual cocktail. . . . his dogmatic ideas are only realized to be such when you are cooled from the first intoxication of his nervous organization. I like him, because I have to be on strict guard not to be taken in. . . .

He comments at length on Leavis and Forbes in another letter:

> F. R. Leavis is an English don, about thirty-something, a light, lithe, nervous, one who sleeps not . . . and is now a seething mass of brains, often very jumbled, I think. Erratic; a man with an immoral glut of books in his study: such an appalling number of books that when I entered I literally thought they must be sapping his mind hour by hour, how could it be else? . . . He is the most personal don I know; brave in the sense that he makes many enemies, slays people right and left. . . . He condemns Lucas, and flouts Forbes. Forbes is, next to Richards, the most vital mind: a crazy looking Scot,

with tremendous enthusiasms, and an electrifying instant vocabulary, which turns on remarkable periods. Forbes, supposed to give a course on a special period, 1770–1805, spends the entire time analyzing two poems by Blake! and builds up his own amazing system of interpretation. Very funny, too, he. But you see the fallacies in Leavis; a biting iconoclast, unbalanced. I have had him for supervisions this year, and go to war about once a fortnight.

In the same letter, he calls I. A. Richards "the profoundest mind in Cambridge, in English, and a tremendous, reserved, human, dominating-by-reticence man," and it was from Richards that he recieved most at Cambridge. In February 1928 he had just had two poems accepted by J. C. Squire for the *London Mercury.* "I am wild with delight," he wrote Squire, "like a small boy with a new drum at Christmas." It was in this euphoric state that he found the courage to send poems to Richards, with considerable diffidence. When Richards responded favorably to the poems, saying he had "got a good deal out of them," Eberhart replied gratefully, and suggested that he had had some trouble in reaching the don: "One might wait all his life for someone to introduce him to God, and when they got there, God would probably be out. Deities need assiduous tracking down." Two days later the Richardses invited him to tea.

In the months that followed, up until Eberhart left Cambridge in 1929, he gave many pieces to Richards, and they often met to "chat" about them.[4] A sense of their relationship in those days can be gathered from the sequel to Richard's remark about Eberhart in a university publication called *The Granta,* where he accused the young man of a tendency, according to Eberhart, to "suck his poetic thumb." Eberhart planned, as a joke, to show the master that there were no toothmarks.

> Mrs. Richards called me Saturday noon for lunch, [he wrote afterwards] so I entered the pleasant sanctum directly opposite Kings; it was a sunny, warm day, and we had coffee after lunch in the sunshine of the window facing the Gate of Kings.

Then we walked, the three of us, for over an hour along the backs, noticing the upsprung early crocuses. . . . I actually showed my ungnashed thumb to I. A.; in an instant he said, wryly, "Oh, so you haven't grown teeth yet!" This reduced me, and my dull brain couldn't answer. Then there was delicious discussion; he asked me what I thought he meant. I said a poetic thumb supposed some ability, but that the sucking idea connoted infancy. He said he meant the figure as a compliment; but still that I was enjoying too intensely, perhaps, my particular poetic lollypop. He said he thought "Caravan of Silence" was the best poem in the book [*Cambridge Poetry, 1929*]. . . . It was highly amusing, to be walking with him and his wife in the sun along the backs, and taking him to task for his criticism.

There is no evidence to suggest that Eberhart revised a great deal under his mentor's criticisms. Richards, guided by Coleridge's injunction, "Let us not impose an act of uniformity against poetry," never had any idea of "shaping" the young poet's work, but simply encouraged that work generally, with attention and praise, and tried to discourage certain tendencies, especially a "content with chaos," a complacency about disorder and unintelligibility in his lines. Clearly, it was this gentle advice, this encouragement, actually simply in the fact of his friendship (a friendship that lasts to the present day), that the great critic gave most to the young poet.

III

Eberhart's career as a poet had already begun when he came to Cambridge and met Leavis, Forbes, and Richards. During the months before he left Chicago, Harriet Monroe accepted some poems for *Poetry*,[5] two of which won honorable mention in *Poetry's* annual competition. He continued to send poems to the magazine and in May of 1928 received a letter from Miss Monroe, saying in part:

I am so glad your muse is taking a fresh start. Of the poems you send me I am keeping:

The Kiss of Stillness (but cutting out the last stanza—or maybe that last three.)
Sumatra Shore Leave (but cutting out 2 lines above the last 4.)
Wentworth Place (a sonnet)
Night Watch on the Pacific (only no. I, or possibly I and II.)
L'Après-midi d'un Faune

When Eberhart complained about the cutting of the poems, she replied, "You asked why these omissions—merely because these lines are poor, they injure the poems; whatever your excellent motive, you don't get it into good poetic form." The poems appeared, with Miss Monroe's editorial liberties taken, in the December 1929 issue.[6]

While at Cambridge, he also had poems accepted by the *London Mercury* and *The Irish Statesman,* and a new magazine at Cambridge, *Experiment.* The high point of his career at Cambridge, when he received some public recognition as a poet, came early in 1929 with the publication of *Cambridge Poetry, 1929,* and of the March 1st issue of *The Cambridge Review.* Eberhart had three poems in *Cambridge Poetry:* "Maze," "Nannette," and "Caravan of Silence."[7] He was not satisfied with this representation. Christopher Saltmarshe had asked for some poems after seeing some of those Richards had at the time. Eberhart

> finally gave in six, on condition that the book would be, as represented, a serious attempt to obtain the best work in Cambridge, to give half a dozen poets a dozen poems or so. The editor didn't have courage . . . thus the book is glutted with bad stuff, and is no better than the general run of Oxford and Cambridge anthologies. Because I am unknown, perhaps a little out of self-protection too, Salty saw to it that three of my poems were cut out; he notified me in January. And it did make me feel as contentious and little-with-wrath as a schoolboy, hurt at the simpering personalism connected with a book.

Whatever the editors' motives, and one doubts that they were as sinister as the contentious Eberhart thought them, the young American's right to better representation was supported by the opinion of F. R. Leavis in a review in *The Cambridge Review*. "It is plain to me," he wrote of Eberhart,

> that he ought to have had at least as much room as anyone. He not only merits more generous representation; he is peculiarly handicapped by not having it. For he is so original, so strongly individual, that we need a good deal of his work in order to learn, and become familiar with, his idiom, his characteristic rhythms, and his habits of imagery. Half of the contributors could have been spared to make room for more of him. . . .[8]

The only other poet in the anthology singled out for comment by Leavis is William Empson.

Most of his work between spring of 1928 and spring of 1929 went into one poem.

> During spring vac I took a ten day bicycle trip, staying in little villages each night at old pubs, drinking with the red-nosed antiquities that lined the benches to find the romance-stuff of their old tales. But mostly the tales dwindled into greetings and goodbyes and refillings of pipes. . . . I had a few immortals along with me, probably out of mistrust of the actual, and at night read Shakespeare, Milton, Donne, Keats, and Chaucer. The result of this ten day trip alone was the unfolding of my first long poem, nameless yet and a recreating, at least an attempt to recreate, various states of mind. It had assumed the length of a thousand lines by the time the Tripos scared me away from it. . . . It is now in the hands of god I. A. Richards for criticism.

He worked on the poem, which was to become *A Bravery of Earth,* throughout the following year. In March of 1929 he wrote his father that it was nearing completion, and by July he was ready to submit it to a publisher. Mansfield Forbes put him in touch with Piers Thompson of Jonathan Cape, and a month later Thompson wrote him:

As I told you, Edward Garnett our reader is very interested in A BRAVERY OF EARTH. He does not think we are likely to do anything but lose money over it but feels that it ought to receive our imprint. I have read it myself and liked the part immensely which derives from your journey around the world. The earlier philosophical part I must admit beats me. . . .

I have talked to Mr. Cape about the manuscript and he is prepared to publish it.

The book came out from Cape's in March of 1930. Cape-Smith imported sheets and published the book in New York later the same spring.

The "various states of mind" that the poem attempts to create are defined as a series of "awarenesses," chronicling the poet's growth from childhood to adulthood:

Into the first awareness trembling,
Girded with mortality;
Into the second awareness plunging,
Impaled upon mentality;
Into the third awareness coming
To understand in men's action
Mankind's desire and destiny,
Youth lies buried and a man stands up
In a bravery of earth.[9]

The first awareness is characterized primarily by a delight in physical sensation:

Tender-coming time, with sight,
Sound, and with smell, touch,
Loosed the actual world, gave
Me increase, brimmed my growth, rushing
Diffusive life. [*p. 16*]

There seem to be two stages to this first awareness. In the first stage the poet seems wholly unaware of death, does not even perceive the realities of existence:

Love without idea, this is,
The voluntary acceptance. [*p. 24*]

The poet is aware of death in the second stage, but insists that:

What man calls death is only
Change . . .
. . .
And we shall change and go,
But life creates for ever.

So in the first stage at its highest development, the poet says,

Through intuition life and death
Were unified. . . . [*p. 31*]

He soon realizes, however, that what he has called "intuition" is a
function of desire, a pretentious kind of wishful thinking; he intuits
unity because he wants to. And yet this realization of solipsism does
not depress him; on the contrary, it gives him a sense of power in
his ability to create his own world.

The mind flashed on me! The mind burst forth!
And the sudden second awareness was come.
Thought with memory fortified
Could subtly interweave
Existing things with things desired
And build illusion out of dream. [*p. 34*]

But this approach to life also fails, after attempts to apply it in various ways, in the face of real misfortune.

There is no appeal from suffering.
Tired Agony with glassy eye
Sits watching the sufferer endure.
Nor is there torment imagined by men
That equals day, on day, on day,

And lingering week, on week, on week,
And month, on month, on moving month
Of pain consuming human life
In stopless march to certain death.   [*p. 43*]

. . .

They carry her slowly to the grave
As the spent sun slopes to the west.
Step slowly. This is a time to be brave.
(O laughing one we loved the best!)
The glad blithe days are gone,
For ever over and gone. Step slowly,
As the coffin curves across the lawn.

. . .

   Forget the rest
With the coffin, stiff in the hands of man
(O laughing one we loved the best!)
Edging between the gravestones. Then,
O then all's lost—and only the smell
Of earth and the touch of earth are known.
Now, nearing the pit, forget how well
The gods confound us, petals blown
By the rude wind, blossoms torn from the stalk—
And all that we know is but dimly guessed.
Step slowly. Be still, be brave as you walk,
(O laughing one we loved the best!)
As you step to the end of all man knows
And stand on the verge of nothing.   [*pp. 47–48*]

From here the poet progresses into the third awareness.

Out of the maelstrom world I groped
To find new freedom through the mind's
Creation of a tangible form
For its desires. And thus I chose
The wilderness hill of art, to climb
Its thorny paths toward the high
Sublime sky-piercing crags and there,
Serene, be summited with visions

Where no chaos is. For art,
. . . .
Defends the lingering god in man. [*p. 53*]

The chief thrust of the third awareness, then, is to re-create the peace
of the first awareness; and although natural creation is sufficient
unto itself, the artist is compelled to will his own creation.

Soon, soon, my limbs in eagerness
Pressed on upon the hill of art;
For waking from that languorous
Brief accord with the natal earth,
That solitude contemplative
That lives more like a pulse of blood
In pulse with rocks and trees, than like
A thrust of thought that gave it being,
Now loosed from this serenity,
As if a dissonance had shocked
The fragile poise of harmony
And it, desire, had been the vibrance
That shaped the ghosts of my creation,
I waking now felt chill and fever
Racking me through with my will's desire
To represent a world less known
Than in that calm.
. . .
I climbed on the hill! Yet the principle
Of growth will gather within the mind
Sometime like sap within a tree;
And it is full with meaning then,
Nor needs its own creation then
To feed it, nourished by the same
Vitality that is in crystal,
Rock, plant, water, beast, and man.
But sun brings on the overflow,
But will creates the urge to art. [*pp. 59–60*]

Then he studies great artists and thinkers of the past from Socrates
to Nietzsche, turning finally to the study of himself; becoming

at last fully aware of his own insignificance from the perspective of eternity, he can seek truth in "the full impersonal."

> But the mind turns upon itself
> With a gimlet eye that drills and drills
> Till the final membrane of being is pierced
> At the nothingness at the end of thought.
> Not freedom freed, but life's negation,
> Like the unconsciousness before birth,
> And the slow death after death,
> The state unequalled till this hour,
> Willed annihilation won. [*p. 68*]
> . . .
> Let the mind break down its passion,
> Let the mind outgrow love,
> Let mankind be called a stone;
> Let thought die out to the last star,
> And the spirit of man be found on the sun
> Burning, out of astounding gloom.

> Into the solemn stillness going,
> Into the fixed impersonal
> I go, where is no human mind
> To fall down on a human woe.
> Beyond our humanness and love,
> To the full impersonal I go. [*p. 69*]

Then, a few pages later, begins the lyrical account of his voyage.

> Dawnward and sunsetward
> The desert stretched from Santa Fe
> To the mute circumference of the world,
> All gold. [*p. 78*]

He is soon on the ship and

> Ten thousand tons of steel
> Slid out to sea like a birch canoe. [*p. 82*]

He catalogues the crew, ending with a sharp contrast:

> "Toothless," the scum, the glory,
> Lord of the sea wolves.
>   . . .
> "Toothless," naked energy
> The brute misery of man
> In the dregs of destiny.
> "Slim," sensitive, conceals
> Delicate humanity;
> The mask is fixed to the fact;
> The face, set to seaward,
> Sees wonder, mystery, miracle,
> Understands, and is silent;
> Sees philosophy in a gull,
> Meaning in the sea rhythm,
> Turns among the sailors firm
> In the one feature of acquiescence.
> "Slim," secret among blasphemers,
> Blasphemes, but the warm stars
> Find him on the nightwatch,
> Light up the tremor of hands
> At the inner joy of the sea,
> Release the surprising culture,
> Moods, deeps, desire, despair.   [*pp. 83–84*]

Then his own work:

> In the nightwatch he went to the bridge,
> Took over the wheel, and steered for a star!
>   . . .
>   And the wheelman felt
> The subtle pulse of the great ship,
> The throb of the iron heart beating,
> Grew sensitive to the slow turn
> Of the prow from port to starboard,
> Wheeled with his arms and shoulders
> The smooth spokes left to right

Anticipating the veer to port
Even before the starboard extreme,
Fixing his eyes on the one star,
Steering the ship for a golden star.

. . .

Green light to starboard, red light to port.
The pilot house bell, the fo'csle bell.
"The lights are burning bright, sir."
The mate cannot know he means the stars!
He makes a trumpet of his hands,
He pours his throat on the wind:
"The lights are burning bright, sir,"
But night smothers his voice
With the rough, gloved hand of silence. [*pp. 85–88*]

Three long passages, finally, seem to embody the poem's conclusions:

The brute propeller slushes on,
Grinds water and the soul,
Clop, clop, clop, clop,
And will not let him sleep,
One, two. What we create
Takes our hot mind and preys on us.
The goalward mechanism, three,
Four, one, two, three,
Four, goalward mechanism,
Preys on its creator, destroys
The peace that has no goal.
The mind creates its own foe.
One, two, " 'Tis destiny." [*pp. 89–90*]

The description of the chain locker comes closer to a poetic realization of the intensity of his sense of destiny.

Down to the chain locker, mole!
Sweat in the black heat, rat!
The din begins, the great chain

Groans to pull up China, the inert
Brute depth of ocean.
Stow her down, "Slim." The monstrous
Snake with metallic fangs
Ponderously looms, horrible,
Down from the skyless hole, writhes
With destructive slowness to the pit.
Our four hands train the head,
The dull, powerful body down
Into the abyss, dangerously
Balancing on an iron beam.
We slave with link in dead link,
The remorseless power and dark,
Overwhelming, force of the chain.
The oppressive doom comes on;
On; on; we sweat in the trap
With muscle and brain, to hold the brute
Thing that noses and unnerves,
Stopless, without change, with fatal
Rhythm and mad noise. [*p. 98*]

Such passages are interspersed with description of the beauties of
the Orient, of which the passage beginning, "The bells of a Chinese
temple sang," reprinted in *Collected Poems,* is a good example, and
the poet seems to take consolation in the working out of destiny
amidst self-renewing beauty. The poem ends on an affirmative note.

A man stark naked firing a boiler!
A god in the hell-hole of a ship!
. . .
The arc of your arm as you swing
Is the curve of the earth;
Shovel in, shovel in time
By the brawny arm-arced shovelful!
Feed the wild demon
The hardy morning earth,
Elemental, fresh,
Palpitant, locked in trees.

Give her the bitter taste
Of volcanic wastelands,
Let her bolt æons
Of sulphurous years.
Shovel in time! quick! quick!
Banquet her hunger with time!
Flex your steel muscles,
Harden your whole being
For the lift of ten billion
Years into the fires!
You quiver with tempestuous
Harmony; you are a thing
Of fire! fire-like! Giant! Giant!
This is the splendid reincarnation. [*pp. 125–27*]

The reviewers agreed with Piers Thompson that the earlier sections of the book were turgid and obscure; and also like Thompson they found considerable delight in the voyage passages, "filled," in the words of one, "with character and colors." [10] Most reviews also agree, however, that the poem as a whole shows promise, comparing it, sometimes favorably, with Wordsworth's *Prelude,* and finding clearly expressed "the development of man's awareness . . . into an impersonal and objective attitude toward life." [11] William Rose Benét finds that "remarkable intuitions flash forth" [12] and another critic that "he touches ecstasy more closely and more often than do most of the poets of this century." [13]

This critical acceptance is, however, far from unqualified. One critic attacks the plan of the poem in principle, suggesting that its "pseudo-philosophical and autobiographical presentation of the influences molding a poet's life" is the unfortunate result of "too much academic study of English poetry." [14] Most reviewers, however, meet the poem on its own ground and severely criticize what they feel to be a lack of control, Richards's "content with chaos." Benét calls the language not "very distinguished;" Edith Walton complains about the "long abstract passages in which the quickening image is lacking; " and Harriet Monroe suggests that one

should "read rapidly" for "general effect and [with] some attention
to rich growths here and there," but step swiftly over "rank patches
of weeds." [15]

None of the reviewers attempts to come to grips with the poem's
content in any but very vague terms: objective, affirmative, optimis-
tic. Only Richard Church has any advice on the relationship of the
thought to the poetry; Eberhart, says Church, while possessed of
richness and complexity of life, "has yet to learn that desolating
emptiness of the poet; that poverty which can render all things
without staining them in self. . . . but his is a fault that contains
great promise." [16] This indulgent, almost patronizing tone, finding
considerable fault but recognizing great potential, dominates most
of the reviews of *A Bravery of Earth*.

IV

Sometime in 1926 or 1927, W. H. Cowley, a Dartmouth friend, sent
some of Eberhart's poems to a young woman named Louise R.
Hawkes, the daughter of a wealthy linoleum executive who later became United States Senator from New Jersey. She was soon in correspondence with the poet, beginning a love affair, largely epistolary, that lasted for two years and reverberated in Eberhart's life for
a decade. They exchanged a few letters during his voyage and his
first year at Cambridge, and by June of 1928 they had established a
rapport which included an agreement not to meet one another, for
as she put it, "The possibility of our communion away from the material world fascinated me as a kind of revelation of intellectual paradise."

They soon set up, Eberhart wrote Cowley, "a great Myth-by-Let-
ter" complete with ideal images of one another with special names:
Ricco and Maia. Had she stayed in America, this arrangement
might have endured, but she came to Europe to write a dissertation
on Italian children's literature, and Eberhart soon became impatient
with the abstraction of the relationship. In October of 1928, he sent
an ultimatum:

... You have bewitched me ... you have torn down my
strength to resist ... you have humbled me, and I have all
the strength of your spirit, the enthusiasms of your mind, and
your feminine grace out of thin air!

Then he demanded "actual companionship" or "complete forget-
ting." But she stood fast; unwilling to sully their Ideal with reality,
and fearing that she would disappoint him, she called his bluff with
an abrupt "Servez-vous, Monsieur."

Of course he decided that he could best suit himself by suiting her
and abided by her wish. Although they were both in Paris at the
same time in December of 1928, they did not meet, but their affec-
tions continued to escalate, though in very different ways. For him
Maia was "a name all compact of sweet heart, lover, beloved, adored.
. . ." And although he had never met her, he became jealous of her
other friends: ". . . the absurd possessive instinct grows on me, even
at this distance. . . ." When he continued to insist on meeting her,
she chided, "Is it that you don't believe in the reality of my unreality . . . or do you fear the unreality of my reality!" A little later, still
enjoying the game, she defined their relationship: "you Seeker after
Heights, and Maia woven beautiful with dreams. . . . I make you
poet-high-priest of my strangely vague and fervid Searching-after-
Beauty." Just a few days before they met, finally, she said, "Anatole
France wrote something about 'his loving with fervor whenever he
found the personification of his ideas.' That's what I think of love.
. . ." She cited this as an argument for their remaining in the great
Symbolic Unreal, for she was still unsure about meeting him; but
"don't you see, dear," he replied, "that for me *real* things themselves
become symbols." That seems to have settled the matter.

In any event, he went to meet her at Taormina on March 25,
1929. She laid elaborate plans to ensure a properly dramatic atmosphere for this entry into reality, leaving careful instructions for him
to take a certain route at a certain time to meet her. He still remembered it thirty-two years later:

I went to meet . . . her at the Greek Theatre where I would have come up from Scylla and Charybdis but she would be facing Etna and I had better look back twice at those waters but she would be wearing green as of the earth with her back turned to me but if I mentioned a certain name it would be at my peril and she would turn. I called. She turned. And the next two weeks were heaven.

After the vacation, Louise wrote recalling their good times, and her letter should be quoted at length, because those two weeks were not only the climax of their romance but also their only considerable length of time together.

Remember? Saturday we had spent in Girgenti, Girgenti of the "tawny gold temples." Girgenti of the red and purple cabbages, the crazy cobbly streets running up, running down, as witlessly as the brigade of young Sicilians who charged, be-clubbed and shouting, around a corner—revival of the "Sicilian Vespers" of the 13th c. . . . . . A crumbling baroque doorway, and a once-pretentious courtyard sighing for the past now and then. A long road moving to the plains that reach the sea, holding the aged-gold temples in their lap, beckoning us down to laugh and pray and live, and come away, we too, more old, more gold.

Under a gray sky we saw the temples, distant shadows of the past. . . . Simplicity and majesty and "fragments of an-other life." A walk along the rocky path beside the catacombs, with "blood flowers" of the tiny blossoms, and sunlight in you and me. . . . Remember the rock you climbed? The view of the gray sea from the terrace before the temple of Juno while I sat watching you in your delight, and praying to the still-loved Queen of Gods to make me more your Maia and less the girl who is Louise. . . .

Easter morning came, Day of all Days, came crowned with sunlight, trailing the earth with a thousand flower colors. What was it made me love you as if it were the first day of my life! . . . . Remember the Easter cake with the lambs of God and the banners and bushes and whirly-gig flowers in sugar-stuff which I had to taste because of the friendliness of our ten compartment-mates? And the receiving line we held as they all climbed out, each shaking hands with us and wishing "Buon viaggio e Buona Pasqua!" We *did* have a good trip and a glorious Easter, didn't we Ricco! I wonder how much their wishes had to do with it!

They continued to write affectionately and she visited Cambridge briefly in June, staying with Mrs. Gordon. He introduced her to all his friends, took her walking in York and Lincoln and punting on the Cam, but the days were crowded with people and events, and it seemed that almost as soon as she got there she was gone. He followed her to Paris for a few days before she sailed for America. He was irretrievably in love, and not with a vision but with a woman:

> I am most sure that I love Louise, because one's senses do not err. . . . A mental loyalty to the Ghost Maia is possible, but it does not mean as much to me, as the present, felt, realized love of you.

But she had a lofty concept which she refused to abandon. "It is with *Ideal* love that we are concerned," she wrote shortly after their Sicilian adventure.

> Why? I am not certain, except that we think ourselves more capable of its realization than many people, because the risk is greater and the task more arduous and renders the Goal more unattainable in its magnificence.

After her Cambridge visit she still wrote of their love as "mystical" and admitted, "I seem to be moving away from you with the same steady, inevitable motion which brought me more and more certainly to you through last year."

They met again at her family's home in New Jersey and she went with him to meet his family in Chicago, on her way to California; but her letters fell off after she started teaching at Scripps College, while he continued through his months in a New York slaughter-house and as a tutor at Palm Beach, Florida. In March of 1930, she wrote, "Maia is asleep. I prefer to think her asleep. I am terribly and wearily American in the rush and routine of my life here [at Scripps], and I see no escape." In April she decided to marry a colleague, and although she changed her mind temporarily, Eberhart was crushed. In July she wrote from Europe: "I shall never marry you, Ricco, and I shall always love you as the expression of what I most aspire to." Three days later he wrote to Cowley,

> The prison walls of money, family, and convention, cast a dank shade around her, which she cannot overthrow, because she has never felt the surpassing warmth of complete freedom.

On June 18, 1932, she finally married Morgan Padelford.

It is impossible to judge just what this romance meant to Eberhart's life. It brought on some poems, including a spate of sonnets, written between May 11 and June 11, 1932, which were published in 1967,[17] and he continued to correspond with Louise and to think about her for many years. As late as 1938 he wrote bitterly that she had just "sailed on another paper voyage to some other tinsel destination. . . . I still can't think of her without wanting to get out a bomb. . . ." A friend wrote in 1939, in response to a letter that is not preserved: "I thought your Maia letter rather tragic, I cannot understand your constant remembrance of something dead and gone."

The intensity and duration of Eberhart's feeling is almost strange in view of the fact that they were never together for more than two weeks, and that their total time together during the whole romance does not exceed much more than a month. Yet these very facts are perhaps the key to what happened. In their long, intimate letters on life and art and poetry and the Ideal, they constructed images of one another that had only a peripheral relation to reality. In all fairness, it must be emphasized that she was much more aware of this than Eberhart. It was not so much that she loved him less as it was that she loved him in a different way. Her feeling for him was largely cerebral, spiritualized, an embodiment of aspiration, while his for her added to all this a visceral urge for total communion. Maia became inevitably Louise, while Ricco remained immutably Ricco, and she had the truth when she wrote in 1940, "perhaps I was right years ago in believing that our medium was the Written Word."

V

For Eberhart's life, the years 1927–1929 represent the final stages of youth's necessary, if temporary, rejection of the ideals of an older generation. He had found sanction for such independence in the liberalism of Dartmouth, and his voyage finished the process. "I have thrown off all creeds," he wrote at the end of his odyssey, "orthodox Christianity, modern ideals of economic success, the desire for worldly acclaim." Even the old Duo spirit did not escape the purge: "There is of course entirely too much organization in the world," he wrote a fellow Duo a few weeks after his arrival in Cambridge.

> Duo may even harm the young by instilling in them this worship of organization, which . . . cheats them out of any understanding of our materialism as it is in true perspective. We have sold our souls to the devil and capitalism.

He also wrote his father, "There is nothing absolute about Christian dogma. All you have to do is go to the Orient to realize this." By February he could write a Chicago friend,

> To be away from America has given me the best perspective view of it that I have ever had—and I am not eager to return. . . . I have renounced the philosophy in which I was born, and will not compromise my ideals with American materialism.

His time at Cambridge provided these ideals, which he refused to compromise. He had absorbed massive doses of intellectual experience as he had before absorbed the sensations and impressions of his voyage. Cambridge convinced him of the importance of poetry to his own life and to the life of man, and allowed him the opportunity to gauge that importance and assess the means of fulfilling it. "Until I came to Cambridge," he wrote Richards after graduation,

> I was too impetuous, and wrote wildly and badly out of fierceness. It can be done. But another and subtler method, a control of awareness in which the mind peers down on one's brain and heart, seems to be better. The leisure of Cambridge gave me my discovery of Milton, a new Wordsworth, and Donne. This same leisure, with the little knowledge it brought, cast upon me that actual terror of the ideal which comes from a love of the masters. I fear one's humility would make one weep, if he did not forget, momentarily, the terror of the ideal, and standing in his unique relation to experience, write as master there, because it is necessary, because everything is new.

"I become increasingly aware that my highest destiny is in the creation of beauty," he wrote his father,

> that what happens to me financially or physically, does not matter so much, if my intellectual and spiritual development can go on. . . . but the star is a high one, I am a rebel anyway, and not conventional, and my greatest love is for what I can create. Thus I expect a hard life, but I will not renounce my ideals, if I have to fall into the gutter of the world, or vagabond to the moon.

In the same letter he speaks of marriage as "a means to comprehensive life, but not an end in itself. Comprehensive life is the end." Cambridge, with its leisure, its cultural opportunities, its constant emotional and intellectual stimulations, seemed to be such a life, and for years afterward it remained what he still called it in 1941, a "dream of life as it ought to be!"

CHAPTER FOUR
1929–1932

On August 10, 1929, Eberhart left England and about ten days later arrived in the United States. He spent three days at the Hawkes home in Montclair, N. J., then met his father and stepmother [1] in New York and went with them to Chicago. He accompanied his father on a business trip to Iowa and found his way to Austin:

> It appeared that I had acquired the character of a legendary hero, and since there are only ten thousand odd (very) souls in the town, I endured a spate of hand-shaking and what-of-Europeing. But when the solemn superintendent of the High Schools formally requested me to "give a speech" on the Constitution before the assembled youth of the town, I fear my introversion was not understood.

In Chicago he met W. H. Cowley, who later declared himself "disappointed" with the results of two years' absence:

> . . . When you strode into my office that August afternoon with your pipe, your three months' growth of hair, your collegiate coat, your unbuttoned neck, you mouthed as pretty a dialect as any Londoner. More than that your mannerism struck me as affected, and your heavy-fisted denunciations of things American impressed me as much too Olympian.

Typical "heavy-fisted denunciations" have already been quoted, and there is considerable evidence that Eberhart's attitude toward his native land at this time was at best patronizing: ". . . to come again into this dense atmosphere of Americanism appalls me, and calls for humour, tolerance, and large laconic smile."

Although this condescension was partly a result of an Anglophilia acquired at Cambridge, it was also very much an expression of his reluctance to return to the necessities of life in the material world. A few days after he had written his father from England that he would not renounce his ideals, he had written to his friend Foster much less confidently:

> You see, I don't have enough faith in my potential future as a "creative artist" (the name mocks) to be entirely self-reliant, entirely inner-dynamic. . . . Yet I am not crass enough to return to the brazen idolatry of some obvious "success." . . .

By September, after he had begun job-hunting in New York, his sense of reality was still more highly developed:

> I am too near the gaunt necessity of making a living to dare any from-ivory-tower ideas about America. Certainly, you can't kick against the pricks, unless you are subsidized, or want to be a complete vagabond. The last presents itself as an heroic gesture of living: but certain things mean so much to me, that my Way lies in the difficult course of compromise, to win the world and win the soul both. . . . O, my insides are all right, I am worth something to myself, but the adjustment to the American world is rather monstrous.

His "compromise" between the world and the soul, however, involved concessions mainly on the part of the world. "You demonstrate," he wrote a few days later to an old friend of his mother, "that one can't have his cake and eat it too, a tenet that I do not as yet live by." He had at least learned by this time, nevertheless, that one could not stand aloof from economic life. As he put it, in another letter, "Not to enter the millrace here allows one the profits of drowning."

He made his first attempt to enter the millrace early in September, when he came to New York with letters from his connections in England, hoping that these would help him get a job in publishing. For days he trudged from firm to firm, gathering regrets and more letters of introduction. One company offered him a job as a traveling book salesman, and Bobbs-Merrill promised to let him read manuscripts at three dollars apiece, but no one had a steady job in publishing. By the end of the month, he was almost ready to give up and return to Chicago, where his brother might have been able to find something for him.

Finally, though "not too keen on the packing house game," he took a position in the New York branch of Adolph Gobel, Inc., the firm for which his father was working, with the idea of starting at the bottom and working his way to some real material prosperity. For almost three months, he went to work at 4:30 every morning in a slaughterhouse, first making production tests on the killing-floor in Manhattan and later in Brooklyn checking hams in and out, sitting "all day on a barrel in a cold place, just above freezing. . . . ," for $35 a week.

> There, there is a symbol, plunged into the maelstrom. The cries of dying pigs, the gleaming rich blood in a strange exultation released from the deft probe in the neck, are cries into the soul, are dear and terrible to know.

Despite the symbolic value of the experience, he felt "stunted, unable to live inwardly, cut off from felicities, sunk in a well of uninteresting work, and impaled upon the spikes of harsh reality all day." He soon came to consider the slaughterhouse "a vision of hell actual."

He did manage to find time to read at least eight manuscripts for Bobbs-Merrill and wrote some reviews for the *New Republic,* at two cents per word, but there was clearly not much money in the work, and he apparently was not very good at it. He once confessed to "messing up" two reviews and added, "but even Richards told me I couldn't write prose." After Eberhart left New York, Edmund Wilson, who was then an editor of the *New Republic* and had evidently taken a liking to the young poet, wrote that there would be no more reviews because, "I will have to wrestle with you considerably over anything you write and get you to revise it," and this could not be done by mail. In the same letter Wilson asked if he was "absolutely broke," and scribbled at the end, "Let me know if you are really up against it. . . .," further suggesting that his poetic promise, rather than his prose talent, were involved in his work for the magazine.

Determined to escape the slaughterhouse, he wrote his former supervisor at Cambridge asking if he knew of any teaching positions that might be open, lamenting that "It seems such a waste of spirit at this age, to undergo a long siege of trial and error, before finding a niche of peace and some power." He also wrote I. A. Richards, who was teaching in China, and only vigorous assertions that there was absolutely no money in it kept him from joining his old mentor. Then his application at an employment agency finally paid off; he got a position as tutor to the two daughters of Mr. and Mrs. Rodney Procter, of Procter and Gamble, from late December to late April in Palm Beach, Florida. On December 7, 1929, he separated himself permanently from the meat packing industry.

He left for Palm Beach about the 21st of December, stopped off to visit the Fosters near Philadelphia, and was in Florida by New Year's Eve. After being "used . . . into a frailty" in New York, he was quickly invigorated by the Florida sun and was delighted with the job. The Procter girls, whom he taught four hours a day, proved apt students, and their parents seemed to be "both fine people, calm, genuine, and very kind." They bought him a bicycle, and every morning he rode down the beach to give lessons, then tennis or swimming in the afternoon.

It was all very delightful, but he soon found he was, as he later put it, "too susceptible to environment," for he was as incapacitated for creative work in the warm, soft life of Palm Beach as he had been in the cold, hard one of New York. After two weeks he wrote Foster, "As for me, I am disgusted with myself. I am no good, and more lax and lost than I've been for long." A few days later he told Louise Hawkes that, although he had read quantities of Chapman and Proust, "I cannot even bludgeon myself into working consecutively and for a long time at any one thing." At the end of January, the Procters took a trip and left him to his own devices, but he did not improve the time: "I wanted these days to be rich with work, but it won't come. . . . Here I dwell with not a responsibility for ten days, cared for, and yet I write nothing."

It is probably safe to say that his lassitude was due in great part to his participation in "the vast and gaudy shows of wealth in Palm Beach." Though "without affectation," the Procters lived "like the lords of the earth, in simple and grand manner," and they were happy to have their daughters' tutor join in. "For a week I have been in the thick mill and press of Palm Beach saasiety [sic]," he wrote, "it is a pleasant, harmless kind of death. . . . for a week I have thrown over all seriousness and attempt, I am nothing but your happiest playboy of the southern world." That he never allowed himself to fall into the habit of considering himself part of this world, however, is evident from some of his descriptions of it.

And Mr. X, glancing at the immaculate moon, found cause to mention Mr. Richard Halliburton's latest book, yes, it was a good money-maker, he hit on just the thing, it took! . . . Mrs. X points to the Gumbo-Jumbos, just over there, they've just arrived, he's just had his portrait done, they say, and given it to the Chicago University. Did you hear her greeting? Really, these westerners! . . . . They are the Mr. and Mrs. Ugly-Muglys, they own almost the whole place. Blue shine the faintly incandescent lights of the Flamingo. As we retire Mrs. Z and Mrs. Ugly-Mugly pay their respects. . . . Then,—but aren't the Q's and the U-G's queer? So many people from the West this year, new comers. Then all the beautiful people go in their grand cars sedately back to their magnificent homes. Mr. Bold is doing so much *good* to put on these entertainments!

Toward the end of his Palm Beach tenure, he remained more or less amused by it all:

> In the midst of all which, see me beaming in final seasonal burst of parties. Barbara Hutton, smooth-cheeked, is said to have 50 millions settled on her heavy breasts: good Pan, what a weight of doom! . . . . Lithe Anne Tilney, 19, as glowing as Youth itself, marrying in June an Adonis, to embark on a year's world-honeymoon, with stops in Africa and Siam to take the mere lives of lions.

A sense of isolation from the luxury of Palm Beach was inevitable as long as his future was so cloudy. For some reason the only colleges where he applied for jobs were Dartmouth and Harvard, with predictable results, and it appeared that at best he would be reduced to another tutoring position. By April, with the leisurely interlude "of tutoring the very Princesses of money kings. . . ." drawing to a close, he began to remember wistfully "olde Engelonde. Surely I look back on your island," he wrote Michael Roberts,

> that sweet two year haven and home. In England, it seems probable one can integrate: Here, all is dissonance. Yet it is a greater task, to attempt this colossus. . . . Only literature and life are cleft as far apart, as I am from money. . . . The overwhelming bulk of real life in America consumes itself in things, immediacies, machines. The artist is a mis-fit, scowled upon by dull Worldlies as weakling.

At the end of his Palm Beach tenure he had apparently saved enough to live on for a few weeks, and he went back to New York to look for work. He was finally offered a very lush tutoring job that would have occupied him for almost a year at a good salary and taken him to Europe for the winter, but "It was a tutorship to a mollycoddle aged 17, and . . . the people seemed crass, vulgar, peculiar. . . . ," so he stalled in hopes of something better. About the middle of June, the parents of Andrew Foster offered to let him use a cottage on their estate in Phoenixville, Pennsylvania, for the summer. It was not a difficult decision, and on June 25th he repaired to the estate, known as Broadwater, for two months of peaceful isolation, reading and writing.

He lived alone in a farmhouse called Walden, and although he saw a good deal of the Fosters, his life was more involved with the natural world around him: "I look out on the earth for the first time. Every cell seems fresh to act." He became closest, apparently, with the local insects:

> Today I fell in love with an insect. First such love. It jumped on my finger, delicate and clean as a straight green twig. A most sweet fellow. Lithe, marvellously patient, and unafraid. As if on stilts, he shifted from right to left with fascinating pause. He stationed himself on his hind four legs, drew up his northern part, and was a Praying Mantis. . . .
>
> I have four social wasps just outside a screen, on a shutter. The wind blows it to and fro, time; they don't care. Only four; never are there more. In one month they've made an abode about two inches across, with many concave rows of caves. Vegetable material, masticated, is used, and they back in, to form each little tunnel, then seem to tap and shape with their mouths.
>
> Only a foot away, a solitary hornet builds his nest, a cylinder of mud. He goes down to the lake-edge and promptly returns with a ball of damp, compact mud, as big as a pea, held in his forelegs. He applies this, then using his head as a mallet, flattens it, shapes it to the nest, splendid craftsman. . . . a considerable hermit hornet.

It was also at this time that he first saw the now famous groundhog:

Jack had thrown a shot groundhog onto a board above ground, flat to the open sun. I surveyed the corpse just now, keeping well out of the wind. The animal had lost all its form, all that we call grace and trimness; it was a seething mass of maggots; the shock of the sea-like motion and swirl of these was at first so great as to give the illusion of the viscera pulsing and moving. One looks at one's face in the glass, and wonders on the eternal question of consciousness. There was intense life, though no longer the groundhog's, in the rotting carcass; but it takes calm reason to stave off revulsion at decay. I think we must come to love that reality of decay, symbol again of the very force of life. Life is the animating principle, and we are nothing but its nurslings.

Just a few days after his letter on the insects, however, he wrote:

Here, by the intrinsic irony of existence, where shines the objective happiness, the leisure, the freedom of time, the lack of restrictions, I . . . do little but read. . . . I grow dull and lethargic for days . . . while all the time I am contented and extremely comfortable.

Contented, extremely comfortable, and decidedly ambivalent, he remained at Broadwater for the rest of the summer.

The following fall he secured another tutorship, this time to the adopted son of the King of Siam and to the son of the Siamese minister to Washington. He was instructed to report to Washington on September 15, 1930; from there he went to Silver Springs, Maryland, to undertake the supervision of the boys and their studies at Southport, the home of Professor and Mrs. Robert W. Bolwell. As it turned out, he was a good deal more than a tutor and lived with the boys almost around the clock. "We work from nine till one," he told his father in October,

usually play tennis in the afternoon; another hour's work before dinner; and that is their day. They are surprising and extraordinary boys, and I am already fond of them. . . . I have a

Buick roadster for my own use and to take them about in. . . .
One's life is so personally connected with everybody here, I
don't get enough time to myself. . . . It is a bit thick to live
on the level of 13-year-olds, but I am liking the job indeed, and
one can learn a lot from the instantaneous youth of the boys.

After a few months, however, he began to tire of the constant drain
on his energies of what amounted to parenthood. ". . . as a matter
of fact, I'm fed up with them both," he wrote the following March,

and will welcome a vacation in April 8–20. In this house one
gets no time to oneself and over a period of months it is difficult either to keep the order or have the sense of humor this
job requires. . . . This kind of life satisfies nothing inner in
me.

In April, the king himself came to the United States for the re-
moval of a cataract. Being unable to find a hospital that could be
put at his exclusive disposal, he settled for the estate of Whitelaw
Reid in White Plains, New York, where Eberhart reported for duty
after his vacation and where he stayed through the summer. Ophir
Hall was considerably more pleasant and interesting than Southport:

this twelve hundred acre estate . . . . the castle as superb as
any I have thought lived in. . . . There are some hundred and
fifty rooms and about two hundred servants. . . . Diplomacy,
that gauze, that sieve, is seen waving as a banner of ancient
decorum in every room.

There is little evidence in the letters of this period to indicate any
intense discontent, but he later wrote that he soon had a marked
distaste "for the King and all he stood for," and that he had to live
a completely dual life, "bowing and scraping while within I was
swearing and fuming." His poem on the sequel to the king's operation, "The Rape of the Cataract," gives, a little more lightheartedly,
an accurate sense of the atmosphere at Ophir Hall in those days.

He completed a year with the Siamese and, finding that he had saved a good deal of money, he decided to take a trip to Germany; he was in Berlin by the beginning of October. He "lived with a splendid German family for the winter, on the outskirts of the city, going into town for lessons in the language from a tutoress." He spent a good deal of time going to concerts and walking.

Berlin opened its many sides to the view, its curious young people with their eternal post-war frustrations, no money, and a veritably infernal state of mind, quite amoral; . . . and the sometimes very beautiful women, women of the North, perhaps Nietzschean blond beasts; its stumpy men, smoking cigars; and the remains of Romanticism still in the feeling for nature, for woods and water, for long walks, of the stolid, pleasant, and intelligent Germans.

Through connections with the Siamese embassy, he made valuable social contacts and attended several delightful balls and parties. Then he

took a trip south, visiting Dresden, Munchen, Augsburg, Nurnburg, and finally Freiburg where I had to wait for God to produce snow in the Black Forest so that I might climb the Feldberg and go skiing.

He also visited the tombs of Eberhart forebears in Wurtemburg and found a statue in Stuttgart "of Eberhart die Greiner or of the Rushing beard, twenty feet high outside the railroad station." He found his family name on many streets and bridges in this part of Germany, and took considerable pride in his "ancestors who ruled Wurtemburg for 300 years" in the late Middle Ages. It was a pleasant few months, but he learned little German and experienced some of the same difficulty that he had so often in periods of material comfort. "This winter is an example of my lack of capacity to master my own time and wayward spirits of power, without some compulsion over me."

This same winter, however, saw his most important publication during what was otherwise a low period in his career. The sales of *A Bravery of Earth* had been disappointing, totaling only a little over 100 copies in England and fewer than 150 in America, and he did not attempt much periodical publication, presumably because, as he wrote in 1929, "there are few journals which I would consider." Both the *Nation* and the *New Republic* rejected poems, and even his friend from Chicago days, Harriet Monroe, returned his manuscripts with the remark that his talent was "getting sidetracked, it seems to me." Then in December 1931, Michael Roberts wrote him,

> But there's another project in the air. The Hogarth press have asked me to edit a sort of declaration of war by Auden, Day Lewis, and a few more,—a rebellion against the sterility of the "detached observer" business which Eliot has done so well.

The letter goes on to invite Eberhart to submit manuscripts, which he did enthusiastically, and he became the only American to be included in *New Signatures,* which came out in February 1932.[2]

In his introduction to this little anthology, Roberts tones down somewhat the sense of "rebellion" in his letter to Eberhart. His most militant statement is that "The poems in this book represent a clear reaction against esoteric poetry in which it is necessary for the reader to catch each recondite allusion." It is clear from his introduction that Roberts's idea was not so much to conduct an anti-Eliot crusade as to announce and encourage a poetry more concerned with contemporary social and psychological problems and more attractive to a contemporary audience, implying, in the words of a *Times Literary Supplement* reviewer, "a necessary correspondence of the poet and the informed sensibility of his age. . . ."[3] The poets in *New Signatures,* according to Roberts, attempt to come to terms with the problems posed by the decline of traditional values in a complex technological age.

> These are not really logical problems at all; they are aspects of an emotional discord which can be resolved neither by rea-

soning nor by action, but only by a new harmonisation such as
that which may be brought about by a work of art. The fact
that each of the writers in this book has solved this problem in
his own way without recourse to any external system of religious belief therefore opens up new poetic possibilities.

He then quotes Eberhart's "Request for Offering" as an expression
of "the delight and amazement that accompany the apprehension of
these apparent contradictions as aspects of a single reality. . . ."

> Amaze your eyes now, hard
> Is the marble pap of the world
> And the baleful lion regard
> With the claws of the paw curled.

There is no evidence to suggest, however, that Eberhart thought of
himelf as part of a movement, and indeed does not consider the
group in *New Signatures* a "school." He has never had the intense
awareness of social problems, moreover, that characterizes many of
the poems in the volume. We shall see that he was relatively oblivi-
ous to the Depression, for example, and as late as 1933 continued to
think that in the fall of 1931 it had just begun "its giddy course",
when it was almost two years old. There is nothing to indicate, furthermore, that he was touched by any of the social or political enthusiasms of the 'thirties, such as the Spanish civil war, which absorbed the interest of so many of his contemporaries, including
Auden, Spender, and Day Lewis. Yet because of his inclusion with
them in *New Signatures,* he had been associated with these poets in
reviews, jacket blurbs, and other anthologies almost ever since.

A few weeks before the publication of *New Signatures,* Eberhart,
in "a kind of panic with the dwindling of my resources," left Germany and went to England to stay for a while with Roberts, living
on the periphery of London's literary world:

> One has come into the orbit of poetry; poetry is talked about;
> poets are bandied about; poetry is used; it is much lived. It is

probed in theory, and enacted in practice. For a time this is good for one. In three weeks, MR's effort at publishing will be out from the Hogarth Press; . . . But one has come into the jungle of London literary forces; at a lunch with a thin, pale man, it turned out to be Hamish Miles. When we passed a lamp post on Charlotte Street, he said last week he saw two men standing against it, one leaning, talking for half an hour; he was Mr. T. S. Eliot, sir. I have met Mr. Geoffrey Saintsbury, whom my host most delicately reduced by logic to a miserable scrap heap in ten minutes. Here, is much talk over Auden, Day Lewis and the rest, Mr. Empson of course, who sends letters from Tokyo including his most recent verses.

. . .

I must go to Cambridge and see if anything can be done.

In Cambridge he stayed with his former don, Mansfield Forbes, "in his new home, 'Finella,' on the backs with Blakean symbols fitted in the ceilings and black marble bathroom to arise from the bath looking Nubian." He went about renewing old acquaintances and finding new ones, attempting to find a job. He visited virtually all his old dons and spent some typically stimulating afternoons with Mrs. Gordon. It was interesting and pleasant, but he was disappointed to find that "people talk about Communism over the teatables, who used to talk about poetry." As the days dragged out with no work turning up,

I am just now tossing on the horns of the dilemma. Should I stick it out here? Or return while I still have enough for an Atlantic faring, though no more? . . . London offers no help, so I suppose I'll come limping back.

A little over two weeks later he wrote Roberts: "I am down in the dumps, failure forever, god be damned for inventing money. It seems I am forced back where I came from. I can't hold out in England; no jobs."

He was apparently surprised to find that there were no jobs in America either, curiously unaware, as he was, of the Great Depression, as long as he was provided for. Upon his return to the United States, however, he began to realize that his trip to Germany had been "a bad move, from a practical standpoint. . . . The depression had just begun its giddy course and I fear I was not astute enough to recognize its proportions." Immediately upon his return, in April 1932, he and Foster went to Hamilton College and Dartmouth seeking a position; failing there he accepted the hospitality of the Fosters' Broadwater for the summer while he conducted a "campaign by letter," assaulting various English departments and other prospects for three months. There was nothing anywhere, and he became progressively more aware not only of the proportions of the Depression but of the importance of a Ph.D. By August he had begun to consider graduate school. He asked his father for the remaining $1500 of his mother's legacy, but it was unavailable. Finally, Mr. Foster offered to lend him the money for a year at Harvard and he accepted, entering graduate school late in September.

His entrance into Harvard marked the end of a pivotal period in Eberhart's life, a period characterized by ambivalence and drifting, moving from one environment to another, certain only that he wanted to write poetry and yet able to do so only infrequently and erratically. As we have seen, under one set of circumstances he raged against the world for its lack of time for creative work; under another, at himself for not working enough. Only one aspect of the environment was consistent and constant: no recognition was taken of him as an artist. However well he was fed, clothed, and housed, he was not encouraged. He had expected this, and part of him bristled in the face of reality and was prepared to fight, to create in spite of it; but he was plagued at the same time by a deep self-doubt, and he found the rewards of alienation meager at last. From this point of view, his drifting begins to show direction. At first the compromises he was willing to make were minimal; he planned to give only so much to "reality" as was necessary to sustain himself. But as time went on, he became more and more dissatisfied with his isolation and his lack of certainty about his future, and more amenable to fundamental compromise. Just before he entered Harvard, he wrote to his father:

> I have always been too impetuous and stormy, too little calm, too willing to experiment with life, to break its usual forms down, but it is about time to begin building something up.

The words must have pleased his father, but the pose of frank self-appraisal and manly resolution does not disguise the fact of capitulation.

CHAPTER FIVE
1932–1940

He began to have misgivings almost as soon as he had matriculated at Harvard. Shortly after opening exercises, he wrote Mr. and Mrs. Foster:

> It was strangely different from Cambridge, where you enter quietly, peaceably, and there is no disconcerting air of efficiency and bustle. There you read to understand, you are left to your own devices, while here the standards of meticulous detail, accuracy, and standardized methods are held up before you threateningly, as if you were still a boy, and had better begin fearing the examinations already. The very air of the students in classrooms, the fact that you have to attend classes all morning on three days a week, and the mountainous laying upon you of papers and theses, is stimulating in the opposite way from Cambridge. . . . it's like being prodded with a bayonet.

While seeing severe difficulties, he assured his patrons that he would try to "screw my fighting spirits up to a sense of adventure." The sense of adventure, however, began to wane as soon as he got into the work.

His most troublesome courses were those required in Anglo-Saxon and Romance Philology, but his others were more interesting: one in Dante, Chaucer, and Montaigne, and another in the Seventeenth

Century. His letters from Cambridge, Massachusetts, however, like those from Cambridge, England, contain much less about studies than about personalities, of whom the most interesting in his first semester was Irving Babbitt,

> to whom I sit (to his green frog's mouth and large head, and a remarkable nervous vitality that makes his fingers continually twitch their pencil over his disordered notes—the while he talks like his books, and every now and then bursts out in a kind of guffaw) militates against all the values of America still.

Kittredge seems to have been the dominating personality of his second semester, at least in his formal studies. He got off to a bad start with the famous scholar, missing the first meeting of his Shakespeare seminar, for which he had signed up at the suggestion of Theodore Spencer. When he approached the testy Elizabethan to apologize, he was treated to a long tirade on his irresponsibility, climaxed by the assertion that he would not be allowed to attend the class; and although better spirits prevailed, Eberhart left making silent, invidious comparisons with the less temperamental dons of Cambridge. Later in the term the professor and the student seem to have won some measure of mutual respect. In April, Eberhart wrote:

> . . . I ran a risk of being squashed by the great Kittredge in going against his kind of scholarship in a paper I have been reading to the seminar anent Shakespeare's sonnets, Empson— or deEmpsonized. I felt his hostility the first meeting, but I have got him around now to agreeing with my theories, a ticklish, skittish, and altogether exciting business.

One doubts that Kittredge was persuaded to change his approach to poetry, but he did give the young Cambridge man an A in the course.

In characteristic unprofessional fashion, Eberhart sometimes attended lectures outside of his field, if the attraction of the man him-

self was sufficient. One such personality was Alfred North White-
head, "a very wonderful form of man, of the greatest kindliness,
and what true energy and what magnificent intelligence."

> Sometimes he, sitting or twitching in his seat, would bring his
> hands, large capable tools, out over the desk like grappling
> hooks, he would force them towards each other as if he were
> squeezing some quite thick object, in the effort to express "the
> curious momentum of the rush of events." He talked with
> oracular serenity and precision, once he could get a start, and
> there was a feeling about his thinking which was poetical, as
> if, even in thinking, he were perceiving, were feeling now the
> world keenly, sensitively, in a new way. "So much of philoso-
> phy would be appropriate before the world were created."
> "The character of things half disclosed." "Why cannot the past
> be the immediate present?" "I am (in one sense) purely sub-
> jective."

T. S. Eliot was also at Harvard at this time, giving "what would
be considered characteristically dry mordant lectures; he is personally a boon to the race, compounded of nuances . . . ." In November he sent a long, grandiloquently diffident request for Eliot's attention. Eliot replied, more cryptically, "Don't be so self-conscious
about it," and suggested that Eberhart ring him up to arrange a
meeting. Apparently, however, Eberhart remained self-conscious, for
it was not until February that he wrote Foster, "I called on T. S.
Eliot this morning, found him dry and most sympathetic, a true
human being." In another letter he was more graphic, remarking
that Eliot "had a Renoir on his wall and a cold sore on his lip."
Eliot apparently kept himself more or less available; in April, for
example, Eberhart told Richards,

> Mr. Eliot was kind enough to help me read [Eliot's] Triumphal
> March recently; it was a wonderful pleasure for me. I had
> missed the Husserl, the Aristophanic and phallic connotations
> of the sausage. I read Christ into Caesar, which he said was not
> intended; but one could have it if one liked.

Eberhart was unable to form the kind of personal relationships at Harvard, however, that he had enjoyed at Cambridge. "The place is cold and unsociable," he wrote Roger Catherwood; compared with Cambridge, "one works harder, but is not allowed to think for oneself. . . . It's a continual nervous twitch for marks . . . and you must only annotate the commentators." He wrote more emphatically in another letter:

> Harvard is fierce; it is the school boy's paradise; he can enjoy being flogged. The quiet acquisition of knowledge as an end worth attaining is beside the point. The point is to enact a "racket" and pull the wool over the professor's eyes. You must beat the other fellow with a club, which is an American mode of conduct. If your club is spiked, you will get A's. This is the criterion. . . . If you do not get A's, you are not only no good, but you will not be allowed to remain in the earthly paradise. I have been appalled at the amount of this kind of attitude prevalent among graduate students. I have also been told that you should not think of teaching at Harvard unless you have a million dollars.

One is tempted to think that perhaps he came closer to the truth when he wrote later, "I suppose I dislike the drier than dusty dust scholars who know the ins and outs of footnote kowtowing because I am not sufficiently accurate myself . . ." and his attitude was undoubtedly colored by his failure of his French and German exams in January of 1933. He mastered the mysteries of scholarship sufficiently, however, to earn a B average in his year at Harvard and there is probably some truth in his remark that he learned to "play up (add quotation marks) to the right people at the right time: I sell my soul to a footnote." It should be added, finally, that his attitude toward graduate studies in the Ivy League has mellowed over the years, for if he could write in 1932, "As for Harvard the dog returns to his vomit," he nevertheless wrote in 1960, in reply to a student who had asked his advice about graduate schools: "I have lately come to a conclusion impossible to me twenty years ago, i.e., that America can afford Harvard."

Whether or not America could afford Harvard, Eberhart himself soon concluded that he could not. As early as October, he wrote to his father, "I would feel better inside if I had a job and were independent; borrowing is not so good." In order to continue, he would have had to borrow again and come under a burden of obligation that seemed to him intolerable, although Mr. Foster was certainly in no hurry for his money (he waited three years as it was). Had he found graduate school more rewarding, Eberhart might have worked harder to find means to continue, but he did not. Early in his second term he began looking for a position, and he soon found that the search was to be as difficult as in the days before the slaughterhouse. "Indeed," he wrote Mr. Foster, "the head of the Appointments bureau says definitely there is nothing to be had, and that a small army even of Phd's is walking the streets." He also wrote to Cambridge to no avail, and Leavis wrote him sometime later that "there are always two or three friends of the right people standing ready to be put in."

The secondary school situation was only a little less bad, but at least there were some openings. He missed one promising position through what might be termed politics. "The young man who was chosen," wrote the head of the English department at this school, "is a friend of the headmaster's. . . . You are wiser, and, I'm sure, a superior teacher—but it was the personal relationship that did the trick." He missed another very attractive prospect, in a public school in a plush New York suburb for technical reasons:

> If the Doctorate is a "racquet"-racket there is a similar iron-collar strangulation device for secondary teaching. I am a candidate for a position in a High School, to teach English to boys and girls sixteen years old. I have a Dartmouth degree, and Cambridge degrees which do no good. Do I have a State Teacher's Certificate? No. Then I must get one. That means 18-hours' credit in an established College of Education, which is a year and a half's work. I must drop my present work,

switch to the Educational School, take courses on Tennyson
and Browning from an anthology I used years ago at Dartmouth; must go to summer school; must get the 18-hours by
telescoping courses in psychology and if it can't be done by
September there is no way of getting a Temporary Certificate
and I can't take the job which would keep me alive, because
I don't know enough about literature to teach the young.

Finally he was invited for an interview to St. Mark's School, in
Southborough, Massachusetts, which he visited on May 3, 1933. Although they were looking for a man with more experience, he had
every reason to be hopeful, until informed that a St. Mark's alumnus
was "being pushed from several angles." He thought for a while
that he had been defeated by politics again, but the alumnus apparently was not pushed hard enough, and Eberhart was finally hired.

II

Eberhart's years at St. Mark's, 1933–40, provided at least the advan-
tages of regular work and regular pay, with summer vacations
which he could spend with his family. On the whole, he taught
courses in which he had some interest, although not of course at the
level he would have desired. Sometimes he also took on courses for
which both his enthusiasm and his qualifications were limited. In
his first term, for example, he was assigned a course in Ancient History, and later another in Modern History, an assignment which he
found almost amusing: "Also, believe it or not, I am teaching Medi-
eval-to-Modern history to Third formers," he wrote to Foster, "and
if they knew I know less than they do about it, my bluff would be
called. Matter of boning up the next twenty pages before they get to
them." He also had at least one tutorial in Anglo-Saxon, for which
he wrote his former teacher at Harvard for a bibliography. Generally, however, he taught standard courses in literature and composition.

It is impossible to tell from the extant records exactly how successful he was as a schoolmaster. The chief criterion at the school seems
to have been the boys' performance on the College Entrance Exam-

ination Board's tests. The only complaint, and it is not a strong one, about his work was that perhaps his sixth form (senior) course was in one term not sufficiently rigorous for CEEB preparation. One of the few surviving letters about his approach to teaching centers on this requirement, where Eberhart notes that in one year the exam emphasized expression, on any subject, "so that Readers [of whom he was one] found themselves trying to judge reports about ions and abstruse generalizations about war. . . ." The kind of superficial process of evaluation represented by the CEEB examinations did not encourage dedication, and it would appear that even they were not used in decisions about teaching assignments. A letter written shortly before the beginning of his fourth year epitomizes, perhaps, his professional life:

> This year at SM looks like a slump. 7 of my 15 A section 6th formers got highest honors on their exams. But the cyclic theory now puts me down: I'm to have only 3 and 4 formers, plus, Helas!, a class in the first form, monkeys aged 12. I don't look forward to it too much. I wish I could have got into a University by this Fall.

Of course he also had extracurricular duties and activities. He attended professional meetings and was faculty adviser to the *Vindex,* the school magazine. He also put in time as skiing coach in the winter and baseball coach in the spring. More to his taste, one presumes, he conducted at least three poetry contests, the entries for which he submitted to his literary friends around Boston for judgment.

Committees and conferences with other faculty members would obviously not leave many records in his personal file, since they were face-to-face meetings, requiring no correspondence, but the fact that he does not mention such work in letters to his friends would indicate that he did not take it too seriously if there was much of it. Aside from such things as recommendations for library purchases, the only surviving contribution to curricular life at St. Mark's is a negative one, but it is worth quoting because it shows how far he had gradually come from his earlier Anglophilia. The issue is Basic English, the approach (developed by his master Richards) to teaching the language. Several months earlier he had suggested that the school look into it as a possibility, providing some bibliography and mentioning that Groton School was trying it out, but by the following December he had decided against it:

> It is good that Groton is lively enough to "do something" about it, but I would be willing to get out my guns and go to war against it for Americans. There is something feverish [in] the way (say Groton) goes about being in the fashion or fad-light of experimental English ideas. Must we always ape England? Is there nothing peculiar to us which we must discover?

Although St. Mark's came as something of a relief after a year of the decidedly inhumane pressures of graduate school, it satisfied his inner life no more than the slaughterhouse or the Siamese court. Indeed, as before, much had to be repressed; he felt himself reduced almost to a professional hypocrite. This attitude is especially evident in his first year. "This year is my first term in a rut," he wrote to some old friends,

> I can cope with the world no more . . . and kicking against the pricks merely ages the bones. I now accept all, I have become thoroughly a social person . . . all for the purpose of slipping small but regular checks into the bank. . . . While the school does not require any higher or special knowledge I may possess . . . it pays me for being pleasant at all hours of the day and night, being diplomatic with the lads, and telling them nothing they should not know, or that their parents do not want them to know. Even in writing this sentence I feel the enormity of the compromise.

The situation is even more emphatically stated in another letter of the same period:

I am returning here next year, which is supposed to be some kind of triumph, for the other new man, the cleric, has been fired: he could not compromise, he had an unbending Puritanical temperament, with Socialistic leanings even, which did not go at all in this bulwark of capitalism. By being "nice" and exercising patience and tact, I seem to have survived. It is not the way of an Eliot or a Pound. For I produce nothing that is intrinsically mine. But my system cannot stand the strain of the despairs and anxieties I used to suffer. I am grateful for the fresh air, the exercise, and the beauty of this place.

The sense of hypocrisy and compromise is still evident in a slightly later letter. "I am paid to keep my mouth well versed in nonsensical data, to accrete poems in secret if I care to," he wrote Mr. and Mrs. Richards, "but not to tell robust truth, and not to offend the rich. . . . And the duality between the cheery greeting and the monstrous evil in the world is not resolved."

His life had compensations, however, besides "small but regular checks." Right on the campus of St. Mark's, for instance, his path crossed with those of two other literary figures. One, W. H. Auden, was already prominent. The other, Robert Lowell, more or less began his career under Eberhart's tutelage. Lowell and his friend Frank Parker, seniors at St. Mark's, started coming to see him in the winter of 1935, and

between then and the end of School Lowell had written about one hundred and fifty poems. I thought this a rather remarkable phenomenon and the man behind the pen promising: I admired his seriousness (and was appalled at the fabulous beliefs the young can have about the infallible and gigantic nature of their own powers) and his incipient ability. I gave them a reading list for this summer. . . . I did not know Lowell well, but tended to suppose that he did not run with the pack. . . . I felt that his strength of mind, his determination, and the apparent seriousness of his intentions were salutary and to be encouraged. . . .

He later recalled the young poet and his developing talent:

> It was on October 19, 1935, that Lowell entered my study and placed on my desk a typewritten manuscript in a rough brown folder. It contained sixty poems, the first fruits and trial of his art as a youth yet in school, produced after some months of talk about poetry and art. . . . That pair [Lowell and Parker] was the soul of spirit. Their minds were at the razor's edge. They leaped over the moon. If anything was certain then, it is certain now: Lowell's mind was heavy, and it was essentially religious. . . . The raw power was there. The forms were scarcely more complicated than the sonnet, which he yet employs, with variable rhyme schemes. And there was a heavy driving force and surd of prose which would bind the lyric flow in strict forms.

Later Eberhart tried to get some of Lowell's work published, but the young poet passed from under his influence, although Eberhart continued to see him and to advise him on both literary and personal problems until Lowell, at the instigation of Merrill Moore and Ford Madox Ford, left New England to study with John Crowe Ransom at Kenyon College. He spent the summer of 1937, however, with Allen Tate, living in a tent in Tate's yard near Clarksville, Tennessee, and Eberhart took some satisfaction in hearing from Tate, "I have great hopes for your pupil Robert Lowell. This past summer he made handsome progress, and I am convinced that he will be a real poet. Besides that he is a fine boy." That Lowell went on to justify the confidence of Ford, Moore, Tate, and Eberhart is of course a matter of public record.

Eberhart's association with Auden was very different from that with Lowell. Auden arrived on these shores in March 1938, with British kudos fresh upon him, and was quoted as saying that he would like to spend some time teaching in American schools. Eberhart sent a note to the headmaster at St. Mark's:

> Appended herewith is notice of my contemporary who seems to have all the secrets of "success." You could hardly do better

than to get Auden to come here, if only for a term; if you don't, I suppose Groton will. . . . If you would want me to write Auden to sound him out, I would be glad to do so.

That same day, "after a talk" with the headmaster, he wrote Auden, who wired that he was interested. More meetings and consultations ensued, and a trustee interviewed Auden in April, upon which occasion Eberhart advised, "Be politic in everything you say to him." Apparently he was politic, for finally an agreement was reached and Auden came to St. Mark's "as a guest member of the faculty for the next few weeks."

Auden took over some regular classes, including one of Eberhart's, and visited all classes at least once. The boys seemed to have enjoyed him a great deal, and he signed a humorous poem he wrote for the *Vindex,* at Eberhart's request, with the name they had given him: "The Feather Merchant."

> He employs very modern and obviously sensible methods— for instance, instead of asking boys to paraphase a quatrain of Gray's Elegy, he will excise key words, put in odd or nonsense words in their places, then ask the boys to hit the meaning of the original as nearly as they can by sensibility (they were too young to have known the poem), i.e. put in "right" words. . . . This method tests their acuteness of perception and has basic merits.

The month of Auden's visit was probably Eberhart's most enjoyable at St. Mark's. They took at least one trip to New York together, and they spent a good deal of time talking over poems. Auden was "totally sociable and electrifying," and Eberhart wrote him later, "I shall never forget the evenings when you sat in pure poetic heaven, oracle to your poems—they came like living things, impersonal beyond the two persons sitting there."

Ah yes, those were good days, when he would make tea, or come in and grab this typewriter and dash off a poem on it (scand[al]ously punctuated, but he would take advice, change pointing of lines here and there), or try to drug me at breakfast with those absurd pills he took to give himself a lift (I never took one), or grow flighty when I would drive, driving from the back seat like any yokel, or wolf his food at some faculty wife's dinner, his plate always empty before the maid even got around the table—dear old Whizz, a truly vigilant man. I liked him best when alone he would intone his poems, particularly the Rimbaud and the Housman. . . . But I digress. You have to be a politico in America, to live: he is good at that. It is too bad for his greatness that he has such an admixture of the Comic. But I believe in him, as much as any.

Eberhart's letter to the poetry editor of *The Atlantic Monthly* gives a further sense of their relationship:

It is fun having Whizz around. We criticize each other's poems. I am delighted you have taken one of his for the *Atlantic*. In that one I suggested that the four lines about generation—I forget them—were of a different tone, they stuck out. He thought perhaps, but thought they were all right. Another he wrote last week I found flaws in, and he had changed lines by the next morning. He is very fluid in this way, changes, revises, cuts, remakes at will. The point of this letter is to show you two poems of mine (again I put them in for consideration, enthusiastically), with his particular criticisms. The long one was written first. The little one afterwards, and had a third stanza which he thought not as good—but thinks this poem "a marvellous little poem" or whatever the phrase was.

The letter goes on with a long list of Auden's comments on various lines and illustrates the kind of discussions they held. It is safe to say, then, that Auden's visit was as profitable as it was enjoyable for Eberhart. However profitable it might have been for Auden, on the other hand, it was apparently not very enjoyable, and he thought St. Mark's a less than perfect atmosphere for writing. He wrote Eberhart later "to thank you for the joy of your company at St. Mark's;

it would have been a bad month indeed without you. But Remember GET OUT OF THERE QUICK [sic]."

Eberhart's experiences with Lowell and Auden were very much the exception to the rule of his life at St. Mark's itself, but he did make valuable connections around Boston. One account of a "dinner on the hill" describes a not atypical evening, and reflects, incidentally, the interests of a man confined largely to the monastic life of a boys' school:

> There was, as perhaps the central eye-delight, a divorcee. . . .
> She was a Cabot. . . . For the past six years she has lived in a
> castle in Florence. She has a son in the first form at Groton.
> She was the most beautiful woman I have seen for a long time.
> There must have been reasons for the Cabots speaking only—
> at one remove—to God. I can see how one might like to speak
> only to her; such blond perfection of face and body pleased the
> spirit. . . . There was another divorcee there, my partner. . . .
> One of her sons may come here next year. Her maiden name
> was Aldrich, she being the granddaughter of Thomas Bailey
> Aldrich. She had not the perfect fleshly seductive charm of the
> other, but . . . a beautiful face, very sensitive and New Eng-
> lish, very intelligent. Dinner, wine, talk.

The brisk cultural and social life around Harvard was also available to him, and he took full advantage, although his memories of Harvard's intellectual pretentiousness distorted his pleasure somewhat. His attendance at a lecture by Wallace Stevens will serve as an example.

> Stevens looked younger than he apparently is, and, as all
> Americans almost, could have passed for a broker or a banker:
> a round, fleshed face stating "a good type," and an utter calm-
> ness in his manner which made you wonder where the poet of
> him was—happily concealed behind thick masks of years, con-
> cealed in some perfection of manners, locked up in the bone
> box of the head. . . . But I did not get too much from the
> lecture; I was depressed to see the audience, and wondered

whether these, indeed, are the lovers of poetry, those on the inside of the tradition—with their sluggish looks, their miserable dirtiness, their absurd note-scribbling, their scraggly heads and fireless eyes. I began to hold the heretical notion that the most obvious healthy football-goers would seem to have an actual poetry of life in them denied to these sallow companions of the substitute pages. But I am probably wrong.

More enjoyable were social events where he could get relatively close to the personalities involved. He made here friendships which were to be valuable both personally and professionally later. In December 1937, for example, he met R. P. Blackmur, who almost twenty years later was to suggest his name for a visiting professorship at Princeton.

I went to John Holmes' where there were more poets together than I had ever experienced before. Practically everybody had had a book out this year. R. P. Blackmur, whom I had not met before, and whose "The Double Agent" (Arrow ed.) you must know as the best essays of these times by an American (barring possibly Edmund Wilson) sat in his small frame with a neat clean brisk face, coming to a point at the chin, and with straight hair, a chiselled kind of look, with hardly any mouth at all, very small and precise, sapped by a little mustache; he had an accent of Maine, and was thoroughly intelligent—he liked to hold forth, like a pocket edition of Dr. Johnson sitting there, and he did not pay much attention to others, although he was quite civil. His triumph, I thought, was when later on he gave a perfect definition of "borage" in [Hart] Crane, with his usual professional grace and not a moment's hesitation.

One more example will give a clearer idea of his personal involvement with life around Cambridge and Boston. It is an account of a tea at Frank Parker's family home, where he met Ford Madox Ford.

He looked too much like his pictures. He talked in a very low drawl. One could see him in London in the nineties adumbrat-

ing some nicety with Aubrey Beardsley. I wanted to get him to
tell about Swinburne, but there were too many people around.
. . . The young poet Harry Brown was there, neat and brisk,
who reported that Auden is in New York and is coming up
this Friday for the performance of "The Dog," done by Har-
vardians in a theater in Boston. . . . There was also a tall,
sombre Finn from Minnesota, a Duluthian once removed from
the original Finnish shores, who is "doing well" at Harvard
and writes verses. Cal Lowell committed an aggression and
stole the lion (plus wife) for dinner alone. Frank Parker,
[Blair] Clark, the Finn and I drove out to Nahant where we
prowled around those wonderful cliffs and felt the knock and
shock of the sea under the stars.

It should be pointed out that Eberhart never really became a part
of this life during these years. He was usually on the periphery of
events, forming few close personal relationships and never being at
the center of New England cultural activity, so that while he found
some relief here from the "narrow and rigid strictures of a schoolmaster," he also became more intensely aware of the kind of life
which a poet might have but which was denied to him. The very
activities that gave him pleasure, therefore, probably contributed to
the tendency to depression that haunted him almost throughout his
years at St. Mark's. In his correspondence there develops an almost
oppressive refrain of self-pity. His developing tendency to brood
over rather than to combat his problems is best judged by Frederick
Prokosch, who finally became annoyed with his melancholy:

You make this statement: "I've been maimed inside for the
last two years." Well, I could talk for hours on such an attitude; but even not knowing the circumstances, I can say that
that reveals a concentration on self rather than a lucid and ra-
tionally discriminating frame of mind. I take exception to that
statement. It is a sort of masturbation really.

In his later years at St. Mark's the expression of his discontent fo-
cuses on money. Curiously, despite his relative security, he had be-

come obsessed with his poverty. In a letter from April of 1937, for example, there is evidence that some of the implications of the Great Depression had begun to dawn on him. "There must be a great decay of the middle classes in America," he noticed;

> now it's either labor or a top crust of the big money. I seem to be another sacrifice to the latter; I exist on the fringe, in full view of material glories, of that rich society, yet obviously I do not belong to it: I do not have the money in the bank. I have no yacht. . . . If I should be bereft of my "job" tomorrow, in three months I would be a pauper. Think of it! To have reached the mid-stream, and to be nowhere.

It is strange to read such letters, in view of the number of people in 1937 who had no job, or who could not expect three months of grace between unemployment and pauperdom. It becomes even worse when he is found almost sneering at his more fortunate friends. In October, 1937, for instance, he wrote his old friend Andrew Foster, who was in Greece working for the State Department: "You have had an easy life and are in Athens because your father got rich. I am in St. Mark's because I have always been poor, and I don't see any way out of it at this point."

These are queer remarks from one who in his first year at St. Mark's was able to save $1600, and who just a few months after the letter quoted above was considering a summer vacation in Europe seriously enough to get a passport. Some of his friends noticed the anomaly too, although they endured quietly a great deal of near-abuse from him. "You think too much about money and relate too many things to it," wrote Andrew Foster's sister Elizabeth.

> That will burn you up and you will say well you don't know anything about it. . . . I'll admit I'm lucky at the present time but I'll also admit that I know a good many people with less than you have who do not think it the only end in the world. Perhaps you don't know how much you do talk about it, and if it's really so important why not find a rich wife and then forget it?

Louise Hawkes Padelford had written about the same thing more cryptically over a year earlier: "There's a lot more to be said about living than the fact that a person has bread and water or cake and wine."

III

Despite Eberhart's obession with the subject, then, his periods of depression cannot really be explained in terms of his economic position, or the direction of his life in the material world. It may be explained, however, in terms of the direction of his literary career, for that career was not developing to his satisfaction. His poems continued to be rejected, for instance, by Harriet Monroe, who no longer found his work much to her taste. In 1935 she rejected some poems and added,

> But then, I didn't like your *New Signatures* group so well as the poems we printed in your [Chicago] days. I am glad you came back to this country—I still think we have much better poets than England at present.

A few weeks later, she rejected some more, including "The Rape of the Cataract," with stronger language: "As the work of a poet of some experience, these things are incredibly crude. I can't understand how you could pass such stumbling halting lines. You must know better." Two weeks later she rejected three more without comment. These were apparently not the only poems she rejected, for when she finally did accept a poem in 1936, Eberhart said, "Harriet Monroe has taken 'Song of the Soul,' after several years of our argumentation: whether it means that her ideas are improving or that my work is deteriorating I don't know." After Miss Monroe's death, he did better with *Poetry*. In July of 1937 Morton Zabel accepted "If I could only live at the pitch that is near madness," "I walked out to the graveyard to see the dead," and "Anglo-Saxon Song." He had held the poems for a very long time, however, and in the interim, "I walked out to the graveyard . . ." had been accepted for the anthology *New Letters in America,* so it had to be deleted from the group, but the other two, along with two more, were finally published in January 1938.

Eberhart's association with European publications between 1933 and 1937, when *Reading the Spirit* was published in America, was only a little more successful. He submitted poems to *The Criterion* in 1934 and 1935, and to *Scrutiny,* but without success. One of the earliest and the most important of his periodical publications during this period, however, was that of "The Groundhog." In 1934 Michael Roberts showed the poem to Janet Adam Smith, who asked to keep it for *The Listener,* the British Broadcasting Corporation's literary weekly. Eberhart was willing, and it was published in the August 22, 1934, issue of that publication. *The Listener* also later accepted "Dissertation by Waxlight," and "1934," both of which were also bought for publication in a collection of poems first published in *The Listener.*

Early in 1935, Eberhart sent a poem entitled "Mais l'amour infini montera dans l'ame," to James Sweeney, the brother of John L. Sweeney, his classmate at Cambridge. Sweeney thought highly of the poem but did not say anything about publication until over a year later, when he wrote Eberhart that he and Eugene Jolas wanted to print it in the first American issue of *Transition,* along with another poem, "Alphabet Book," which Eberhart had written as an exercise for I. A. Richards. In its review of *Transition, Time Magazine* quoted two-thirds of "Mais l'amour. . .," calling it "one of *Transition*'s few intelligible works." [1] Since some of the stanzas quoted by *Time* could easily be interpreted as obscene, Eberhart fully expected repercussions at St. Mark's, but in August he wrote Jack Sweeney:

> About *Transition,* I have had no criticism whatsover; perhaps "your best friend won't tell you" and some have evaded me as odious. I have not myself shown the piece. But several persons have been praiseworthy in that I "made Time."

He did not include "Mais l'amour," however, in his second book, for which he submitted a manuscript to Cape at the end of September, 1935. After it was rejected about a month later, he wrote for advice to Roberts, who replied,

> Good news that you are being sensible and going to bring out a book. . . . You've no reputation worth speaking about over here, but your book would be reviewed pretty carefully, I think. Things are rather better in the reviews than they were.

Eberhart apparently then sent a copy of the manuscript to Roberts, for the next surviving letter to him says,

> I had hoped to hear from you before now about my book. . . . The Richards think the mss. ought to be cut down and I went through with a fell swoop the other day, knocking out about two out of every three poems. Please let me know what progress there is, whether Chatto is interested.

Less than a month later, Roberts reported that Chatto and Windus was ready to offer a contract: "I see no reason why you should not accept, and we'll get on with the job of putting the book in order."

The most important part of putting it in order was the selection of poems to be included. When Eberhart submitted poems to an American publisher in April, he wrote a letter which illustrates that process:

> On Mr. Parsons' [a partner in Chatto and Windus] list, on Roberts', and on mine, for inclusion, are the following poems:
> No. 1. Maze
> No. 2. Request for Offering
> No. 7. For a Lamb
> No. 9. Cynic Song
> No. 11. Caravan of Silence
> No. 10. Necessity
> No. 18. Four Lakes' Days
> No. 19. Ode to Silence
> No. 22. Dissertation [by Waxlight]
> No. 28. The Groundhog

No. 35. Death is indescribably [much on me]
     No. 35. 1934
On Roberts' list and also on Mr. Parsons', poems which I have
agreed to and included are
     No. 3. World's mere environment
     No. 17. New Year's Eve
     No. 6. Fragments
And on Roberts' list, but not on Mr. Parsons', but now put in
are
     No. 8. Maya and the Hunter
     No. 16. You, too, are coming up
Mr. Parsons wanted one poem, When Doris Danced, which I
have deleted. Roberts wrote to ask if I would pass those first
18 poems as a basis for the book, then add ten or more of my
choosing. I have built the book as you now see it, with 38
poems; but I am instructing Michael on, say, 5 which can be
cut if they so desire.

In an earlier letter, Roberts asked Eberhart to side with him, presumably against Parsons, on the inclusion of "Mais l'amour . . . ,"
but Eberhart insisted that the poem be "kept out for political reasons." The other poem which he had published in *Transition* was
excluded for another kind of "political" reason: *"Alphabet Book*
would have done you a good deal of harm," wrote Roberts,

> even if the Introd. had jabbered about it. People here are sick
> of Paris-Transition-Experimental-Lindley [?] Writing, and re-
> ject good and bad experiment alike unless they've learned to
> trust the writer first.

They exchanged several lists with comments and argument, and by
April 27th Parsons had approved a final selection, after "long-dis-
tance cornered machinations over inclusions."
     The other major consideration in preparing the book was Rob-
erts's introduction. They early decided that he would write one, and
in March he sent Eberhart the first draft:

. . . improve its spelling, syntax, rhetoric and sense as you will: it is your book in which it must appear. Remember that my intention is persuasive—an air of intelligent but infectious enthusiasm is what is needed. But all the same, I don't want the note to look silly in five or ten years' time. . . .

Eberhart returned the draft with minor suggestions and went on:

The thing you don't do as a critic is to make an attempt at evaluation. You might compare a poem of mine with one of, say, Auden, Empson, CDL or Sp and have something to say about me in relation to these: it would fit in with New Sig. etc. and would catch the eye of some readers more happily. . . . You could make the Empson an[ti]thesis, show the lack of Eliot and Pound, or show some likenesses to Yeats. The variety of the work (scope) ought to be stressed.

A few days later he was having still more reservations about the introduction.

I have shown it to several people; there is no unanimity of opinion. Some think it snows under the poems. . . . Others think it good. I am wondering how nearly you can prognosticate its value to the readers. . . . What does Chatto think of it? I recount many books of poetry in the last ten years, and none of any importance with introductions. I recall some where the introductions hurt the books. . . .

To these letters Roberts replied:

Introduction recast. . . . But as for dragging [in] Auden and Empson, I'm writing an Introduction that may have to stand for 20 years, not a review. Your work stands on its own feet: I'm willing to justify it by reference to Blake and Wordsworth and Whitman, and let who will justify Auden by reference to yours. The fact that it is easy to write a critical introduction without mentioning Auden or Eliot is the best certificate of your independence.

And a few days later:

> Pound and Marianne Moore were introduced by Eliot; Hart
> Crane by Allen Tate; and so on. My word hasn't their weight,
> but people don't seem to resent the practice. I was against it
> myself, but Ian Parsons all in favour: He liked the first draft
> too.

On May 8th, Eberhart replied, "The introduction is excellent as
now set and I quite approve and appreciate the changes you have
made in it."

Since Parsons declared the work "ready for the printer" on April
27th, the question was by this time theoretical. Eberhart had hoped
to publish by June 1st in order to have copies for sale in Hanover
for his class reunion on June 8th, but printing was delayed, and on
June 6th Parsons wired that he thought it best to postpone publication until the opening of the fall term at the British universities.
The first set of proofs was corrected by Roberts; then that set and a
corrected set were sent to Eberhart, who returned them with further
corrections and comment on July 22nd. Accompanied by very little
further correspondence, the book went slowly through the presses
and appeared in London, under the title, *Reading the Spirit,* on October 1, 1936.

His search for an American publisher for the book was much
longer and more difficult, and was probably the most important single factor in his discontent during the 'thirties. In January 1936, he
took a manuscript to New York and gave it to E. F. Saxton of Harper's, without success. In April he tried Harper's again, sending to
another editor both the poems and a section of a projected novel.
He was advised that ". . . there is some doubt about the selling
chances of the books," but that the editors would like to see more of
the novel; but the novel, a heavy, labored, near-parody of Henry
James to begin with, was never finished. In the same month he tried
Random House, only to be told that publication, while desirable on
the merit of the work, "would be a luxury that we must deny ourselves. . . ."

In June he sent a set of the Chatto proofs to Prokosch, who declared himself "absolutely delighted! Beautifully selected and arranged. So I'm now writing to Harper's very violently ordering them to do them—! I do hope they will." So Eberhart sent a copy of the London edition in October; by December he grew impatient. "Harper's have had it over a month, but are so slow that I sent an ultimatum the other day and expect to be turned down right soon." He was. The editor spoke of the limited market for poetry and regretted, ". . . I doubt whether we can do well enough with the book to make the venture a satisfactory one for either of us."

Two weeks earlier, Random House had contacted him again, asking to see the novel they had heard of "via Chatto and Windus." Eberhart stalled until he heard from Harper's and then, probably since they did not find the novel publishable, sent a copy of *Reading the Spirit* alone. He went to see the editor about it, apparently during Christmas vacation, but they were not interested in the poetry without a salable novel, although the editor whom he had met bought the submitted copy for his personal library. A few days later he submitted it to Harcourt, Brace and received his rejection a month later, followed in March by a rejection from Arrow Editions.

In April and May he tried Macmillan, and the ensuing exchange is worth quoting at length because it illustrates both the attitudes of American publishers and his response to them. He visited the Macmillan offices in April, and received a letter early the following month:

> We have had the book read by several of our very best advisers. . . . They have characterized the verse in this book as having great individual strength and striking perception in repeated instances. Despite this appreciation of the unusual aspects of your writing, however, it was the considered opinion here that on the whole, the book might find a somewhat narrow audience in this country. . . . As you know, the market in general is a fairly restricted one so that like other publishing firms, we are obliged to limit somewhat our seasonal list in this field and cannot undertake a very large number of books of verse in each season:

Eberhart replied that he "appreciate[d] the spirit in which you exe-
cuted your charge," but he had by this time heard so much about the
limited market for poetry that he could not resist going on:

> If I am right . . . there is something rotten in the state of
> Am'urr'ican letters. It's a racket, they say. Publishers who want
> to pride themselves on quality are content to take quantity on
> the grounds of the smallness of appeal of strict writing. The
> strict is the only kind that lasts. The bally hoo books are ob-
> viously no good. It is the poets themselves who strive to raise
> the level of culture, seemingly never the publishers—for them
> the lined pocket is more important. Maybe it was always so.

The editor's reply had the merit of a little more candor than his earlier letter:

> . . . in spite of the many outstanding merits which our advisers
> saw in it, they liked certain of the poems much better than
> they did others and in the end there seemed to be no other
> alternative but to regretfully decide against undertaking the
> collection. It is our feeling, in all sincerity, that to do justice to
> a book the publisher must have complete enthusiasm for all of
> it. . . .
> I hope you will forgive my having stressed perhaps too
> much, in my letter, the market problem, which seemed to us
> to arise in some degree in view of the particular nature of
> poetry.

Eberhart's answer, the last letter in the exchange, sums up his feelings about his experience with American publishers. He apologized
that he "did not mean to be querulous," and went on:

> Points I would make:
> "complete enthusiasm" of publishers about a book of poems
> I should think impossible; if a number of men are "completely
> sold," the poetry must be bad. It could only be mediocre poetry,
> that which would appeal to considerable numbers, which would
> meet with the approval of the publishers. You will recall that

even the best men could not decide on "The Waste Land" for
ten years.

publishers are in to make money; even from poetry perhaps.
Yet time tells that there is no or little money in poetry. Poetry
must be carried by the general success of the firm. I then cannot
see why American publishers do not become idealists for once
and try to publish the best verse available, instead of the usual
mawkish volumes. I am pro-English in this regard, for in England they have that much sense; they do not intend to make
money on a volume of verse (they intend it to go in the black,
of course), but they will go out of their way, in fact they will
exercise the greatest discernment to publish the best poetry and
quell the less good.

. . . Better say frankly why the work is not liked. I would
give a great deal for exact and precise criticism; poets have
much to learn from everybody's opinion of their work.

He expressed his ideas somewhat more explicitly in another letter at
about the same time:

I, myself, I confess, have tried several publishers for *Reading
the Spirit,* without American success. Such obtuseness on the
part of our dear American brethren stirs up my bile. They
publish tosh for the subway girls, the gum-chewing stenog-
raphers; they take on certain poets almost certainly mainly for
personal reasons; but they remain beautifully ignorant about
poetry as poetry; "you're in the racket too," Auden has said
about them.

It is interesting that the only editor willing to "say frankly why
the work is not liked" was in the company that finally published it,
the Oxford University Press. On January 16, 1937, Oxford's D. S.
Fairchild wrote him,

I've only just seen a copy of the book of poems you did for
Chatto and Windus—it *is* good! And what a pleasure to read
poetry that is strong *and* articulate as well! What has been
done with the book in America? Will you let me know soon?

Eberhart replied immediately to tell Fairchild of his difficulties with American publishers and to assure him that "I should entertain any interest you might have in *Reading the Spirit* with pleasure." On the next day, Fairchild wrote that while Oxford would like to see another group of poems,

> *Reading the Spirit* has been rejected. We went through it time and again—all agreed as to you *as a poet* but couldn't come to terms on this as an Oxford book. . . . Your book interested us, gave us pleasure to read—but we can't honestly see a market for it.

As he had Macmillan, Eberhart wrote asking "to know exactly why you turned the poems down. . . ." Fairchild's response was the only open and helpful letter he received from an editor.

> You ask what poetry *is* marketable: I say the poetry the editor likes. Auden and Spender sell. Also Frost and Millay. . . . The reason we rejected the book—tradition cries "Hold, enough! Say nothing," but why not say?—as it stands "Reading the Spirit" is too varied, not all you. It has a sharpness . . . where there should be assurance, and an abruptness of wording, a choppy effect . . . that in other spots is more expert.
>
> We had an idea of doing an edition of fifty copies—but what good would that be to you—or to us? So, it seems best to not do this book . . . and to sit back and wait for a new MS from you, or does that seem wrong?

Before this exchange with Fairchild, however, Eberhart had written of his troubles to Ian Parsons, who responded commiserating in February and added, "The O.U.P. man's name is Paul Willert, and I hope he may have got into touch with you by now. If not, by all means write to him direct." Since no correspondence between Willert and Eberhart in the spring of 1937 is extant, he probably went to New York to see him, and apparently Willert liked the book enough to sway the rest of the editors, for it was accepted, and work was begun on it the following fall. Sheets were imported from London, a new dust jacket and cover designed, and the book came out in New York on December 2, 1937.

The reviews of *Reading the Spirit* come to no general agreement. Indeed, their polar judgments are occasionally almost amusing. The reviewer for *The Manchester Guardian,* for example, finds that, "Apart from the well-assimilated influence of Hopkins he is, in form and substance, singularly clear of influences; is, in fact, a strongly individual poet," [2] whereas C. Day Lewis, writing in *Life and Letters,* asserts that the book is "surprisingly imitative. Faithful but flat echoes of Blake and Hopkins still haunt his work." [3] The generally hostile tenor of the Day Lewis review makes an interesting contrast with a still more hostile one in the American *Poet Lore,* by one Rex Hunter, who apparently read little further than the jacket blurb's mention of Eberhart's rather fortuitous association with Auden, Day Lewis, and Spender. He mentions the blurb, then quotes "The Groundhog" and "Job," concluding, "It will then be seen that Eberhardt [sic] has sold his lyric birthright to the triplets Auden-Lewis-Spender for a mess of dubious pottage." [4] A similar example of the operation of prejudice is *Poetry Review's* notice, which begins with the statement that *Reading the Spirit,*

> if one may judge from the journals and anthologies which, as he records, have published some of them, appeal to those who read poetry as if it were a crossword puzzle, preferring the difficult, the obscure, the unintelligible because it flatters their self-esteem . . . to discern a meaning where ordinary people fail.

This evidence plus the quotation of fewer than twenty lines from two poems are considered sufficient to damn the book. [5]

John Peale Bishop, in *Poetry,* is typical of several reviewers who get bogged down in their concern for the influences upon the poet. Bishop centers on Blake, "And William Blake, for all that he is among the great poets, is also among the worst influences." He then goes on to connect Blake with more recent forces:

From the practice of his predecessors Blake does indeed depart, but his ear has been trained by them. . . . The corresponding influence in Mr. Eberhart's case would appear to be the more or less forgotten Georgian poets; his natural ear is, to say the most, uncertain; and it has been trained in an inept school.

He then goes on to attempt to prove his point, never finding anything that is uniquely Eberhart's.[6]

There are, on the other hand, several sympathetic and discerning reviews. Clifford Dyment, in *Time and Tide,* summarizes nicely the poet's strengths: "his gift of sensuous description," he writes, "his clarity of statement, his unsentimental perception, the virility of his images, and the delicate fanciful quality of his imagination are all apparent. . . ." [7] A précis of his major thematic direction is attempted by Janet Adam Smith in *The Criterion:*

> All his poems are stretched between opposites: in moments of Passion the body seems to grasp reality, but the body corrupts and decays; Job is good and Job's head is full of bubbles; when two people are most close in love, then they are most alone; life is only given a meaning by death. Existence is a tight-rope walk between these extremes; and it is only by experiencing both, denying neither, by thinking *and* feeling as honestly and as passionately as we can, that any kind of harmony is to be reached.[8]

Perhaps the most balanced British review, however, is by F. R. Leavis in *Scrutiny.* He suggests that Eberhart's development since he knew him in Cambridge has been disappointing. "But it is pleasant to be reminded that he has, after all, produced what is, comparatively, a very respectable sheaf of memorable work . . ." He remembers the Eberhart of the 'twenties:

> If one thought of Blake it was perhaps because Eberhart, if a "romantic," was so unlike Shelley. It was also, no doubt, because of the peculiarly individual quality of that sensibility, the

definition of which, in his strange rhythms and elusive prose-
sense, is so sharp. . . .

The later poems, however, did not keep faith with that sensibility,
in Leavis's judgement:

> He had none of the cerebration and wit then beginning to be
> cultivated by young poets. Later alas he entered into rivalry,
> and we have verse that is difficult in a different way from his
> best and characteristic. "Dissertation by Waxlight," for instance,
> aims at the metaphysical and much of the later verse that can
> only be said to be in manners of his own seems to me unsatis-
> factory too.

One senses here the presence of a bias, an a priori assumption of
what poetry ought (or more precisely perhaps, ought not) to be, but
the review is at least thoughtful, well-considered, and sympathetic.[9]
   The most understanding review published in England appeared
in the *Times Literary Supplement*

> In his first book, "A Bravery of Earth," Mr. Eberhart traced in
> a single poem the progression of awareness from the sensory
> to the imaginative through which he and mankind must grow.
> And in this new volume of thirty-one exceedingly individual
> poems he is primarily engaged in working out his own strug-
> gles at the point of development at which the analytical reason
> and the earth-loving senses are in continual conflict. It may
> be urged that a poet should express the harmony which is the
> resolution of such conflict. But in a time so jarred with inner
> conflict as ours it is perhaps inevitable that the most vital poetry
> should crystallize the prevailing tension as Mr. Eberhart's does.

The reviewer goes on to describe the poet's "continual conflict" that
seeks "the equilibrium of conflicting elements," and "moments of
balanced tensions." The review is interesting because it is probably
the earliest application of such terminology to Eberhart's work, but
more importantly, it is perhaps the most disinterested review of

Reading the Spirit to appear on either side of the Atlantic, attempting to describe briefly and sharply just what happens in the poems.[10]

The two reviews which did the most to come to terms with both the power and the problems of the poet were by Americans: Philip Horton in *The New Republic* and R.P. Blackmur in the *Partisan Review*. Horton uses a good deal of space on the influence of Blake, Hopkins, and the metaphysical poets of the seventeenth century, giving examples which he sees as "highly derivative." But he goes on:

> It is greatly in Mr. Eberhart's favor that his poetry is most successful when it is least derivative.
>
> On increasing intimacy with the verse, it becomes clear that Mr. Eberhart has his own integrity, one which in his best work creates its own speech and idiom. The essence of this integrity seems to lie in a sensibility vividly aware of the world and yet curiously isolated and self-centered. There is an insistence upon the first person throughout the book that is almost frenetic at times. It is as though the poet had reversed and adapted Descartes' proposition to read: I am, therefore, I believe; and adopted it as an article of faith:
>> Leave me. Alone I can pluck up a looking-glass,
>> And say my own eyes to my own eyes are, now.
>
> I suspect that many of the defects of the verse are due to an exaggerated awareness of this introverted sensibility. . . .

Horton then suggests that in many poems, especially in the latter part of the book, Eberhart managed to solve "the conflict of his locked-in sensibility and the world," and he quotes "In a Hard Intellectual Light" as "one of the most perfectly achieved poems in the book." "It is this intelligent control of sensibility . . . ," he concludes, "which gives memorable power and precision to such pieces as 'The Groundhog,' 'Caravan of Silence,' 'Necessity,' and 'Dissertation by Waxlight.' "[11]

Of Blackmur's review, Horton wrote Eberhart,

He [Blackmur] confessed that he was a little apprehensive of how you might take it. . . . it doesn't shower you with bouquets by any manner of means, but much better (I'm sure you'll agree) it analyzes some of the flaws and weaknesses with considerable acuteness. . . . The great trouble he took in writing it (and he told me it had been quite a struggle) shows that he thought the work eminently worth taking pains about.

Blackmur's basic approach in what Eberhart justly called "the best review of all" is set forth immediately in his first paragraph:

Mr. Eberhart is not an easy poet; he is too energetic, which he luckily cannot help, and he fails at critical points to complete his poems either as examples of perception or as examples of craft, which is a failure that, luckily, he can help. It is his predicament, and ours, that his talent has seldom in the particular poem either found a satisfactory medium or discovered its governing limits. We feel him keep sensibility on the stretch in the struggle to get out of the predicament. . . . What matters is that in this struggle . . . a great number of images, insights, and vitalizing observations are struck off; rich material of everyman's dilemma is exposed; and the general body of his work has the look, the feel, the twist, of poetry.

In elaborating his thesis, Blackmur suggests that Eberhart's failure to realize a consistent and "continuous mastery of craft" results from the fact that "he so far lacks a theme adequate to his ambition as he sees it, or perhaps it would be more accurate to put it that he has never so felt a theme as to require his utmost in craft." He then goes into a discussion of "Four Lakes' Days." Considering the poem as a whole an imitation of Hopkins, he suggests that the passages where the poet has a comprehensive grasp of his subject "are imitation genuine and digested, and it is flattery to point them out." Where this grasp does not obtain, however, the imitation is "gross" and "is its own punishment." He concludes:

It may rather be that Mr. Eberhart wants to put more into his verse than he has got ready in imaginative form, and that he also employs imaginative devices beyond the scope of the material he actually does have. If he *himself* wrote the passages complained of above, and others in other poems drawn from Hopkins and Eliot, not only would the source of complaint disappear but the poems would be far more objective. That he could do this is demonstrated by what he has done; that he wants to do it is either obvious, or I am wrong entirely about what I feel as his sense of his profession. . . .

Blackmur's review is open to several objections, the most important being that he makes flat statements about his examples without submitting detailed evidence, but one can only prove so much in the space allotted to a review, and the piece is nevertheless important in two respects. First, it is the most careful examination in print of Eberhart's major weakness, a lack of control which other critics have mentioned but never studied. Secondly, and more importantly from a historical point of view, it was his first serious and thorough examination by a critic of real stature.[12]

At the same time that *Reading the Spirit* was being published so reluctantly and reviewed so generally unenthusiastically, Eberhart began applying for funds to the Guggenheim Foundation, which turned him down for four successive years. He submitted his first application in the fall of 1937, stating as his primary objective simply "to write poetry," but adding that he had an unfinished novel and an idea for a verse drama. His plans were somewhat vague, though eloquent:

> I desire primarily to test myself against Imagination. To put it more bluntly, I want to live (for the period of the Fellowship) totally as poet. This can only be done by complete devotion to the art, which I have found impracticable under the exigencies of my present position. I desire leisure for prolonged, deep contemplation of life.

To his statement of intention he added a bibliography (and later sent copies) of his published work.

Only his first two applications differ in any important respect; namely, in the people that he named as references. I. A. Richards and Frederick Prokosch (himself a Guggenheim Fellow) were the only undeniably literary people on the list. Ralph Thompson was then book review editor for *The New York Times,* but it is doubtful that he knew Eberhart's work well. The others were President Hopkins, George Swift, Philip Russell (a Wall Street attorney and friend), and Andrew Foster, by then with the American consulate in Athens.

In his second attempt, however, he took the advice of Blackmur, who told him to "stick to literary references. I don't see what good a vice-consul or a broker or a partner of Mr. Swift packing butter can do." Allen Tate wrote, "I will be delighted to put in my word for you," but warned that none of his nominees in recent years had won a fellowship, and advised him not to be sanguine. Besides Blackmur and Tate, he added to his list of sponsors Horace Gregory, who agreed to recommend him, warning that it seemed to him "like applying for an Irish sweepstakes." He also sought the endorsement of Mark Van Doren, but Van Doren declined on the grounds that he was *hors de combat,* since he was himself up for a grant. In the same letter, however, he commented extensively, and for the most part favorably, on a group of poems that Eberhart had sent; and Eberhart, on an impulse, "a wild spurt," sent a copy of the comments to the Guggenheim Foundation, a move which "delighted" Van Doren.

On his third try, he added the names of W. H. Auden, John Crowe Ransom, Michael Roberts, and Theodore Spencer, but still to no avail. In 1941, finally, Henry A. Moe, the secretary of the foundation, suggested that he "present a complete application *de novo,*" but Eberhart did not want to bother his previous sponsors, and he had no new ones, so he let the application stand, and again failed to win a grant.

IV

Eberhart's chronic low spirits, then, are explicable only in the context of the slow progress of his literary career. The reluctance of editors to accept his poems for magazines, the long search for an American publisher, the lukewarm reception of *Reading the Spirit,* and his failure with the Guggenheim Foundation, all combined to produce his sense of poverty. "God, what a cost it has been to try to live for poetry," he wrote after several rejections of *Reading the Spirit.* "I have lost everything by it—got very little along in that art itself." The intimate relationship which he felt at this time between literary success and economic success is suggested by a somewhat later remark, just after he had been turned down by a leading review: "I begin to feel that only poets with established incomes should continue. MacLeish with his Chicago merchandising house, Prokosch with his prosaic thousands. They get on." This attitude took its most insidious form, however, during the months before *Reading the Spirit* was accepted by Oxford, when he came very near turning on his friends. The tendency is apparent in the letter to Andrew Foster quoted earlier. The fact that it was related to his lack of literary recognition is clearer in an even more acid letter written at almost the same time to Jack Sweeney, then living in the fashionable Plaza hotel in New York, who had tried to soothe his pique at an adverse review; Eberhart replied:

> There's nothing like actual hardship to bring out the gall—but you have never known material hardship. Your superiority to reviewers, etc. is a Plaza touch. It's easy to sit in the Plaza and be superior to the contemporary scene; I'd like to be able to do it myself. I'd take the income any day, and let the reputation remain problematical. Your words come from pride and economic security.

This could stand as perhaps the most unfortunate letter he ever wrote, had he not written a still worse one to Elizabeth Drew just a few months later. She had written him:

it saddens me that you are so disappointed about the book. You shouldn't be, my dear, for were you Donne, Blake and Hopkins rolled into one, the response to your poems would be exactly the same. What response did the last two of those get anyhow, not to mention fifty others. The public for serious poetry is *tiny*. You say you have had three good reviews. I call that *good* fortune not bad, if they were understanding. You say to be a "successful poet" (hateful description!) you must advertize yourself, but who is successful in that way? Spender and Day Lewis are quite exploded reputations now, Auden has come into prominence by his dramas, not by his lyric poetry . . . but who else is a pin better off in reputation than yourself? No one!

She then goes on to suggest that he has cut himself off too completely by teaching at St. Mark's and that he should, among other alternatives, have completed his work at Harvard. In an incredibly obtuse reply to this sincere effort to help him, Eberhart centered on this suggestion:

I am rather amused at the way you mock and fleer at my solemnity. Some say style is all and yours is a grandmother's manner. . . . You talk about "success" almost like an American. I revolted against certain successes long ago, they were so horrible. You must know all the facts before you can lay down the law. You say I should have stayed on and got my Phd. at Harvard. . . . As it happened, I had to borrow 500 lbs. [sic] for that year. . . . There was no money in sight, no jobs; I had had help from my family earlier, now (then) I should be helping them. What an ignoble position not to be able to do so! . . . It has taken me three years just to square off that debt. Think that over a while. . . . To have been fated to have a fortune or an income would have made all that you seem to have desired not only possible but possibly easy.

These letters are the clearest possible illustration of the extent to which his sense of failure had distorted his vision, not so much by what they say as by their relationship to their epistolary context. Sweeney's "pride and economic security" were irrelevant to his advice about reviewers, and it is inconceivable that Miss Drew's letter could be interpreted as a mock; and his assignment to her of his own concern with "success," finally, could only result from an almost unhealthy egocentrism. More important, however, it becomes clear that he did not renounce the common norm of success for the sake of poetry, but embraced poetry as a substitute for that norm. We find again and again that he is willing to give up economic security, indeed economic luxury, only in return for a kind of literary recognition that is every bit as worldly, as tangible almost, as money itself. The full significance of this will not become clear, however, until later, when we shall see that he regained his spirit before attaining either wealth or any substantial recognition, suggesting that both stood in the place of some more comprehensive goal; but before the goal could be even partially attained, he would have to come still closer to reality in very concrete ways.

CHAPTER SIX
1937–1946

On January 8, 1940, Eberhart was informed that his services would not be required by St. Mark's after December of the same year. The only available record of the reason for his dismissal is a letter from the headmaster written in May 1941. Enrollment was down at the school, and the headmaster expected that "we shall have to cut our budget next year by $10,000 or $15,000," and he could not ask to keep Eberhart "when I should have to report at the same time that the English classes can be managed without you." As soon as he was informed of his dismissal, he began what was to be an eighteen-month search for a new position. "The Harvard Placement Bureau was duly solicited," but nothing was forthcoming from that quarter. He also "tried Theodore Morrison in re English A [at Harvard]. The first thing he asked me was my age. When I told him, he folded up like a clam." This was but one of almost a score of rebuffs he received between January 1940, and June 1941. Only in a few cases was he even able to entertain hopes.

The first of these was at Kenyon College. At the suggestion of Merrill Moore, he wrote John Crowe Ransom, who replied that there was a possibility that a new post, though not a very attractive one, was to be instituted for the following year. In February, Eberhart met Ransom, who was in the area to deliver a lecture at Yale and who invited him to visit Kenyon. So during St. Mark's spring vacation in March, he drove to Gambier, Ohio, and spent two days with Ransom, discussing the possible position and meeting Kenyon's president G. K. Chalmers. He came away encouraged, writing Moore, "I gathered the feeling that Ransom wants me." His personal qualifications, however, turned out to be irrelevant, for Kenyon finally decided not to institute the post. The following year the proposal was taken up again but finally tabled. When he wrote Eberhart about it, Ransom added that he had checked for him with Randall Jarrell at the University of Texas, but "They regard him as extra-curricular. . . . and keeping him salves their conscience that they are generous with creative and contemporary letters." The situation was similar at Vanderbilt, which Ransom pronounced "mad on Ph.D.'s and scholars." The best that he could suggest was that Eberhart join the armed forces for awhile.

At about the same time as his first application to Kenyon, he wrote President Hopkins about the opportunities at Dartmouth. Hopkins responded sympathetically, but emphasized that it was almost exclusively a departmental decision and told him to apply to the department, which he did. It turned out that there was a vacancy, but it was primarily for a man qualified to teach advanced courses in Shakespeare, "and in all modesty I had to admit my deep ignorance of Shakespeare, much as I have read him, and much as I should theoretically have liked to grow into such a position."

The cases of Kenyon and Dartmouth were typical of his year and a half of job-hunting. Every college he wrote had either no vacancy at all or none for which he was qualified according to prevailing professional standards. Of course his status as a practicing, published poet was finally irrelevant, although it gave him the backing of such people as Moore, Ransom, and Mark Van Doren. By spring of 1941, therefore, he was considering work far afield from his most basic interests. He almost took a job as a diplomatic courier with the State Department, and even considered selling insurance.

At about the same time, he began looking for a post in another preparatory school. His friend Dudley Fitts had left Choate, for example, making a vacancy there, but instead of replacing him with a man of equal qualifications, they shuffled the staff and "appointed a combination athlete-junior English master, still a senior in Amherst, who will of course come here for next to nothing." He also tried several other secondary schools and was finally taken on by the Cambridge School, in Kendall Green, Massachusetts.

The Cambridge School post came not a day too soon. His terminal sabbatical was almost over and his savings were nearly exhausted, although he had spent much of the first few months in 1941 rent-free in a New Hampshire cabin owned by a St. Mark's colleague. More importantly, he was weary of uncertainty and ready to effect a permanent rapprochement with reality. He was thirty-six when he was told that he was to leave St. Mark's, and he wrote Foster, "I am coming to the age where I would give much for security, enough money, the possibility of a family." His poetry was not among the things that he was prepared to give up, as we shall see, but he did say, in 1941, "To live for spiritual ends is to invite the empty pocket," and a few weeks later he declared to Ransom that

> when I was 25 I hated security with all the force with which I now desire it. I threw myself gladly on, around, and above the world. But now if one could only be secure, work hard, and get on with the real job of teaching.

This statement was probably the result, in part, of some lingering hope of work at Kenyon, but the general desire for security and stability was the logical conclusion to the direction of his life for the previous decade. It was also related, finally, to his growing interest in a young lady whom he had met the previous fall through her brother, Charles Butcher, then business manager and master of mathematics at St. Mark's.

II

Helen Elizabeth Butcher was born into the upper middle class of Cambridge, Massachusetts, in 1914. Her father and his brother were partners in the Butcher Polish Co., which they had inherited from the founder, their father, Charles Butcher, and which provided the family with a comfortable, although not luxurious, income. While attending Smith College, Elizabeth (who does not use her first name) did various kinds of social work in the summers, most notably as a courier with the Frontier Nursing Service in the mountains of eastern Kentucky. She found the work rewarding and majored in sociology for her B.A., going on the following year for a B.S. in social work at Simmons College.

She then worked for a year in the Neighborhood House in Roxbury, Massachusetts, but the frustrations in the work outweighed the satisfactions. She had gone into community work rather than individual casework because she felt that she could thus attack the roots of social problems on a broad level; but she soon found that the Neighborhood House project was designed not fundamentally to change conditions but merely to make them tolerable. She was convinced, for instance, that some of the same people who sponsored the Neighborhood House drew at least part of their income from the property in the slums which the House was supposed to help.

So she decided to go into teaching and secured a position in the fourth grade at the Buckingham School in Cambridge. She was working there in October of 1940, when her family gave a small dinner party for the birthday of her brother, who invited a poet who was his colleague at St. Mark's. That was about all she knew about him. Since Mrs. Butcher was a pacifist, it had probably not been mentioned that he had recently completed a Business and Professional Men's military training course instituted at Fort Devens, in Ayer, Mass. after the fall of France. So Elizabeth was somewhat shocked when, as she came down the stairs and into the parlor, she found their guest holding a walking stick and lunging as if with a bayonet at her mother, who shrank back in her chair and protested, "Yes, yes, Mr. Eberhart, but we won't defeat Hitler *that* way!" The martial atmosphere quickly dissipated, however, as they moved from introductions to dinner and to the theater for *Life With Father*.

Before the end of the evening, Elizabeth was in love, and when Eberhart invited her out to dinner a few days later, she dusted off her college anthology and prepared herself to ask intelligent questions about Tennyson, Brooke, and more successfully, Robert Frost. The only other thing that the Eberharts remember about their first evening alone together is a slight misunderstanding that temporarily relieved the Butchers of their one misgiving about their daughter's poet-suitor. Mrs. Butcher, observing Elizabeth's growing enthusiasm for Eberhart, reminded her that poets generally made little money and often inhabited uncomfortable garrets in seamy sections of town. So when Eberhart, whose *Song and Idea* was soon to be published in London, mentioned that he hoped the Germans would not sink the "sheets" he was expecting from England, she was happy to be able to tell her parents that, besides being a poet and teacher, her new beau was also an importer of linens.

When the truth about his sheets came out, she nevertheless continued to see him. He came in from St. Mark's as often as he could, frequently picking her up at the Buckingham School, where fourth graders who saw him coming quickly informed their teacher, ten years his junior, "Here comes your father, Miss Butcher!" They continued to meet throughout the winter and spring for dinner or the theater or, very frequently in fair weather, for walks in the Middlesex Fells. Eberhart often took along photograph albums and they would sit on a boulder while he explained the virtues of all his relatives. Elizabeth was moved by this uninhibited love of and pride in his family, and was delighted when she was invited to Chicago in the summer of 1941 to meet them all.

They had begun to talk about marriage long before this, but Eberhart remained ambivalent. He was thirty-seven and ready for the emotional security of family life, not to mention that he was in love. On the other hand, he feared the effect on his poetry of this loss of freedom. ". . . I made a deep wager I would never give up my creative gift," he had written early in 1940, "and have never seen the proper connection between that and usual married life. . . ."

And just two days before he proposed, he wrote his sister, "I question how I could further my career as a married man." Even a few weeks before the ceremony, his doubts persisted: "Maybe marriage will kill off the poetry, who knows?"

This was the central issue in their discussions of marriage, and they both realized that it could not be resolved by talk. Eberhart's brother, Dryden, always more forceful and certain of his opinions that his speculative brother, also realized it, and he took Eberhart to lunch one day and unequivocally laid down the law that honor demanded that he must either marry the young lady or else free her for other possibilities, preferably the former. The young lady herself, meanwhile, began to feel that her continued patience would compromise her dignity. Her resolve was further strengthened by an incident that occurred on their way home one day from a visit to Chicago's Brookfield Zoo. They stopped to talk by Lake Michigan, and she became so upset that she got out of the car and walked away into the shrubbery. When Eberhart could not find her, he became frantic, easily believing that she had thrown herself into the lake. Thoroughly annoyed at this demonstration of self-esteem she informed him that evening that she planned to leave the following week to visit friends in Indiana and then return to Cambridge. If an ultimatum was not explicitly stated, it was clearly implied.

The following Monday, July 14th, he asked her if she would like to visit the planetarium. "It was a high clear cloudless full midsummer day. I had planned a poetic act at the planetarium, under the constellation of Mars and Venus, but the place was closed." On the way home they saw a place where for fifty cents they could ride in a speedboat full of people far out into the lake and back. They got in, and when they were almost as far from shore as they were going to get, he slipped his mother's pearl ring set with diamonds on her finger and kissed her. At first she was not sure of the exact meaning of the gesture, but the other occupants of the boat had no doubts, and cheered.

A few days later the future Mrs. Eberhart returned to Cambridge to prepare for the wedding, an elaborate affair for six hundred guests, with a week of festivities preceding the ceremony, which was held on August 29, 1941. They "honeymooned in Maine on the Cranberry Isles, Big Cranberry in fact, and had a seductive cottage on Dead Man's Point." They later stayed at Castine, on Penobscot Bay, for a few days before returning to take up residence in a faculty apartment at the Cambridge School.

Eberhart began his new job immediately, while Mrs. Eberhart retained her post at the Buckingham School. The Cambridge School operated under the then relatively new system known as "progressive" education, and Eberhart was wary of the unfamiliar methods, "Feeling a bit skittish whether I know enough for the new kind of teaching, and not knowing how to study for it (any suggestions will be welcome)." The headmaster reassured him: "You'll have to discover your own way of doing it, by trial and error;" his only other advice was that "to catch the spirit of it," Eberhart might read some Dewey. He remained rather nervous about the project, but soon found that the school was much to his liking. "Well, I begin the new estate with much pleasure I must say," he wrote Dudley Fitts:

> The school is totally opposite from SM: the opposition is part of the pleasure, I intimate. From the freedom allowed here, the former abode was little else than Nazi tyranny. Here boys and girls smoke when they will (almost), make up their own rooms, work communally together on all manner of projects, never say "sir"—except for the smoothies two years at St. George's . . . —wear what clothes they will, escape church and stiff collars, and this noon I heard a cute p. g. girl rattling off the names of the Cummington boys—Blackmur, Tate, D. Schwartz—, a kind of people never heard of at SM, especially by those of 17. Also there are assortments of German and English refugees, Czechs, and what-n-tots to make you rejoice in the name of democracy. I shall probably discover a good deal of dumbness, but have already found a spirit entirely alien to my former abode. . . . We are gradually fixing up our little apartment. . . .

III

Eberhart had hardly had time to become accustomed to his new position when the Japanese struck Pearl Harbor, raising the prospect of military service. He had had some small taste of military life in the Business and Professional Men's Battalion at Fort Devens in the summer of 1940, and the following fall he had been part of the "cadre" that supervised "a course in military drill and instruction" at St. Mark's, but for all that he was not pleased when he had to register for the draft, and despite the fact that he was almost 38, he fully expected his number to come up. Then, early in 1942, he found an opportunity to serve in a capacity that would make some use of his training and experience. A friend he had known at Fort Devens told him that a group of men with teaching experience was being gathered to be trained to teach gunnery for the United States Navy. He made inquiries and was finally advised to apply for a commission under the program, which he did on June 12, 1942, receiving a commission as a lieutenant in the Naval Reserve, on August 10, 1942, to begin active duty on August 15th in a six-week course in gunnery at Pensacola, Florida. The commission was of course welcome, but there was one slightly ironic note: his commission made him unable to respond as he would have liked to an inquiry from the English department at Tufts College about just the kind of position for which he had been looking for almost ten years.

The Navy certainly had its compensations, however; Mrs. Eberhart was able to join him in Florida, and in October 1942, at the end of his training course, they settled into a comfortable home in Hollywood, Florida, for his first assignment, as Theoretical Gunnery Instructor, which involved

> long hard hours, from 6am to 4pm, and a most interesting new teaching experience. We hope we will be retained here indefinitely as it is such a beautiful town. We have bananas, oranges, grapefruit, and papayas in the garden: I plucked a grapefruit right off the tree for breakfast this morning.

In a letter to *Common Sense* written during his tour at Hollywood, his enthusiasm was a little qualified:

> Being an instructor in Naval gunnery at an air station in the South is, at this season of the year, about as pleasant a way of serving in the armed forces as one can imagine. That is not to speak of sand flies, mosquitoes, spiders, cockroaches, all manner of tiny enemies; or of heat rash in January. As a change from teaching in a private school in the North it is an agreeable occupation if for no other reason than that the students want to learn since their lives depend on it, instead of being constrained to learn by parents and by custom.

Later in the same letter, he touches on a problem that was probably very important to him:

> Personally, I have come to the conclusion that I would rather see a large body of men absolutely determined to do their best under every test of war, without dispiriting insinuation into the ultimate meanings of life, fate, and death, than men constantly at war, not with the adversary, but with themselves over what all the shooting is about. This represents a change of view I have undergone since entering the armed services. There may be more than one way to skin a cat, but the essential business is to get the cat "skun."
> . . . . The fermentation of ideas must be sought elsewhere.[1]

In May 1943 he was transferred to the Aerial Free Gunnery Training Unit in Dam Neck, Virginia. For the first few weeks they lived on the base in Norfolk, but they moved the following summer into an apartment in Virginia Beach, "a block from the Old Ocean." The move was timely, for in September an accidental explosion destroyed the building where they had lived in Norfolk, killing 26 people and injuring 250.

Although some of his work was very similar to that in Hollywood, there was more variety and greater responsibility. "Being in the Navy, in aviation gunnery, is always interesting," he wrote in

January 1944, "sometimes exciting, and in any event it takes most of one's time and energy. The mobility and changefulness of everything to do with the Navy makes it life-like to me. . . ." His most interesting work at the Dam Neck unit was the development of a pocket-sized manual, *Free Gunner's Hand Book,* which he sponsored in the summer of 1943. Although Eberhart says in one letter that the booklet "was a cooperative effort," he apparently bore primary responsibility. Designed as an easy reference for airplane gunners not only during training but also in combat, the manual was published on August 6, 1943.

Later that same year, Eberhart "understudied the office[s] of O[fficer] in C[harge] Instruction and Training Officer" and was given the responsibility of the former office early in 1944. He enjoyed this taste of authority and wrote in March, when his tour at Dam Neck was almost up, to try to retain or improve his position:

> . . . I came into the gunnery program because I had been a teacher for many years. I have been intensely interested in it as a teacher, but I want an opportunity to change over to the administrative end of the gunnery program; if possible, I want to be groomed for a chance at OinC or Training Officer when my next change comes. After a year and a half of teaching, I want the refreshment of administrative duties. . . . I am doing administrative work here now, and it is for this reason that I want very much to remain here in the capacity of OinC Instruction as well as OinC Sighting.

He was allowed to remain an extra six months at Dam Neck, and in September he tried again for a bigger job. The letter summarizes his career to that time:

> My duties. . . . include being scheduling officer. I have had about ten months of administrative duties, over and above previous activities as sighting instructor. . . . At AFGTU I have served, in addition to the above mentioned capacities [OinC Instruction and OinC Sighting], as acting Training Officer, Training Officer, and Officer in Charge.

Little more than a month later, he was informed that he was to become "fourth in command and Training Officer" of the Naval Air Station at Wildwood, New Jersey. He assumed these duties in the latter part of November 1944, having been promoted to lieutenant commander on October 17th.

"I miss a certain rough, breezy, and frontier feeling about Dam Neck," he wrote from his new station back to his former colleagues in the South, but it is doubtful that he in any way disliked the bigger and rather more comfortable arrangements at Wildwood, or the "unheard-of leniency here, a half-day off per week in addition to Sunday." Mrs. Eberhart was of course able to join him, and the ready accessibility of Philadelphia from their apartment in Cape May, New Jersey, surely compensated for the missed breeziness of Dam Neck. He was even able to function, in a slight way, as a man of letters, appearing to read his poetry before the Wildwood Ladies Aid.

More important, his work held more variety, interest, and responsibility than he had known before. "I have enjoyed my Navy Career to date," he wrote Auden,

> a complete refreshment from the stuffiness of literary people, literary attitudes. Up to this station I succeeded in Jekylling Mr. Hyde so that everybody thought I was a right guy, if none too salty, but of late I have been found out, by some of my own enlisted personnel! I have flocks of WAVES under me, one of my titles is "Synthetic Training Officer." Who would have thought one would become such? I am also officer in charge of CARTU: Combat Aircrew Refresher Training Unit; Senior Member of an Examining Board; and o in c of a "Basic Educational Program" where we get 56 illiterate grown males from total illiteracy through 4th grade. I am 4th in command of the whole station numbering several thousands.

He continued to enjoy these many roles until fall of 1945. In July he had the pleasure of being told, "You are badly needed in the 12th N.D. [on the west coast] as OinC of one of the ground schools at an outlying activity," and the letter goes on to list several places where he might go, not including the naval air station at Alameda, California, where he was finally sent. "The orders came through a week before the end of the war," he recalled later. "I was sent anyway." The Eberharts moved into a two-room apartment in a converted motion picture theater in Oakland and settled down for their last tour of duty. "The war is over," he wrote in November 1945,

> but training goes retardingly on. I find myself the officer in charge of a school. I have 15 officer instructors teaching everything from Calculus to Carpentry to 365 students. . . . I teach a course in College English so called; rejoice in the alertness of some of the waves and older men; enjoy playing with words and helping the writers to determine synechdochy and metonomy.

In March 1946, however, he was made Officer Personnel Officer, helping to process officers who were leaving the service. "I like my new work," he wrote Jack Sweeney,

> I am now personnel officer, the paper navy sailor of the rubber stamps, signing my name a hundred times a day to documents supposedly important, and satisfying the demands of eleven frantic female secretaries.

With the war over, however, the pressure of work was considerably less intense, and the Eberharts had time for frequent trips around California and some social life. The latter was especially active after they met Kenneth Rexroth. At the suggestion of James Laughlin of the publishing firm, New Directions, Rexroth invited them to supper at his apartment one evening. Eberhart appeared in uniform only to find that his elegant gold braid made a bright contrast in a group of ardent bearded pacifists and anarchists. Rexroth and his friends were tolerant of the Eberharts' militarism, however, and mutual interests in art and literature cut through political differences, with the result that the Eberharts became part of the active, if frequently offbeat, literary activity of the area. In the ensuing months they saw a good deal of Rexroth and his wife Marie, and the two couples often went together on excursions into the countryside. Mrs. Eberhart wrote her brother and his wife of a typical adventure; Rexroth took them rock climbing one weekend:

> he's an enthusiastic if not confidence inspiring climber. The first thing he did was to hand the end of a rope to Dick, tell him to stand with his back facing out over a 50 foot drop to jagged rocks below, and then to "bounce" down as they call it. I was watching nervously from below thinking to myself that it wasn't going to be any bounce but a splash of Eberhart all over the country-side. "Go on," says Rexroth, "bounce. What the hell are you waiting for?" Dick was obviously waiting for the world to come to an end, an eclipse of the sun or anything to distract Rexroth so he could climb down like a sane human being. Marie, Kenneth's wife, was urging K. to let Dick try a shorter place. "Will you keep quiet," says K. getting peevish, "just because you have what you call a weak knee. . . . doesn't mean Eberhart's afraid to go down." Well personally I knew Eberhart's knees would have been shaking if they hadn't been too paralyzed. All of a sudden, however, the old stubborn streak in RGE came out and then I thanked God for what I curse at other times because I knew that no matter how K. argued, Eberhart would stand firm. . . . After that Dick climbed several very steep places as well as Kenneth did, and climbed down one facing out, so his honor was redeemed.

Their close friendship with the Rexroths during their months at Alameda was also responsible for less strenuous adventures; through Rexroth, directly or indirectly, they met many literary and academic people, and Eberhart more and more came out from behind his uniform, as it were, and appeared as poet. He held, for instance, at least four public readings or discussions. "A week ago yesterday I had a totalitarian experience," he wrote in March, 1946;

> I had been invited to give the annual poetry lecture at Mills College, but the totalitarian part was that all 600 girls had to

attend; they were to be exposed to a poet once every few years, as they are to other experts in other fields. Had I not been tipped off, I should have been amazed when after I took the podium they all with one will arose! I read a paper and quite a few poems, at the end waving before these luscious, or perhaps gangling youngsters a Chinese paper snake given me by Muriel Rukeyser in the same Chinese restaurant where we dined, and then read a recent poem on the subject, as if to prove that poetry can be spun out of anything, a paper toy become the spirit of very evil. Later we were cocktailed by the Dean, where a member of the state department just back from Russia and just to return thither held forth informally on Russian affairs. . . . I sat between the etcher Roy Partridge and the guest refugee composer Darius Milhaud. The girls gave me a spread in the paper and want to go flying kites.[2]

A month later Josephine Miles asked him to the University of California to talk to her class:

She had had some poems mimeographed, and I had had others done at the navy, upon which I had written critical notes. The sunlight was resplendent; Chinese students lolled on the lawns by the campanile. I enjoyed the hour, but an hour is much too short a time to do anything but warm up. The students in their appearances are far different from Cambridge or Harvard types. I suppose they think they have their own type of sophistication, but they are a wild-west looking gang, some gangling tall men with full dirty beards half an inch long; some with plaid shirts; many without neckties; most intently smoking Manxman pipes. The women also look different, but I don't know quite how. They asked intelligent questions, however, and seemed interested. . . . Then we went to Piedmont to the Society for Aesthetics, whose meetings I have much enjoyed; the Hungerlands live in a huge old place, a castle of Suburbia. Helmut discussed his paintings last time; this, a paper by one Fischman on Tovey's music criticism, with vociferous argumentation by members of the Mills and UC faculty thereafter.

At about the same time that he was planning his appearance at Mills, Eberhart found out that he had added to his roles of poet, teacher and husband that of prospective father. Although they were both delighted, the news presented some problems; they had intended to drive back to Cambridge, but now the doctor advised against any automobile travel for the expectant mother. Finally they decided that she should fly home, which she did in June. Eberhart's brother, his wife, and two of their children came to California, and they all left San Francisco on June 28th to drive to New Mexico and visit their sister. Eberhart, now a civilian, drove home from there, arriving in Cambridge in plenty of time for the birth of Richard Butcher Eberhart in October. In November he wrote a friend

> that since seeing you I have become a father. Butch is three weeks old today. He has already begun the ancient process of pushing his parents into the grave. He pipes loud, is terrific in rages, in total protest. What a dynamo! It is entirely likely that he will never write a poem. At present he keeps me awake half the night and quite definitely puts me in my place. I see what they mean by the child being father to the man. . . . Needless to say, being forty-two I take some pride in this achievement, or more properly happening.

Although this letter had of course its own special origin, its tone of contentment and "some pride" is typical of Eberhart's letters after 1941 or 1942. His friend Sweeney stated the case nicely when he wrote, in February 1943,

> Your letters seem happier and more whole than I've ever known them to be. I suspect that the transfiguration is chiefly due to your extraordinary wife, though part of it comes from the new, more outward focus of your eyes.

This sense of happiness and wholeness cannot be accounted for either by his economic position or by the progress of his literary career. Although after their first year of marriage money ceased to be a serious problem for the Eberharts, they were scarcely wealthy, and although after 1939 his literary career did progress considerably, as we shall see, he could hardly be said to have had a spectacular reputation.

As suggested earlier, these considerations seem to have been subordinate to the larger issue of his relationship to material and social reality. Since 1922 or 1923 he had always been essentially alone, partly causing and partly caused by the introversion alluded to obliquely in the letter quoted above. His life at St. Mark's had its attractions, as we have seen, but it was a life of considerable psychic isolation. When he married he assumed, for the first time in twenty years, a vital role in a family, a role to which his identity as poet was not irrelevant, since it was as such that Mrs. Eberhart first thought of and loved him.

When he became an officer in the Navy, furthermore, he assumed, as he had never been able to as poet, a vital role in society. While teaching at St. Mark's he had always had the sense of being a servant, a minor worker on the fringes of wealth, while as an officer he was able, as he put it, to "use individual initiative," to exercise his will in a socially important function, whether designing training aids, running a school for illiterates, or sitting as a senior member of a court-martial. The profession of poetry was on the whole separate from his identity as a soldier; but as a person, at least, he could feel as integrated into his social environment as when he was president of Duodecim and captain of the football team. Although the poem is not overtly about himself, something of the contrast between his life in the 'thirties and in the 'forties seems to be behind the first two stanzas of "An Airman Considers His Power," especially in the first two and last two lines:

> I was in the days of peace
> Of warlike tissues made,
> And that was a strange man
> Fighting in a shade.

> All things by opposites go,
> Truth has there his lease,
> Peace has come with war,
> War that came with peace.

He had neither the luxury of Burr Oaks nor the recognition he was later to receive, but for the first time since his mother's death, he had finally acquired, in his marriage and in his work, a "niche of peace and some power."

IV

At about the time of the American publication of *Reading the Spirit,* in December 1937, Eberhart began for the first time to send out his poems in large quantities to various magazines, beginning a practice which he has followed ever since, simply knocking at the door until someone opens up. At first he was not very successful, but gradually he began to be accepted, so that by the 'forties he was publishing a great deal, not only in little magazines and anthologies, but in *The Kenyon Review, The Southern Review, Partisan Review, The New Republic, The New Yorker, The Atlantic Monthly,* and others.

In his early attempts, the editors of reputable reviews seem to have found him sufficiently accomplished to encourage but not quite ready for publication. When he submitted the long poem "A Meditation" to *The Kenyon Review,* for example, John Crowe Ransom wrote him,

> It is certainly far above the common run of manuscripts we have been receiving. . . . We don't like it enough, though we like it very much. Won't you please send us some other poems to see?

Eberhart replied with a two-page commentary on the poem, including the comments of his friends Prokosch and Sweeney, and submitted more poems. Ransom held the poems for a long time but finally reported:

> I hate to be so finicky, but I don't like the poems quite well enough. I think they lack mainly a sort of finish, or slickness, which applies to the structure as much as to the tone. You certainly have plenty of stuff. . . . Your very great variations of

styles might imply uncertainty in settling down to your metier, whichever style that is to call for.

A few months later he returned another batch:

> I don't [know] anybody who writes poetry with more insistence on making the words mind you; sometimes the verbalisms are dazzling; always they are new and fresh enough. But the effect for me is generally harsh; I miss what I have been used to think of as poetic tone. I like these little ones, however, best of those of yours I have seen recently. I can't like any of them quite well enough.

The Kenyon Review was the last of the important reviews to accept him, but Ransom finally received some he liked and published them in 1944.[8]

Partisan Review also finally accepted poems, but only after a long period of trial, beginning near the end of 1937, when F. W. Dupee wrote him, "We should be very glad to see poems or prose. We hope wherever possible to print longer poems or groups of poems; but we shall be happy to see anything you care to send us." Eberhart immediately sent some poems, calling attention in a postscript to a recent radio broadcast of his poems over a New York station. Dupee replied a little less than a month later,

> I am sorry that we have kept these poems so long, but there are six of us and each of us wanted to read them very carefully. Many things about them we like very much. . . . but we felt that they didn't quite represent your work at its best.

Eberhart accepted their judgment of course: "However, I don't see how six people ever combine to like a poem." He added further poems, which were likewise rejected. "I hope these two rejections won't discourage you from sending us other poems," Dupee wrote in rejecting them. "If only we could get something as good as 'The Groundhog'. . . ." Eberhart remonstrated,

I never liked the Groundhog as much as it seems to be liked
by some; when I wrote it—especially in the last few lines—I
thought it verged on the sentimental, however necessary, exact,
and strong-oncoming were the lines, "given" in a rush. I have
been surprised to see how it has got about; another example of
the oddity of poetic reputation. You ask for something as good
as the Groundhog. Here is something better.

Dupee disagreed:

All that I can say is that, to my lights, "The Soul Longs . . . ,"
like the poem in construction [rejected earlier], doesn't achieve
form. . . . Naturally I am sorry that we haven't been able to
accept your work so far, that we don't seem to agree on the
nature of poetry.

This seems to have ended his submissions to *Partisan Review* for
over a year, until Dwight MacDonald "cordially invite[d]" him to
send some in. He accepted the invitation, only to be rejected again.
Less than a year later, however, the editor relented and printed a
poem in the fall 1940 issue.[4]
    Eberhart was a little less active in his submissions to the "slick"
magazines. After *Harper's,* for instance, rejected one batch of
poems, signing the judgement impersonally, "The Editors," he apparently did not submit any more for several years. He was more
successful with the *New Yorker*. In September of 1939, Merrill
Moore wrote him,

Why don't you send some of your things to the New Yorker?
I have a feeling while reading it that a poem of yours ought to
appear on the next page. Do you want to psychoanalyze that?

Had he wanted to psychoanalyze it, Eberhart might have suggested
that Moore had subliminally noticed a poem which had appeared in
that magazine two weeks earlier.[5] Eberhart had begun submitting
poems to the *New Yorker* several months earlier, and one group
was rejected in June with the comment that they were "a little too

cerebral for the *New Yorker,* which of course is not a literary magazine." A little over a month later, however, he was able to write Foster, "I have descended to the *New Yorker,* which will print one of my poems one of these weeks." An interesting little controversy developed over the title of this poem, which is reprinted in *Collected Poems* with just the first line as title. Eberhart had simply wanted to call it "Poem," but one of the editors wrote him,

> Mr. Maxwell . . . asked me to write saying that the title POEM is not one we can use on the poem beginning "Go to the shine, etc." Apparently he did a vast amount of research and conferring to learn that The New Yorker would have to establish a whole new set of traditions before doing anything so revolutionary as to use this title.

Eberhart replied, defending his title and suggesting that it might be less revolutionary to leave the poem titleless, or that it might be called "The Lyric Absolute," or "Light Physicist," or "Light Physics." Barring these, he authorized the editors to pick their own title, which they did: "To a Poet," a title which Eberhart judged "odd but interesting."

The Atlantic Monthly required a longer siege. The editors had much earlier rejected "The Groundhog," with the comment, "This isn't for our gentle little circle." In May of 1938 he had gotten far enough that the Assistant Editor kept five poems for Editor Weeks to scrutinize. "What I like about these five," she wrote, "is a greater clarity of both feeling and imagery. In some of your poems your skill in making images and music seem almost to run away with you." The senior editor did not agree, however, that these poems were any better, and the *Atlantic* continued to reject his work for many months, always adding friendly comments and asserting that they were "borderline" decisions.

Later he assaulted Weeks himself, who replied, "You are in the position of having a good many friends in the *Atlantic* and yet such friends as never seem to help you materially," and went on to say that several of the poems he had submitted were very interesting but that some among the editors thought "that your poems are un-necessarily oblique." A year later, Weeks rejected "A World-View," which Eberhart had written for an appearance before the Tufts Chapter of Phi Beta Kappa, but was encouraging to the extent that he said it seemed "one of the best bids you have made so far." Eberhart replied:

> I would like to read you a lecture on your duty to serious poetry as an editor of The Atlantic Monthly, but find myself too amiable to do it, and appreciate both the failure of your refusal and the futility of my wrath. Being a contemplative individual, I also appreciate the rightness of your refusal and the wrongness of my protest, if I had any to make.

He then proceeded to make a protest and to read a lecture, suggesting that Weeks

> ought in all conscience to lead rather than to follow the atti-tudes of your readers, into the highest expressions of the age, rather than the mediocre; which would be an act year in and year out of effort and daring worthy of the [*Atlantic's*] high traditions of the last century.

Weeks of course disagreed:

> You are tempted to lecture me on the duties of an editor, and I, you, on the duties of a poet. It seems to me that in this crucial year [1941] when people are searching more earnestly for truth and guidance than at any time these past two decades, the curse which above all a poet must avoid is that of unintelligi-bility. I question whether these lines of yours—which suffer from a ponderous title ["A World-View"]—have either the strength or the clarity which they need to have if they are to be meaningful to a general but not uneducated audience such as ours. When I say this I am not thinking of . . . the more sensitively attuned of our readers. I am thinking of thousands of men and women in middle life who love poetry and who

have followed with progressive difficulty the cryptic intricacy of so many young poets whose work is in some measure derived from Hopkins and Eliot. This is not a time for art to be esoteric. . . .

You abjure me "in all conscience to lead rather than follow the attitudes of your readers." As I look back over our record to the first of this year, it seems to me that more often than not we have done just that. Certainly it was not the conventional thing to publish Auden's poem of 1600 lines in January and February, but I have no misgiving whatever about devoting so much space to it. . . . Of course we don't hit that level every time, but I think we do it more often than you have been willing to acknowledge.

Eberhart was indeed willing to acknowledge very little:

I appreciate your problem as an editor, but I have the profoundest respect for poetry as a vital resource of life; the fact that I respect The Atlantic Monthly is the reason why I am now willing to pursue my ideas further. I suppose a cranky idealism may be at the back of this. . . . You were lively and expert to have printed the long Auden poem, but a severe critic could say that it took no courage; it would have taken courage to print Auden about 1933, when he was just getting under way: he could say you embalm him now safely in his fame.

He goes on to suggest some measures for correcting the *Atlantic's* conservatism; for instance,

You might steal the thunder of journals like those above mentioned [Kenyon Review, Southern Review, etc.] and print from time to time a little anthology of poets under thirty, or under twenty five. . . . for instance, there is now in this country an English poet, George Barker, to whom Poetry (London) is giving a "Barker number," whose selected poems are forthcoming from Macmillan. . . . If you will look at Yeats' last letters to Dorothy Wellesley you will find mention of Barker

as the only young poet Yeats cared for, that is as a very young
poet. My argument is that people like Barker, whom I hap-
pen to know, do not usually send poems to The Atlantic
Monthly, or at least that is my impression. They have been
told that it is no place for them.

Weeks apparently did not answer this letter, but six months later he
wrote again:

> I am hoping to bring together in time for the March *Atlantic*
> selections from the work of some of our new American poets,
> and if you have a fresh manuscript to send our way I shall be
> happy to read it within the fortnight.

Eberhart had some fresh manuscript on hand and sent it in; a little
over a month later "The Atlantic finally broke down, but with im-
mense reserve and becoming modesty selected an eight liner." [6]
   During this period Eberhart was also solicited by many little magazines from all over the country, as he has been ever since. There
was *Pulse* in Los Angeles and *View* in New York; the short-lived
Trend at the University of Chicago and *Palisade* in Indianola,
Iowa; his "To Evade the Whirlwind" was printed in *Fantasy* in
Pittsburgh, and three others were accepted by *Diogenes* in Madison,
Wisconsin; another solicitor was *The Little Man: The Magazine
of Tomorrow,* in Cincinnati. Other magazines begun about this
time later became relatively important and have published a good
deal of Eberhart's work, among them Theodore Weiss's *Quarterly
Review of Literature* and Kerker Quinn's *Accent.* Another little
magazine, *Vice Versa,* "a sort of American *New Verse,* rather brisk,
rather flip, and quite unaccommodating," was edited by Harry
Brown, whom Eberhart had known well when he was editor of
The Harvard Advocate in 1938 and 1939, and whose "Ode to Richard Eberhart" was printed in the *Advocate* in 1940.[7]
   Many of these little magazines were of course based on college
campuses. The diffidence of Eberhart's first letter from David
McDowell, editor of *Hika,* at Kenyon, is typical, except for its men-

tion of Lowell and Moore, of requests he has often received ever since:

> It is with a sense of guilt that I begin this letter, and I am sure that you will easily understand why, inasmuch as you are concerned. I am writing to ask you a favor, and on top of that a favor that I am afraid I have little right to ask—hence the sense of guilt—I want to ask you if it would be possible for you to act as *guest contributor* for our literary magazine here at Kenyon? I spoke to Cal about it at the beginning of the year, but he seemed to think that at the time you would surely be too busy. However, since then I have read your book—and may I say that I admire it—and also gotten a letter from Merrill Moore, who suggested very strongly that I get in touch with you. Therefore I refuse to wait any longer.
>
> Of course, I realize that this is asking a lot to expect a writer to *give away* a publishable piece of work, but we are trying to shoot high, and I feel that that is the most important thing. It seems better to me, even in this small magazine, to shoot high and perhaps miss than never to try at all.

Eberhart sent a poem, and the following spring, when Auden was at St. Mark's, he sent another to go with one from Auden. Then the following year McDowell again asked the same favor, "realizing . . . that it is a considerable one to ask of a writer who must consider his expenses before his altruistic impulses." Eberhart's "altruistic impulses" prevailed again, however, and he sent four early pieces.

Eberhart had a much closer and more interesting relationship with the young editors of *Furioso:* James Angleton, a law student at Yale, and his undergraduate roommate, E. Reed Whittemore, later editor of *The Carleton Miscellany*. He met the editors, probably through Dudley Fitts, early in 1939, and submitted a long section of "A Meditation" for *Furioso*. The result was "a furious controversy" among the three of them which could not be resolved, and they finally published other work instead.[8] During the discussions of "A

Meditation," however, Eberhart sent copies of the comments of I. A. Richards and Jack Sweeney. Finally the poem was published along with these letters in the third issue.[9]

Correspondence between Eberhart and the editors illustrates some of the ends and means of magazines such as *Furioso*. In September 1939, for example, Eberhart advised,

> Several people have commented on your No. 1 disliking the somewhat "smutty" tone, if that is the word (it probably isn't); I mean, you should keep a serious poetry magazine absolutely serious (or absolutely humorous if you print humorous or light pieces). But you know all this.

He also suggested in the same letter that each issue, or at least an occasional issue, should "feature one writer a time, with a dozen or so pieces." Angleton had just returned from Italy with ideas from Ezra Pound, to which Whittemore referred in answering Eberhart:

> And tales of Rapallo. Pound says Cummings [whose "Dirge" was in the first issue] will keep no. 1 on the bookshelves . . . , saying that only Cummings can equal Catullus, so. He wants the third issue to be [a] memorial to Ford Madox Ford—and undoubtedly something good might come of that.
>
>   . . .
>
> I agree with you that variety magazines are not good. But variety is better than the wrong policy. One poet can be over-played, however, and one school. If, however, there was one writer or school in *each* issue as you suggested, we would be following up perhaps the wisest Poundian directions Jim has received, that of making each issue stand out distinctly from every other.

Later letters from Angleton show the forming policies of the magazine and some of the reasons behind them:

> For the next issue I don't know Dick [sic]. I have been thinking of printing more unknowns, and so far I haven't re-

ceived any support or interest from many of the old steadies. (That's a badly expressed sentence and you mustn't read too much into it.) What I mean is that I have discovered certain poets out in Calif. who I believe show not only po[?] but enthusiasm for *Furioso*. We have a difficult choice to make. We either have to go along as we are and fold up eventually, or we have to take note of new blood. You are not ancient but poet enough to get into most any mag. However there are hundreds who don't stand a chance. They constantly rap at *Poetry*'s door, "unwept, unhonoured, and unsung," and I believe that they have effected a fusion of internal and externals which our vast amount of contributions fail to do. Excepting you and a few others there are few poets of promise. The stamp of the "Waste Land," which is hardly their own, dominates our Eastern poets.

In the same letter he outlines specific approaches to reaching a wider audience:

Now I have tried to appeal for co-operation from *Furioso* friends, to help on circulation, interest etc. Perhaps this is asking too much, but can we live on letters and contributions alone? At present I haven't hardly a dime and yet there is another issue which must appear. . . .

In spite of this I have several new ideas which I shall put through. For the next issue there will be a long article from I. A. Richards. His Department is interested in the reception and interest provoked by reviewers and English Departments. They will no doubt give me all the co-operation necessary at Harvard in a little plan I have; namely, to print some 6,000 copies or more of Furioso which will be distributed to all classes in modern thought, criticism, poetry, etc. in American Universities. A sample copy should place before them the best in contemporary poetry. . . . I believe that Gregory will tap all those interested at Sarah Lawrence, Carmen at Bryn Mawr, E. Swan and Troy at Bennington, Richards & Co., at Harvard etc. Once the ball gets rolling for the next issue we should be able to hit all 48 university students of poetry.

An apparently later letter indicates that *Furioso*'s continued success gave the editors a strengthened faith in what amounted to a literary mission:

> We are going on with *Furioso* after we leave Yale and we are going to have a better and more appreciated magazine than all the others. I know this as a fact. I know that we will mold a large audience and that they will support us. I know also that we are going to improve to the point where we shall [have] all the best poets wanting their material in *Furioso,* not because of payment, but because we will have the more informed and appreciative audience. . . . I have a vision of that audience and it will be one which will go to an organic community of students and people not over thirty from here to California. Poetry has too much of the East coast appeal, it has been too long the private property of the Gotham Book Mart. But there are over a thousand schools and universities in the middle and far-west and that is where we're going to take poetry.

Angleton and Whittemore were able to continue their pursuit of this vision until the war interrupted publication and ended Eberhart's close association with this important little magazine.

It was also during this period in the late 'thirties and early 'forties that Eberhart began to be included by anthologists, among the most important of whom was Oscar Williams, whom Eberhart first met in the winter of 1940. Williams wrote him in October asking for poems for *New Poems: 1940,* in which the editor hoped "to devote the great majority of the space to poetry written with at least a consciousness of the state of the world." Eberhart, who was then looking for an American publisher for his third book, immediately sent poems and added,

> I am glad that you are doing the book, and doubly glad you have a publisher . . . who is willing to do it at perhaps a loss—you yourself will know the hardships of authorship, the constant fight it is.

After the end of term at St. Mark's, Eberhart went to see Williams in New York, and further correspondence ensued. Williams wanted to use "The Virgin" along with two other poems, but Eberhart remonstrated:

> I do not wish to have The Virgin in unless you should insist. I know the last line or lines must appeal to you particularly (something like your wild feeling), but I do not think the poem too good as a whole.

Williams did not insist, and "A Meditation" was substituted.[10]

The friendship that began with this meeting and this correspondence lasted until Williams's death and deserves closer examination, because Eberhart appeared in almost every anthology that Williams edited. The letters of this period indicate that their friendship, like Williams's inclusion of Eberhart, resulted primarily from a mutual respect for each other's work. In response to a friend who had called Williams "a very *bad* poet," Eberhart wrote in May, 1940, "I . . . like his work. We'll have to go to bat on that. He may not be ultimately good, but he is exciting, refreshing, and throws in a certain newness to letters.

The evidence of Williams's genuine regard for Eberhart's work is still more substantial. In early 1943, for example, when Williams was assembling poems for *New Poems: 1943,* Eberhart sent several groups of poems for his consideration, only to have Williams ask for more. At first Eberhart readily complied: "You were right in returning my mordant pieces." But two months later he became impatient:

> My book tells me I have sent you twenty-three poems. You seem to reject all these with merciless abandon. . . .
> There is simply no use of a poet's trying to justify his work, especially to a friend. You have the poems. If you don't like them for God's sake send them back and forget about it.

Williams's wife's reply suggests that, far from favoring his friend, the anthologist was setting unusually high standards:

You're the only poet over whom he's so suffered that I myself have finally gotten exasperated. . . . He expects from you
truly major poetry, which he doesn't from most of the others.
. . . So, over every one of your things, all-day long stewing.
. . . Dick MUST have some really great poem, complete, perfect in every line. Then, back to you what's on hand with cries
for a new batch.

In 1943 Williams decided to give up the *New Poems* series, and his
wife's explanation indicates that he rarely included people for
merely personal reasons:

> Oscar yells "Tell Dick why I gave up the anthology." That
> is a rather long order. Well, in the first place, the book has
> become a respectable literary property and the publisher gets
> ideas that take time to eradicate, such as putting in the Millays,
> etc. Also, Oscar has lost most of his friends through his in-
> ability to publish them, and so many poets known and un-
> known come around and raise rumpuses because they aren't in
> that a rather unpleasant atmosphere has been created around
> the thing for Oscar. . . . The first two books were of interest
> only to the poets themselves, but the third is selling, making
> money, etc. That involves a great deal of bother that has little
> to do with the actual editing, making the book an actual
> chore. . . .

This is not to suggest, however, that editorial decisions were entirely irrelevant to friendship; indeed, in one letter Williams states,
"I've included you in all 4 [anthologies] because you are a *poet* and
a *friend.*" It is to suggest that editorial decisions were very far from
being dependent upon friendship. That this was so is clear from the
correspondence surrounding *New Poems: 1944,* which Williams
finally undertook after all. Williams originally accepted four poems
from Eberhart, but "On account of the publisher insisting that I cut
my book down (paper shortage, and what not)," he had to cut
Eberhart's selection down to two: "Dam Neck, Virginia," and "The
Fury of Aerial Bombardment." Eberhart responded with friendly
but very strong language:

I have been for you since I first knew you and do not anticipate a change of heart in this regard, but you do make me mad sometimes. . . . What a terrific oddity or worse, dichotomy, in poets. They are supposed to be devotees of Truth, yet most easily they break all the rules in the book. Their word is not worth a penny. . . . I think you have been anthologizing long enough so that you should keep everybody "at the tentative" until you decide—but you should not give the old double-cross like this. . . . But I suppose if I were in your shoes, doing the book, I would be worse than you! So do what you please, I'll not go back on you.

Williams remained amiable, calling Eberhart one of "the few O very few of the very very very best poets," but stood his ground:

Poets are a selfish lot, and there is no getting around that. . . . Your drive toward publication, getting published, is shared by the writer of this letter. An excessive drive toward publication presupposes a consciousness or lack of some kind of merit on the part of the poet, or else, why the drive? I am in total sympathy with your position. But that position is [a] real flaw in both [of] us. . . .
As for you doing worse if you were in my shoes, I agree with you there.

Eberhart accepted this gentle rebuke, though disagreeing, and concluded, ". . . I suppose all these things come down to one's nervous organization, to complexes too deep for words." They remained friends.

His increasing publication in periodicals and anthologies did not make it any easier for Eberhart to find a publisher for his third book, *Song and Idea.* In January 1940 he sent a manuscript to Ian Parsons of Chatto and Windus, including the comments of Auden, who had helped with the selection of the poems. It was of course a very bad time for all the English, and Parsons himself had joined the Royal Air Force. It wasn't until the end of March that his partner, Harold Raymond, wrote. He apologized for Parsons and went on:

I know he had intended to write you before leaving, but did not manage it. He did, however, write a pencilled scribble in a train in France, containing several paragraphs which I was to hand on to you. . . . He says about the poems: "I've read and re-read them and soaked myself in them these last few weeks, and I can't tell you how much pleasure I've had from them. To read contemporary poetry that's so fresh and vital and original is exhilarating at any time, but now it's more than usually stimulating and refreshing. I really am grateful and full of admiration."

. . . "Somehow or other we have just got to do this book. Things are damn bad in the book trade over here and we have been compelled to cut out all 'prestige' publishing—of good books which we know are good but which are almost certain to make a loss."

Raymond then goes on to suggest that he and Parsons

fix up some satisfactory arrangement with you . . . to guarantee us against loss.

To judge from the fate of "Reading the Spirit" [200 copies sold in England; 250 sheets sold to the Oxford press] it would appear almost certain that the new book will involve a loss and it would therefore seem simpler if we published the book for you on an ordinary commission basis. . . . The sum I would suggest is 30 pounds. . . .

Eberhart himself had mentioned the possibility of a guarantee contract, but he had not really considered the idea very seriously and had to think about it for a few days before writing Sweeney for advice:

. . . they recognize the force of my work, and want to find a way to print it again.

We change of course. I should not have welcomed the suggestions they put forth, some years ago. . . . Do you not think, reality being what it is, that I ought to accept; that I ought to have it put out as soon as possible?

Sweeney agreed, and Louise Hawkes Padelford wrote that she would like to be his patron, to "invest in your spirit with alacrity and even more joy and confidence." He accepted both her offer and Chatto's arrangement, and the book was published on November 7, 1940.

His efforts to find a publisher in America duplicated those for *Reading the Spirit*. He contacted Oxford about it three times while trying elsewhere. The book was rejected by them first in the summer of 1939, and then a year later Eberhart wrote Raymond, "The Oxford Press news is pretty stuffy. I saw Vaudrin, whose position I appreciate. They are willing to make a dicker if I lay something on the line, but I shall peddle the book awhile. . . ." Four months later he tried Oxford again:

> I am naturally hopeful that the work will come out here; and I was never morally satisfied on your refusal to go along with me in my career. I trust you are really not satisfied either, although I quite appreciate a ruthless look at dollars and cents.

Vaudrin forced him to take another "ruthless look" and insisted that Oxford simply did not have "the wherewithal to publish verse." They had already discussed an arrangement similar to Chatto's, and when Eberhart finally capitulated in April, Vaudrin immediately sent a breakdown on the cost of importing sheets, binding, etc., totalling about $130.

Eberhart agreed and the order was put in with Chatto, but because of the war, there was no word until the following October that the shipment was even on the water. Then a month later he heard from Raymond that the ship had been "sunk by enemy action." [11] They reordered and waited for another shipment. The original arrangements had been for 300 copies, but Chatto had only 188 left, and they did not arrive until June. Publication was then set for August 20th, and Eberhart received the first copies on August 10th, the same day he received his Naval Reserve commission.

Late in 1941, Eberhart asked James Laughlin of New Directions, who had published some of his work in his annual anthologies, if he would like to see a selection of poems for one of his "Poet of the Month" pamphlet series. Laughlin agreed, but asked him to seek some help in making the selection: "I think you write some damn fine poems now and then, but I also think you can't yourself tell which ones are best. . . ." When he had seen Eberhart's submissions, he was ready to do the pamphlet, but he still said, "I think you a mixture of more vitality and more sloppiness than any other good poet I can think of." On February 10th, nevertheless: "Fine, I've put you down for February, 1943." But in July, he still could not find enough poems that satisfied him: "What I have strongly in mind for your P of M is a really STRONG selection from your work." Eberhart replied:

> I have written to Oxford to see if they will charge for poems as of a selection of the kind you keep mentioning, and will report when I can. My objection to this kind of a volume is that not only is ND as a house supposed to uphold experimentalism and the advance guard, but the P of M books are also supposed to do this, to show in a certain compass what a poet is doing at a time.

Laughlin answered that he had misconstrued the purpose of the pamphlet: "I am absolutely no longer interested in publishing 'interim reports on a poet's journey through his workshop,' if you see what I mean. . . . Experimental stuff goes in ND" (the annual anthology). He soon found, however, that he was as incapable of making a selection as he thought Eberhart was. "I'm sorry to make further delays," he wrote in August, "but I must confess I am quite unable to decide which of your poems are the best."

By November he had set the schedule back to "about July or August." Eberhart remonstrated:

> It was not for nothing that I began *almost a year ago* to ask you for a p of m book *Jan.* or *Feb.* of 1943. There was method

The house at Burr Oaks, Austin, Minnesota, built in 1916 by A. L. Eberhart. There were ten acres of lawns, orchard and thicket on high land, and thirty acres of lowland pasture.

Eberhart's birthplace at 811 North Kenwood Avenue, Austin.

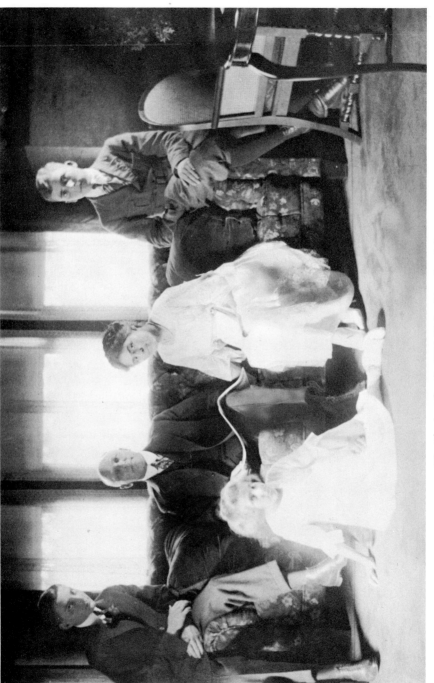

The Eberhart family, 1918. Richard is at far right.

The Duodecim Literary Society.

On the porch of Alpha Delta Phi House, Dartmouth.

On board the *Etha Rickmers,* Indian Ocean, 1927.

Hollywood, Florida, April 1943.

With a kite used in aerial free gunnery instruction, Virginia Beach, 1943.

Christ Church, Cambridge, Massachusetts, August 29, 1941.

In Maine, 1965, with Philip Booth, Daniel Hoffman, and Robert Lowell.

: the Library of Congress, May 1960. *Left to right:* Oscar Williams, Robert Frost, Richard erhart, Carl Sandburg, L. Quincy Mumford, Hy Sobiloff.

YALE UNIVERSITY NEWS BUREAU—ALBURTUS FUND

: Bollingen Prize Committee, Yale University, January 1953. *Left to right:* W. H. Auden, nard Eberhart, Louise Bogan, Malcolm Cowley, Leonard Bacon.

The Poetry Office, Library of Congress, 1960.

The Eberhart family, Washington, 1960.

of that; I have never had a book out at the spring of the year. . . . You definitely promised me Feb. of 1943—now you push it off to July or August. What's the idea?

Laughlin answered, "I think we could advance you to March, perhaps," and went on to reiterate the importance of careful selection: "I feel you . . . love equally well everything that drips from your deathless pen." Further delays ensued, and Eberhart sent "a perfected list" on February 21, 1943, at about the time that the book was originally scheduled to come out.[12] They had by this time decided to use poems from former volumes. On the 25th, Laughlin acknowledged receipt of the list and cited his work with his Utah ski resort as reason for his procrastination:

> I'm apologetic as hell about the long delays. I hoped to be able to get everything lined up a long time before this, but just never seem to get to it. I am busy out here from morning till night with every sort of mechanical nuisance from busted sewer lines to meat rations, and just never seem to get a chance for literary labors.

Then Eberhart did not hear from him until July, when he apologized again for the delay, and in October he wrote still again that he "simply cannot make a choice among them." So by January 1944 Eberhart had ready a still further refined list, which Laughlin accepted in March. On June 1st he wrote, "We are under way," but in October they were having new troubles. Eberhart's letter states the case clearly:

> I asked you for a wire acknowledging mine making essential corrections. . . . Our relations over this book I would not call too savory. . . . Your failure to allow a decent lapse of days in case your addressee were out of town, or unable to attend to the matter in hand, is violent and unnecessary conduct, especially when it relates to the printed word which cannot be retaken once committed. This summary haste in sending the order to the printer to go ahead, without my sanction, is the

more deplorable in view of the incredible delays you allowed
yourself over a period of two years theretofore, in some cases
ignoring my letters in regard to the book for six months. . . .
Nothing could be in more execrable taste than to publish a
book in one year, but advertize it as of another: your relegation
of the book to 1943 after I had received first proofs recording
and listing it at the head of 1944, was an impressive blow. . . .
In many ways, I think you are giving me a pretty raw deal,
but there is of course the Olympian attitude: this is just a little
book for a few from Laughlin's private printing press.

Laughlin's response shows both that Eberhart was not completely
aware of his problems and that he, on the other hand, was not then
in a position to sympathize fully with Eberhart and others like him,
"for whom," as Laughlin himself wrote years later, "my delays and
sometimes even eccentric publishing procedures must have been a
heavy cross to bear." For at the time he was clearly annoyed:

> All of the things which you say in your letter of the 19th
> are quite true. But you should realize what the matter is with-
> out my having to tell you. The damn thing has grown too
> big. I can't keep up with it. In an ordinary business of our
> size—that is—doing the number of books—there would be
> four or five people to spread the work over. Here there is just
> one—ME—and I am obliged to put half my time on the ski
> hotel to make the money to pay the deficit of the books. You
> see we have grown in length of list but not in volume of sales.
> There never will be a large public for this sort of stuff and there
> is no use kidding ourselves about it.
> I have just been too soft about accepting books. . . .
> So . . . [sic] a new program . . . [sic] doing fewer things
> better. Your letter had a great deal to do with my coming to
> this decision so you should feel a certain satisfaction. How the
> writers whose books I am refusing may feel is THEIR worry.
> From now on I am going to stop killing myself for the mythi-
> cal ideal of literature whatever the hell that is. For six years I
> have worked four or five nights a week till 12, and dropped
> eight to ten thousand dollars a year in deficits . . . [sic] but
> NO MORE. . . . So, finita la commedia, as they say in books.

Copies of this troublesome little book, *Poems, New and Selected,* finally became available on January 28, 1945, almost three years after the idea had been approved; and even then, according to Laughlin, "the jackets were printed ass backwards."

In the reviews of *Song and Idea* and *Poems, New and Selected,* there is no longer the interest in influences that dominated the reviews of *Reading the Spirit.* The observations of the best reviewers of the earlier volume, however, begin now to crystallize into what amounts to a critical consensus. Conrad Aiken's review of *Poems, New and Selected* is representative:

> His "Groundhog" remains one of the most remarkable of contemporary poems, its Blakeian intensity and fierceness of vision unimpaired by the wanton roughness of form, the perverse metrics; and the variant of it that appears in "Triptych," recast in the key of Jacobean canting and ranting, is almost as good. But Mr. Eberhart . . . makes the not uncommon mistake of establishing violence and perversity as his norm, with the inevitable result that where everything shrieks and clashes, the uproar at last cancels itself out, and it is as if nothing had been heard at all. . . . if he could only be severe with himself, and canalize his gifts, instead of simply going hell-for-leather at his Idea, with capitals, he could be one of the very best of contemporary poets, as he is already one of the most exciting.[13]

If the reviews of these books agree on their description of Eberhart's work, however, they do not agree in their evaluations of it. On one side, John Malcolm Brinnin's review of *Song and Idea* uses a pose of respect to mask thinly a fundamental hostility. Eberhart, he writes, "must be accepted, almost literally, as a medium gifted with words." Once one makes this concession and gives himself to the poetry, says Brinnin,

> Convention drops away and a reader feels the immediate record of free sensibility. . . . Here poetic realization comes . . . with the silent explosion into meaning of charged symbols.

Brinnin continues, however, to suggest that this is a rare experience because acceptance comes hard: "who for instance, can remain sober under even a voluntary spell when he comes to the line, 'When I think of her the power of poetry arises'?" In such lines, it is averred, "innocence is crowned with absurdity and a reader's whole faith badly shaken." [14]

In a much more sympathetic commentary, John Crowe Ransom, also writing of *Song and Idea,* concedes that Eberhart's "workmanship is crude," but insists that "The man's fundamental attitudes and strategies are right." He agrees with Aiken when he says, "Extreme energy is his mark," but he does not agree that this energy establishes a norm of violence: "Sometimes it is riotous and tasteless, but the man has, every time, a comprehensive poetic experience." The worst that he can say about the poetry is that it is characterized by an obscurity that leaves the reader uncertain and unwilling to commit himself. After quoting the poem, "In prisons of established craze," he writes,

> Responding to this verse one reader will say, Blake, and another will say, Stevens, while a third will say it is just nonsense verse. But so many of the images and ideas make a connection with categories in my own mind that I am reluctant to give it up as does the third reader. . . . But perhaps most of us will be afraid to say what the meaning is that we have acquired, because it may not be the intended and official one at all.[15]

Yet what some readers call absurdity and crudeness, others call "fearlessness," as does Kerker Quinn in the *Herald Tribune Books*

> His word-inversions, his coinages, his ellipses, . . . win the stubborn reader over. It is pleasant to find a poet who is susceptible equally to tradition and experiment and employs neither for its own sake.[16]

A more important index to the growing respect for Eberhart, however, is that some critics read carefully enough not only to ob-

serve the poetry's roughness of form but also to attempt to account
for it. Typical of this approach is W. H. Mellers's review in *Scrutiny* of *Song and Idea* and David Daiches's in *Poetry* of *Poems,
New and Selected*. Mellers, in the longest and most probing of the
reviews of either book, finds an "extreme, even excessive, sensitive-
ness, to nervous experience," at the heart of both the strength and
the weakness of Eberhart's verse. "In all of it there is a quality of
suffering—nerves exposed and jangling, agitated by contrast with
the outside world," he says, and it is this quality that is "communi-
cated in the queer nervous rhythms and in the characteristic verbal
juxtapositions." [17]

David Daiches's sympathetic review of *Poems, New and Selected*,
finally, defines Eberhart's problem as "a certain disparity between
language and insight." He calls Eberhart "a sensitive and accomplished poet whose impressions and intuitions tend to be a little too
subtle for his technique." He examines carefully several verses to
prove his point; and then like Aiken he points to the "Triptych"
version of "The Groundhog," showing that the poet occasionally

> has succeeded in aerating his language, in breaking down some
> of its oversolidity, so that each line and stanza responds more
> delicately to the idea which prompted it and which in turn is
> prompted by it.

It is interesting to note that Daiches considers this version of "The
Groundhog" superior to the earlier, better-known form.[18]

Although no important critic has only unqualified praise for either *Song and Idea* or *Poems, New and Selected,* the reviews have
nevertheless come a long way from the patronizing of *A Bravery of
Earth* and represent an advance from the influence-hunting in comments on *Reading the Spirit*. Most reviewers of the later books
make, as only Blackmur had earlier, careful and respectful examinations of both strengths and weaknesses and conclude, with Mellers,
at least that "Mr. Eberhart remains one of the few poets whose future work may still be worth reading."

CHAPTER SEVEN
1946–1952

As Eberhart's naval career drew to a close, he was determined not to go back to secondary school teaching. His wife urged him to make an all-out effort to secure a position in a college or university, but he was convinced that he had no future in such a position without a Ph.D. The Harvard Appointments Office had several positions on file, but they were almost exclusively beginning instructorships in English composition, from which, he felt, he could not advance to the kind of teaching that really interested him unless he returned to graduate school, which he was not, at forty-two, prepared to do.

He decided, therefore, that if some promising position could be found in the business world he would take it, capitalizing on his administrative experience in the Navy. Then, several months before his discharge, they found out that neither Mrs. Eberhart's brother nor their cousin William wanted to go into the Butcher Polish Company at that time. Since both Mrs. Eberhart's father and his brother William were well along in years, there was some danger that the company would pass out of the family. As this situation developed, attention naturally turned to Eberhart, and he was finally hired in 1946, with the idea of training him to take over the company after a few years.

He stayed with the company until 1952. He first worked in and studied the processes of production, from the basic formulas and raw materials to the finished product. Then, after about half a year, he moved into administrative work and learned that end of the business. By the end of 1947, he was ready to go into sales, to go on the road and learn the old markets and try to open new ones. He took long trips during 1948 and 1949 into Maine, Connecticut, New York, and New Jersey, selling and making contacts. Then he returned to the office in Boston to train new salesmen and for other administrative work.

Eberhart's work with the family firm and his developing literary career were thoroughly separate. His correspondence centers on the latter almost exclusively; but he remembers being enthusiastic about the business as well. He found considerable appeal simply in the idea of a family business, the idea of integrating the most basic social unit with a fundamental economic complex. It was primarily this idea that moved him to join the company, and in 1949 he responded negatively to three separate inquiries about attractive teaching positions because "I am committed to a family business and have a moral responsibility to it."

There is no doubt, on the other hand, that he spent a great deal of time with literary work and literary people, time which, had he taken over the entire management of the polish company, would have had to go for the fast-growing business. Since "everybody knows my main interest is poetry," furthermore, there was some opposition within the company, especially from William Butcher, Sr., to his becoming head of the business. So everyone was relieved when Charles Butcher, II, agreed to come in and take over, after a time, with Eberhart working immediately under him. Although a little ambivalent, Eberhart seems on the whole to have been genuinely satisfied with the arrangement; he knew he could get along with his brother-in-law, whom he had known since the 'thirties, and recognized the latter's superior business talent. "So he is coming in April," he wrote his family in March 1951.

Even if I were a world-beater at business I suppose I could not "beat" this situation. But actually I do not want to beat it and heartily welcome him, inasmuch as the elders cannot get any younger and this will be best for the future. I will be on the board of directors and will be an administrator, but the idea is for Charlie to learn to take over. . . . It looks like a good thing all around, and I am delighted to have Charlie come in. I am always a divided nature; with one part of me, my pugnacious part, I take it as a sort of defeat, but with my more enlightened side I see that I am betraying my best interests to put all my energy into something I do not like 100%.

Charles II's entry into the firm turned out to be timely in several respects. Within little more than a year both of the elder Butchers were dead, and Eberhart was able to take advantage, because young Charles was there, of the best opportunity he had ever had as a poet, as we shall see.

If he did not "like 100%" his work in the Butcher Polish Company, he nevertheless enjoyed his hours outside the office to the fullest, for in Cambridge the Eberharts were at the center of the cultural and social life that Eberhart had watched from a distance, as it were, in the 'thirties. By March 1947 he could write Laughlin of "shindigs with fiedler, brinnin, moss, burr, wilbur, sweeney [sic] et al (Al who?) over the week-end," and in June he wrote Josephine Miles:

> We seem to have had a parade of interesting people in the last few months. . . . There were Nicole Cartier-Bresson, a beautiful 21-year-old French poet who gave an accomplished lecture on the resistance movement, at Harvard, and her sister-in-law, Eli, the wife of Henri Cartier-Bresson who is now tripping the US with Brinnin doing a photograph-prose book.

Richards was now teaching at Harvard, and he met Eliot again:

> At Harvard Commencement last week Richards and Eliot both got honorary degrees, the former giving one of the four speeches. The Richards had us for cocktails afterwards. Ivor and Tom were up on the roof having pictures taken when we ap-

peared; when they descended Ivor had on his gorgeous Cambridge robes, which I had not seen him in for so many years. Mr. Eliot remembered me, to my astonishment. When I said it had been fifteen years ago when I last saw him he instantly asked and averred that it had been fourteen. He congratulated me on my forthcoming Chatto book, that is on the mere fact of its publication, which he needn't have done at all. When Richards said that no man can get to the top of his profession without "Political ability" or some such phrase (jokingly referring to their degrees of the day) Eliot remarked with a smile and a chuckle, "You would certainly be the one to know, Ivor." Ivor told Eliot that Conant's citation referred and compared him (Eliot) to Milton. And so it went, a delightful hour.

Such anecdotes are scattered through Eberhart's correspondence between 1947 and 1952, and they make up a picture of a rich and varied life dissociated from the polish company. In 1948,

Marianne Moore read at Harvard last evening, was spirited and charming, but cut the audience off after half an hour. We went to Harry Levin's where she was delightful at cocktails.

And a few weeks later:

Sir Osbert and Edith Sitwell are in this country on a lecture tour. . . . We had the pleasure of having them for dinner recently: they were perfectly delightful—Edith wore a great turban and an enormous pair of Tibetan hand-beaten silver bracelets.

And the following spring,

Wm. C. Williams was up and read his poems, as then did Wilbur. Frost came over one night in high fettle; we were able to introduce him to Bowra just before he went back to Oxford.

It is clear that the magnet and catalyst of these personalities and events was Harvard University, which no longer seemed the Prussian labor camp that Eberhart remembered from the 'thirties:

> Cummings read at Harvard recently, almost entirely from
> 1 X 1, eschewing perforce the typographical extravaganzas; he
> sat in New Lecture Hall all through his hour with his left
> lean-fingered hand supporting his eggshell head, a beautiful
> continuity of poise. Meanwhile talking sometimes, when being
> particularly rough and "American," out of the side of his
> mouth in guffaws. Then Frost came again and packed the hall
> top and bottom; he is a credit to the human race, has now de-
> veloped a persuasion of the colloquial: from his tall years he
> holds forth wittily, descending occasionally to the reading of a
> poem, then breaking off abruptly when some new idea comes
> into his head. He puts one hand against the flat open other in
> a gesture of communication—as if even words could not do it,
> you had to use the whole machine. Then Spender read his
> Goethe lecture in that ghastly now ghostly Memorial Hall
> dedicated by James Russell Lowell long ago; we had a short
> time of talk and I liked him, his charm and ease, his good
> looks.

Wallace Stevens was also among the many luminaries who passed
through the Eberhart home during these years, and a record survives of his response when Eberhart showed him the New England
Poetry Society's Golden Rose, which Eberhart had won the previous
spring; John Holmes wrote him about the award in April:

> The honor it brings you can only be measured by knowing
> those who have had it before you, and you do know them all,
> although you may not know they have been awarded this
> trophy.
> Ted Spencer, May Sarton, MacLeish, Ciardi, Robert Frost,
> and more than I can remember over a quarter century. You
> know I would like more resounding honors for you, the Pulit-
> zer, the Bollingen. Or are some of the best most quietly given?

The reply from Eberhart, who was later to win both the Pulitzer
and the Bollingen, is respectful but amusing:

There is a certain tenderness about the tradition of such things; the idea gives off a certain nuance. There is also something comical about a golden rose as a poet's trophy, but I have thought about it and can find no better symbol, since it is general and central. A golden thistle? No. A silver canister, as just drained of mead? An actual beaten copper laurel wreath? A platinum flute studded with sapphires? An ancient Irish or Greek harp or lyre made of sandlewood or maybe teak: Invisible strings? No, no doubt a golden rose is as good as any and valuable perhaps in 2050 in some museum—but still far away from poetry, as if we had under eye a platter used at the Mermaid, with names inscribed—but still the poet is elusive, existing in the imagination.

The Rose is a gold medal which the recipient keeps one year and then passes on to the next winter (Richard Wilbur won it the year after Eberhart); Stevens saw it one afternoon after the Harvard-Yale football game:

> Our party turned in from Mt. Auburn St. to Hilliard St. and Wallace Stevens met us at Hilliard Place [where the Eberharts lived]. He had gone to the Signet for lunch and then to the game alone. It was so nice of him to come. We had martinis. He said he had never met Eliot, was asked to stay over for the Advocate Party tomorrow, but was going . . . back to Hartford. We had a warming time. I showed him the Golden Rose to see what he would say: he said, "You can wear it on your cowboy suit."

Probably the most celebrated visitor to the Eberhart household, however, was Dylan Thomas, who spent four days with them in the spring of 1950. He was in Cambridge early in the year to give a reading under the Morris Gray fund at Harvard:

> Dylan appeared like an amorous leopard, shocked everybody, and we finally got him to bed at 2am (after his Gray reading there was a do at the Advocate, then Matty [F. O. Matthiessen]

and him to dinner [)] we appeared later with the Wilburs and
Frank Parker and wife, and finally eventuated at the Wilburs.
Dylan is a rolly [sic] poly lovable child, an inspired alcoholic.
He reads masterfully. Well it was a wild time.

It was apparently on a second visit that Thomas stayed with the
Eberharts, "where he ate only a piece of bacon in three days," because it was not until May that Eberhart wrote Parsons, "Dylan
Thomas has just departed as house-guest—off for more readings—
and left a wake of affection, whimsies, great warmth and jollity."
He also left a coat, and Eberhart lent him his at the airport, never
to see it again. He tried, through Brinnin, who was traveling with
the poet, to retrieve it, but couldn't. "No matter now—" he wrote
Brinnin in July; "we are both sacrificial yeomen to the singing
farmer. . . . burly Dylan."

Probably the most pleasant part of life in Cambridge, however,
was the regular, week-to-week association with other poets, sometimes even in an organized way. In the fall of 1948, for instance, several poets in the area began, at the suggestion of John Ciardi, to
gather for "reading and strict criticism of poems, no holds barred.
And the pleasure of any considerations of poetry." It began with
just Ciardi, Eberhart, and John Holmes and later added May Sarton, Richard Wilbur, and occasionally others, including Archibald
MacLeish and Robert Lowell. They met at varying intervals until
the spring of 1950, when they apparently became too involved in
other activities. Eberhart remembers only one poem which the
group criticized, "The Horse Chestnut Tree," which some members
felt should end with the narrative part, deleting the last nine lines:

> If I had left them off I am sure the poem would never have got
> into one anthology. . . . I recall driving Dick Wilbur back
> from John Holmes' that night. We allowed as how we enjoyed
> the rigorous criticism of our lines but mutually confessed that
> we would be damned if we would change a line of ours for
> all that.

Much more highly organized was The Poets' Theatre, one of Eberhart's most interesting activities when living in Cambridge. It began in June 1950, when

> Lyon Phelps came to our house in Cambridge, Massachusetts, wanting to enlist Molly [Mrs. Mark deWolfe] Howe's and my support toward starting a Poets' Theatre. Several interested poets decided to try their hand at the new form and report any progress in the fall.[1]

They met again the following September and, finding that they had among them written a good deal of verse drama, began to plan their first production. In a little over four months they were ready to stage their first bill, a series of four one-act dramas, on February 26, 1951, at the Parish House of Christ Church in Cambridge.

> It had John Ashbery's "Everyman, a Masque," with music by John O'Hara. My "The Apparition" followed, directed by Molly Howe. . . . Intermission. . . . Then came "Try! Try! a noh play," by Frank O'Hara. Finally, "3 Words in No Time," by Lyon Phelps.[2]

A little less than a month afterwards he wrote Karl Shapiro an account of the evening:

> The play evening was more of a success than anybody thought it was going to be. At least it generated a lot of enthusiasm and talk. The small theater was packed and spectators were stand[ing] 4-deep at the rear. Some said later it was the liveliest Cambridge audience they had seen all year. I presume half students and half oldsters.

The letter goes on to describe the production of each play, but the most memorable event of the evening did not occur on the stage:

> However, the laughter at [O'Hara's] play (or with it?) became almost excessive—the whole spirit of the evening was of ebul-

lience and pleasure. Right after it Thornton Wilder got up impromptu and made an historic speech. It would have taken courage in anybody but one as aggressive as Thornton. He kept talking about the "grass roots," about how this could not have happened 20 years ago (nothing since Baker left), but all of a sudden he threatened the audience with a long aimed arm and finger and lit into it like an irate schoolmaster, ridiculing the spectators for their "bad taste"—"you are acting very badly," etc. It was embarrassing to listen to; at one point I thought he was not going to bring it off. He lectured, cajoled and rebuked the audience as if it were all composed of sophomores. The idea seemed to be that poetry on stage should be listened to with reverence for the glory of language; he seemed to think the boys were laughing "at" the plays to show sophistication toward [a] situation which they did not really possess. He chilled us to the bone. Then he lightened up and ended so enthusiastically that everybody cheered. A pretty unusual occurrence, talked about considerably thereafter pro and con.

The following summer Miss Violet Lang, a member of the group and the author of several verse plays, wrote Eberhart that her father had suggested that if they hoped to solicit funds from individuals or foundations, they would have to have a formal organization to take responsibility for the use of such support. "We have the petty officers of execution, Matchett and me," she wrote,

> and I suppose Lyon *should* be called Manager, Director, or somesuch, but we have not thought in geometric terms of Reassuring Definition or Connotation like having our own note paper or whathaveyou with a list of sponsors and/or directors. Do you think Wilder would like to be (or would consent to be) a "director"? Would you? Would Molly? Would Dick Wilbur?

The other members of the group agreed, and they established a legal corporation:

To produce and present, with the assistance of volunteers . . . experimental plays not likely to obtain commercial production . . . to encourage poets to write for the stage and to educate them in the techniques of the theatre.

The board of directors included Mrs. Howe, John Ciardi, Archibald MacLeish, John L. Sweeney, and Richard Wilbur. William Match- ett became treasurer and Miss Lang secretary; Lyon Phelps was vice president and Eberhart the president.

The organization put on 20 plays, including Eberhart's *The Visionary Farms* on May 21, 1952, between its inception and the spring of 1952, when Eberhart was called away from Cambridge and his close association with the company's productions ended.[3]

Eberhart's activities during these years between the war and his first academic appointment also included public appearances, and records of several survive. He read his poems, for example, to a meeting of the New England Association of Teachers of English in Springfield, Massachusetts, on November 7, 1947. Dudley Fitts was apparently responsbile for this appearance, as well as for one in Andover at about the same time. Almost exactly a year later he sat on a panel discussion at Bard College with William Carlos Williams, Robert Lowell, Richard Wilbur, and others, to which Wallace Stevens came as a special guest, and the following February he spoke under the auspices of the Morris Gray Fund at Harvard, when he was introduced by his old mentor I. A. Richards. The following year he appeared in March at the YW-YMHA Poetry Center in New York, where he had read his poems for the first time in January, 1947, and in May at Dartmouth, along with his classmates Marshall Shacht and Richmond Lattimore. Then in February, 1951, he appeared for the first time with the Institute of Contemporary Arts in Washington, D. C., and at a writers' conference at Indiana University in July. In April of 1952, finally, he delivered the Founder's Day address at Wheaton College, in Norton, Massachusetts, appearing in full academic regalia to give a speech which would be of considerable benefit to him later.

A different kind of recognition was afforded by various poetry contests. He had hardly settled in Cambridge after his return from San Francisco when he was informed that he had won *Poetry's* Guarantor's Prize of $100 for some selections from "The Kite" in the July issue.[4] Four years later he won another $100 from *Poetry,* in the form of the Harriet Monroe Memorial Prize this time, for poems published a few months earlier. In 1951, finally, he won the Poetry Society of America's Shelley Memorial Award, which carried a stipend of over $800. Perhaps more important as an index to the rising respect in which he was held was that he was asked to be a judge in several contests himself. In March 1951, for example, he was one of the judges of the Poetry Center Introductions at the New York YMHA, and a year later he judged the *Atlantic's* Poetry Contest for College Students. Most importantly, he was asked in the spring of 1951 to serve on the committee for the Bollingen Award, which he did for two successive years.

II

While it is clear, then, that his work with the Butcher Polish Company carried considerable responsibility and required much of his time, Eberhart nevertheless was able to take part in a good deal of more or less literary activity. He was also able, of course, to continue writing and publishing poems. Although he still had more poems rejected than accepted, his contributions to periodicals continued to be numerous. He maintained his relationships with the journals which had printed his poetry before, such as the *Kenyon Review,* renewed those with magazines with whom his association had been interrupted by the war, such as *Furioso,* and added many to his list of markets, such as the *Sewanee Review,* the new *Hudson Review, Botteghe Oscure,* and others. And of course the various very little magazines, such as *Circle* in California and *Nine* in England, continued to come and go. He also published two single poems in elegant little special pamphlet editions: *Brotherhood of Men* (which was reprinted in *Selected Poems*) in 1949, and *An Herb Basket* in

1950. Most importantly, of course, he published two books between 1946 and 1952: *Burr Oaks* and *Selected Poems.*

Probably because of the amount of his work that was being printed in periodicals and anthologies, or perhaps because of improved conditions in the publishing business, Eberhart did not have to go searching for a publisher after the war. In early January 1946 Ian Parsons wrote him, "Harold Raymond and I both feel that it's time we had another book of yours on our list. . . . I think a new book would go well here now, and would be best for your reputation generally." What was better, he also had in mind for Eberhart still another book to follow: ". . . . a bit later and when paper is more abundant, we could do a really representative "Selection" from all your books, including the new one." Eberhart was of course delighted at this unsolicited request and promised to gather a manuscript as soon as he could, but he warned that it would be at least a month, because he was still in California and would have to search periodicals for his work. By the 25th of February, however, he had a group ready to submit under the title "Sighting:" "I was for two years a Sighting instructor in the war; in time the warlike connotation will fade, but there are other meanings." There were of course more poems than could go into the book, so Eberhart marked his preferences and asked Parsons to select what he felt would best go in. He was sure only that his war poems should definitely be included.

Parsons took almost four months to make his preliminary selections, and in the interim Eberhart wrote Philip Vaudrin at Oxford University Press in New York:

Some months ago Chatto and Windus wrote asking for a new book of poems. . . .

I believe in the integrity of such continuity. . . .

Another Press wants to do this book. I suppose that the idea of a continuous tradition is not necessary in this country, although I have always favored the notion. I don't know

whether Oxford has any policy or serious feelings about it
and write to find out.

Vaudrin had nothing to say about the traditions of continuity, but
did say, "I think there is no doubt about our wanting to take sheets
from Chatto and Windus of your new book," and asked to see
a manuscript. It was as easy as that, a sharp contrast with the struggles of 1936 and 1941.

On June 27th, Parsons sent his first list of preferred inclusions. He
apologized for the long delay:

> This has not been laziness or the result of that bromide "pres-
> sure of work" (though there is plenty to do), but because I
> found myself quite unable to make a selection from the ex-
> tensive manuscript you sent without reading and re-reading it
> several times, and indeed soaking myself in the poems gen-
> erally.

This letter, along with Eberhart's answer, are the best illustrations
available, within a small compass, of the process of selection and the
importance of having a sensitive editor in the publishing house. Parsons's second paragraph:

> Decision was made the more difficult by the fact that I found
> myself at variance with your own order of merit in so far as
> many of the poems in Sections 1 and 2 were concerned. Several
> of these struck me, and after careful consideration still strike
> me, as "ideas" for poems rather than as realized poems. I may
> be wholly wrong about this, and having been away from books
> and poetry for six years I'm conscious that my eye may be
> completely out; but one can only go by one's own "inside feel-
> ing," and mine didn't respond as it should do. In too many
> cases I was aware of the experience you were trying to pin
> down, recognized it as poetically valuable, but was not moved
> by its expression because of a constriction, an abstractness, in
> the presentation.

There follows a list of his selections, and then he points out an interesting fact about the poems:

> The only thing that makes me think my selection may not be altogether arbitrary is that I notice that most of the poems I have chosen were written before 1936, or from 1942 onwards. This may be pure chance, but it just might possibly reflect some significant change which was taking place in your work in the interval, and had not quite crystallized out.

This letter reached Eberhart on his last day in San Francisco, and he answered it from Las Vegas, indicating the considerations he thought important in decisions about selection:

> Your selection is fine and I agree, with only a few points following. You lean to the conservative side, but I understand that you have to sell the book. For instance, The Human Being has just been taken by *Circle,* the liveliest little magazine in the U.S., which would turn down some of your selections.
>
> . . .
>
> Leave Me My Golden Horn of Hours, excluded, was used last month at the University of California for final examinations. But I don't know how good it is, and agree to exclusion.
>
> I have a certain shyness away from out-stating poems like The Full Weakness of Man. I have preferred The Magical (just published at Harvard [in *Foreground*]) and Of Truth, which has already been anthologized. Keep it your way if you are sure, but please read these three again. Maybe you could use the other two also, but I am perfectly willing to accept your choice if you still wish it. Maybe *FWoM* is good, how does one ever know?

Later in the letter he wonders about other poems:

> I am glad you like TRIPTYCH. I have read [it] publically several times with exciting results. It may be strung out a bit, but I don't know how to cut it yet.
>
> . . .

Again, I have "blushed" to publish, and have not yet published, An Airman Considers. Is this meretricious? Or does it have a core of truth?

Three weeks later he wrote again and, sure that the selections would be satisfactory, spoke of the physical makeup of the book:

I have often thought, since so many poetry books are advertized the same way, that it would be interesting to have one without the dubious benefit of a blurb whatsoever. Blank inner flaps, nothing on the back except perhaps a notice of my other books. Is this too risky a notion? No ballyhoo, let the work talk.

Parsons answered both letters on September 2nd with a new list of inclusions, coming to terms with Eberhart's comments: he agreed about the blurb: "I am all in favour of your suggestion to cut the cackle and let the book talk." He did not agree, however, about Eberhart's title and hoped for a new one. In less than three weeks Eberhart complied: "Title: I propose BURR OAKS. Enclosed is a poem by that title, written last March. I like the strong feel of those words." Parsons liked both the poem and the title, and since they had settled on inclusions, it appeared that they were ready to go to press; but in January, Eberhart had another poem that he wanted in:

Books are so important to the author, and so seldom with me are they put forth, that I wish I were sure that every poem was my best. Horace Gregory in *A History of American Poetry* (Harcourt) speaks of my "unevenness" and Rodman, in a too flattering note in his *New Anthology of American Poetry,* Revised Edition (Random) just out, restates the same point. I learned something Saturday night, when I went to New York to read my work; I read to a critical audience, and was amazed when they burst out in applause at "At the End of War," and again, though a little lighter, at "A Ceremony by the Sea," enclosed. . . . the gist is that I would like the Ceremony in, hoping of course that you like it.

Parsons did like it, and they happened to have two extra pages to fill, so "Ceremony by the Sea" was included. That concluded the initial editorial work on *Burr Oaks,* and proofs were ready in March, but "owing to the chronic state of congestion in the printing and binding trades," Eberhart did not receive the first copy until September 2, 1947, and the book was not officially published until October 16th.

While waiting for Chatto to complete publication, Eberhart dealt with Oxford about its edition. He was clearly not satisfied with the breadth of dissemination of his work in this country, and pointed to the sales of *Poems, New and Selected* to show what could be done:

> Be sure you do what is right [in regard to permission to reprint poems] with respect to Laughlin's book (sold out, I gather, or except for a few copies). Laughlin printed 1500. It is obviously good to sell poetry as he does for .50 to 1.00. You can't go so low, but I think the less you can get the retail price to the more you may dispose of. I wish you could advertize it more fully, as you might take advantage of "snowballing" in the past few years.

Vaudrin agreed in principle, but was "afraid that the economics of Laughlin's business are somewhat different from the economics of the average commercial publisher"; he planned to keep the price to $2.00, however. The Oxford edition was therefore almost identical with Chatto's, except for an errata slip, and was published on November 28th.

In his initial attempts to publish his next book, Eberhart was at first discouraged. He sent a large manuscript to Parsons in August 1948. Reception of the poems was acknowledged by Raymond, but he did not hear from Chatto and Windus again for almost a year; then in July 1949 Parsons finally wrote to apologize and to explain that the market for poetry had decreased considerably, and that although they had hoped this to be merely a reaction after the boom in books during the war, it had not turned out so. "And now I don't at all know what to say to you," he went on, beyond giving you the depressing news that costs of producing any book are steadily mounting, while the sales of books of verse are so small as to be almost non-existent. Even the most established poets have taken a knock and, for any but the favored few, a sale of two or three hundred copies is the very best that can be hoped for. In these circumstances we must, I fear, say "no" to the possibility of a further volume of yours at this moment, sincerely as I regret this. Perhaps in a year or so the situation will have changed and it will once more be possible to put out a book of verse without incurring more than a reasonable cash loss—a thing we have always been glad to do in the past for authors in whose work we believed. The trouble nowadays is that the loss is a three-figure one every time.

That was the end of it until the following fall, when Eberhart suggested, to Vaudrin of Oxford this time, that they plan two books, one a selection from all his work and then another of poems written within the last five years. Vaudrin felt that it should be the other way around, and he hoped for another joint venture with Chatto. In any event, he clearly wanted Eberhart to remain on Oxford's list:

I should like, of course, to see you stay with us, even though the record to date has not been too exciting as far as sales go. It has been exciting to me, however, in terms of your growth as a poet, and I should hate to see you go elsewhere.

Within a few days, however, it became clear that the opportunity to go elsewhere was precisely what Eberhart was to have. John Ciardi wrote the day after Vaudrin to express the Twayne Co.'s interest in a selection: "The time is really right, and I'd love to be the one to do it." On the same day Eberhart asked Laughlin if his New Directions press would be interested, and Laughlin answered in the affirmative. Eberhart's reply deliberated the alternatives:

As you know I have had a good "lash-up" for years with Chatto-Oxford NY and I don't know that it should be broken—

but they don't *boom* one's books, and as you well know I have always been enthusiastic for what you have done for your writers—Kenneth [Rexroth] perhaps especially. I think, from preliminary report, Oxford would want me to get out another "regular" book first, put off a Selected for 2 or 3 years. In the meantime, Ciardi is very eager to get a Selected for his new Twayne outfit. He is a swell guy and his persistence is pleasing. But let's have a talk when you come up. The point about waiting too long is—how long do we live? My doctor gives me a clean bill of health, but I get melancholy every time I think on being 45. The heart has a way of stopping abruptly, as if to say—Nix, brother, life isn't what you thought it was—we want you for the Eternal Worm.

Finally he laid his cards on the table with Oxford and told Vaudrin about both Twayne and New Directions and said he would

do nothing without consulting you, and favor you for either or both books—and much appreciate your wish to hold onto me. If the world were only arranged so that one could give one's entire time to art!

On December 8th, Vaudrin wrote that he had consulted Parsons about the project, and less than two weeks later passed on the reply from London:

Parsons is prepared to go ahead now with a volume of your Selected Poems on the understanding that we would take 500 copies from him at the outset, but he would prefer, as I originally told you we would, to see a new volume come first. We are both, however, quite willing to go along with what I take your wishes to be, viz., to do the Selected Poems now and to follow up later on—say, within a year—with a new book.

Eberhart responded quickly to this very new experience of having three publishers (four, counting Chatto) in pursuit of his work and wrote on New Year's Eve to discuss the various pros and cons of each alternative, and to offer a suggestion that would take advantage of the reliability of the long-established houses in New York and London: he asked for a contract for both books. Vaudrin's response must have been gratifying:

> . . . we will definitely follow up with your new book, and eventually we shall certainly want to do your *Collected Poems.* So can't we settle this business right now? . . . We should be very unhappy indeed about letting you go elsewhere now, either in part or as a whole, after so long and so pleasant an association with you—indeed, "unhappy" is scarcely the word for it.

Eberhart could hardly turn down such an arrangement and wrote Laughlin, not without some exaggeration and, one suspects, some satisfaction:

> Oxford has risen up in wrath and anger and in transatlantic aggression will not let me go. I am sorry to report this. Your invitation to be in your New Classics Series with a Selected was mightily enticing—it gave me a big rosy glow to think of all those ads you sport your men withal! . . . . But the lash-up (mark the Navy) with Chatto-Oxford has endured three books now and they want it to go right on to two more, a Selected at once and a 1946–1951 follow-up regular volume; and promise an eventual Collected.

His next few sentences might have been addressed to almost the whole publishing industry:

> What I really regret, Jay, is that you did not take me on full scale about ten years ago. Then I wooed you but you would not wed . . . you would not let me play in any way of exploiting whole books, the possibilities of future books.

Laughlin clearly harbored no ill-will:

> They would be out of their heads if they let you go. Yes, I too am sorry I did not snap you up a long time ago, but I am some-

times slow in arriving at my judgments. At that time I was not entirely sure. Now I am. I have arrived at this valuation on my own, and not by anything that anybody told me, so you can be sure it is sincere and sound.

Laughlin had to wait fifteen years, therefore, to publish a New Directions *Selected Poems;* and Eberhart had to wait a year and a half for the Chatto-Oxford selection, which finally came out, after all the usual delays with selection, proofreading, printing, binding, and shipping, on March 19, 1951, in England and on June 29, 1951, in New York.

In reviews of *Burr Oaks* and *Selected Poems,* a broadly perceptive and generally favorable critical consensus begins to emerge for the first time. Few reviewers were quite ready to go so far as Eberhart's friend John Holmes, who had long admired his work and ventured a prediction about the pieces in *Selected Poems:* "The poems have been read these twenty years: this book will be read many times twenty more." [5] But neither was Selden Rodman's review typical; Rodman, who is also an old friend of Eberhart's and who collaborated with him in the editing of an anthology during World War II,[6] reads more like the reviews of *Song and Idea* or *Poems, New and Selected* in that he gives as much space to what he feels are the weaknesses of the work as to its strengths. He says, for instance, that

> "Triptych," an argument between a poet and a practical man, fails to come off; one's sympathy is all with the latter who can hardly open his mouth without being overwhelmed by a deluge of whimsy.

One is reminded of Aiken's review, quoted above, in a slightly later passage:

> Eberhart is an inventive poet, with a healthy urge to let violence and exuberance "shock out over the teeth," and the consequence is that the poems of ideas tend to fly apart like a revved-up machine without a governor.

On the whole, however, Rodman concludes that such passages "are not typical. Eberhart can write straight, even sparely, and for the most part does." [7]

Howard Nemerov, writing in the *Sewanee Review* of *Selected Poems,* also has some complaints:

> the longer, discursive poetry seems to me very often diffuse and turgid, operating either by too many particulars too little imagined ("The Brotherhood of Man" [sic]) or by a rhetoric too enlarged for the feeling ("The Soul Longs to Return Whence It Came").

Nemerov seems also, however, to find more to admire than Rodman. More importantly, the very "roughness" that for other critics is a fault now becomes a means to a valid end:

> Mr. Eberhart's cadences, his combinations of sound, often wrenched and twisted to a *deliberate* awkwardness, remain attached to the artificial part of poetry by the minimum means, and produce from the old forms a special and new energy. [italics supplied]
>
>   . . .
>
> Altogether this book has been a source of great pleasure to me; a difficult, unfashionable poetry which is above all things alive and intelligent.[8]

Arthur Mizener, writing of *Burr Oaks* in *Poetry,* takes a closer look at the faults that many reviewers have found in Eberhart's poetry:

> His trouble has always been that his faults are very obvious and easy to feel superior to, because they are as unmodish as it is possible for faults to be; they are Victorian faults. That Mr. Eberhart also has the Victorian virtues is easy to overlook. . . .

Mizener suggests that both the faults and the virtues are the results "of a remarkable honesty," and that in his successful poems, therefore, "he achieves a kind of direct rightness of feeling toward central experiences which is about the rarest thing there is in contemporary verse." This "rightness" is achieved, moreover, "in a language as simple and perfect as you could ask for." He then quotes the short "Rumination" in full and avers, "A writer does not earn that kind of simplicity, as Mr. Eberhart has obviously earned it, easily." [9]

A still more emphatic endorsement of Eberhart's work is in a review of *Selected Poems* by Babette Deutsch, who, after critiques of "The Groundhog" and "The Fury of Aerial Bombardment," suggests that this poet "demands that the doors of perception be cleansed." Miss Deutsch concedes that "the book is uneven," but she is just as sure that "there are things here that in their concentration of thought and feeling, their intensity, be it somber or radiant, are as eloquent as any English poems of our time." [10]

There are some reviews, furthermore, that are characterized by consistent, unrelieved praise, as those of G. P. Meyer in the *Saturday Review of Literature,* who says of *Burr Oaks,* "Ecstacy and awareness are never far away," [11] and of William Arrowsmith, who calls *Selected Poems* "a selection of some of the finest romantic verse —a rarity in itself—written in America in the last twenty years." [12] There were two reviews, however, which were at once enthusiastic and unusually perceptive; they were both by M. L. Rosenthal: his review of *Burr Oaks* in the *Herald Tribune,* and of *Selected Poems* in the *New Republic.* The most remarkable thing about these two reviews is that Rosenthal, rather than simply finding the work uneven, shows a greater catholicity of taste than other reviewers and writes about the different kinds of things that Eberhart does. In the *Burr Oaks* review, for example, he discusses "Triptych" at some length and comments that "this poet is especially distinguished by his fine wit and unabashed fancy." Rosenthal's ability to respond to these qualities co-exists with a recognition of the value of others:

> More important are his use of nostalgia and memory in the title poem and elsewhere and his gift for uniting bleak philosophical realism with these qualities of imagination as well as with the kind of humility and pity found in "At the End of War." . . .

In his review of *Selected Poems,* he concentrates on one aspect of the poems, the treatment of death, writing that Eberhart has "no incantations to ward death off, or ingenious proofs of its irrelevance, or outcries against cruel nature," but instead a "vision of the futility of, yet necessity for, heroism, wisdom and mystic vision—human buffers and constructs against time." The idea is that poetry transforms reality, and

> Sometimes an Eberhart poem is pitched in so high an emotional key that the vision of transformation and the catastrophic knowledge are fused together, seen as equally valid perceptions of the whole truth.

Even in a review that concentrates on a single theme, however, Rosenthal finds space to remark another aspect of the versatile poet's work:

> Again, the rich complexities of wit and imagination evoked in the life of the free intelligence may force grimmer recognitions temporarily underground, as in Eberhart's "Ode to a Chinese Paper Snake," [which] views our culture and its history in ironic perspective.

Although most reviewers of *Burr Oaks* and *Selected Poems* are not quite as sympathetic as Rosenthal, most would agree with him that "Here, for a change, is a strong, original mind that is up to the subjects it considers," [13] and with these two books Eberhart's stature, as measured by critical response, began to be established.

III

In 1950, from July 5th to August 5th, Eberhart had his first visit at Yaddo, the artists' colony on the palatial Spencer Trask estate near Saratoga Springs, New York, a visit that was important in several ways. He slept in a large bedroom in the mansion and went each day with his tin lunchbox "to an idyllic studio in the woods where one stays (except for maybe lunch with the next studio neighbor) until the end of the day," at 4:00. "The evening meal is a big formal affair for the 25 or so artists here. . . . Then there is croquet or later ping pong." The greatest attraction of the place is of course the abundance of silence and solitude for work. He took with him the idea for a poets' theatre

> and was so vitalized with the new possibilities that I wrote about one hundred pages of verse drama in three weeks. W. C. Williams was in the next studio; his typewriter sounded little arpeggios through the pine trees as he completed *Paterson IV*.[14]

It was also here that he began to put together the selection that became *Undercliff*, his next book after *Selected Poems*, putting the poems in rows on the floor of his studio cottage to "walk around among them trying to get their feel in certain relationships." On the 29th he wrote Mrs. Eberhart:

> I worked like hell for three weeks, but suffered a reaction then and have not been doing too well since—however, I gave my pages to Doc Williams who is reading them, and already thinks they are swell. I see it is essential to have so much time that you literally steep in memories and potential recreated feelings. . . . I see from this experience that we, all of us almost as Americans are obsessed with action; we can hardly sit still. This often makes for shallowness, going around a daily tread-mill like a squirrel in a cage. Not to have to hurry or do any-thing but what you want to conduces (up to a point) to what-ever self-realization you may have. You can stew in your own juice—hopefully for somebody's delectation.

Even during the first three weeks, however, he did other things as well as work:

> I had no sooner arrived . . . than Roethke, Harvey Shapiro and Wagner, the latter two young poets, suggested going over to Bennington for a term-end party given by the literary maga-zine staff. . . . The rich Bennington girls had supplied a whole

case of liquor. It was the usual party of talk dancing and drinks. The President was there, although I did not meet him. . . . Also the Nemerovs, who have just had their new baby. . . . nobody seemed willing to depart, so we stayed on into the small hours. Shapiro's girl, an attractive senior, very practical and capable, got us all lodged for the night.

They also took occasional trips into Saratoga Springs to visit the spas or go to the races or explore the various nightspots. Besides Williams, Eberhart's closest association that summer seems to have been with Theodore Roethke, who accompanied him on many of these junkets. One letter records Roethke as pilot of one of the huge target kites that Eberhart had started flying as a hobby during World War II:

> The rules are not to have visitors until the end of the work day at 4 pm or make any noise, but the wind was blowing at 10:30 in the morning so I got Ted Roethke and Harvey Shapiro and the 7 foot kite and a 5 footer. We went out on the broad front lawns almost down to the formal fountain. The 7 footer went up OK just enough wind, not nearly as good as Maine, too many trees. After a while I put the reel on Ted (who weighs 230, a huge man) and let out a lot of line. Then the wind died, so before I could get control the 7 footer was lodged up in the top of a 50 or 60 foot pine tree. We pulled and pulled from all angles. I never thought we would get it out at all but after a while it came out with hardly a scratch! Then we tried the 5 footer and I had a Turkish bath workout as there was just enough to get it up with work. At one point it swooped down to the ground; Hans Sahl hit the earth and it came a foot from his head, which caused much amusement.

It seems clear, then, that Yaddo was, for one of Eberhart's temperament, at least, the perfect place for both work and play, and his month there went by quickly before he had to leave and drive home, giving Roethke a ride to Boston. A few days later he wrote

Elizabeth Ames, the director of Yaddo, to thank her for "the large sympathy of the place:"

> Nothing could be more characteristic of America than that, leaving Laddo, I have not had a minute to write to you for almost a week, having been hurtled violently into the world of yammering action. The transition was hard. Ted and I found a summery field overlooking the high Berkshires; here we sat among flowers eating our Yaddo sandwiches.

It was in the realm of "Yammering reality," however, that the rewards of the summer of 1950 were to be especially important, though that did not become apparent for two years. In the intervening time, life rolled on at an increasing pace: The Poets' Theatre began, young Charles Butcher entered the polish company, both Mrs. Eberhart's father and uncle died, and, as if in compensation, Eberhart's second child, Margaret Ghormley Eberhart, was born in the spring of 1951. In the spring of 1952 Eberhart was promoted to vice-president of the company at a substantial increase in salary, but he was not to get much benefit out of the advance, for on June 24, 1952, he received the following telegram from Robert Heilman, chairman of the English Department at the University of Washington: "Can you teach Theodore Roethke's courses next academic year . . . please wire collect." Eberhart wired that he was interested and asked for details.

Heilman replied:

> Roethke (who, as you would guess, will be on leave next year) finds that his schedule of work [two classes; ten hours] allows him a good deal of time for writing. In seeking a poet to replace him, we have had the hope that there might be some attractiveness in a teaching load which should allow a considerable amount of time and energy for the teacher's own writing.

Eberhart agreed that there was, to say the least, "some attractiveness" in the arrangement. "We have considered the matter," he wrote Heilman, and feel rather giddily that we would like to accept the position, spend a year on the coast, and do a type of work I have not done officially. Thanks very much for the offer, which I trust will allow time for my own work, as you suggest. . . .

It happens that I am Vice President of a family business. My brother-in-law is now in it, his father and uncle having died within the last year. Since I have worked in it since 1946 I am able, thanks to their liberalism and understanding, to take a sort of "Sabbatical" year off from business and then return to it. This makes the project possible at all.

Heilman replied:

I hope that your letter of July 4 definitely means that you have taken the position here, for we would very much like to have you. You alternate somewhat between *would* and *will* in your verbal system, but on the whole it seems to me that the *will's* have it, and I hope I am not wrong in proceeding accordingly.

He was not wrong, but Roethke had not yet gotten the word when he wrote on the 14th: "I'm delighted—we all are—that you are seriously considering coming out here." He goes on to discuss housing possibilities, then:

All this started, I guess, when you remarked on our trip from Yaddo to Boston that you might like to do some teaching again. The boys (the committee) put you No. 1 on the list; they particularly liked the fact you belong to no "school" or faction.

Eberhart wrote to thank him for his interest and explained, "Betty's brother being in the business now turned the trick. . . . I feel that I can take a year off and be refreshed with new life." The letter goes on to ask for "pointers in regard to teaching" and to discuss again housing opportunities and ends with a mention of other possibilities he had passed up; then: "Your post is right on the nubbin, to be wanted for what you are and given pretty free rein. I get euphoric thinking about it and thank you again so much." Although he did not know it, he was to continue to be wanted for what he was from then on, and would never return to full-time work in anything but poetry and teaching, which was what he had wanted to do for almost a quarter of a century.

CHAPTER EIGHT
1952–1961

In the fall of 1952, Eberhart left Cambridge with his family on his third trip across the country to the Pacific. They stopped in Chicago and visited his brother Dryden for a few days, then went to Austin and turned west through the Bad Lands and the Black Hills to Yellowstone and Old Faithful and to Lewiston, Idaho, the home of Dryden's wife's family. Finally, after a 4000-mile drive they arrived in Seattle and "secured a furnished ranch-type clean, neat house (a row-house of a new sort) seven miles north of the city, apparently the only one available—it's a boom town." The massively beautiful scenery was of course the first thing they noticed. When the weather was clear they could see Mt. Rainier, "very abrupt and startling though far away," from their front door, and across Puget Sound from their back window loomed the Olympics, which presented them in the evening with "fabulous, Japanese-like sunsets." Occasionally they could glimpse Mt. Baker, a hundred miles away.

They did not really get to see the country, however, until the following May when Mrs. Butcher came to visit and they went out with her for

> four spectacular week-ends, visiting Grand Coulee Dam, which made by man, was less impressive than the vast Dry Coulee and Dry Falls made by God millions of years ago in a shift of the ice age.

They also visited the Olympic Peninsula and Neah Bay, the farthest northwest tip of the United States. Then they went to Victoria, British Columbia,

> the nearest I have been to England lo these many years, marvellously calm, dignified, restful, with well-dressed ladies in plaids and old Englishmen in knickers with pipes. Rather unbelievable.

His new job was equally congenial in many ways. He was welcomed by the *Seattle Post-Intelligencer,* for example, with a poem in the Sunday magazine that ended with

> Play us the harp a lover hones, keyed to that pitch near madness;
> Search every ditch for groundhog bones: gladden us with sadness.
> For Richard and for poorer, then a welcome to our doors—
> Rare the bard who can wax poetic and/or floors!

More importantly, he found the university itself

> Most interesting, 16,000 students—a huge English Dept. of 60 or more members. The students are very liberal and individualistic. I am enjoying my two classes very much. . . . The life is much easier than business, as to hours and intensity. It is really charming and there are many interesting people to know.

Certainly he had nothing about which he could complain in his course load. He met one class in Modern Poetry and another in Creative Writing between noon and two o'clock every day, with the rest of his time more or less free. "I am enjoying the courses very much," he wrote Roethke,

> They are lots of fun, the students various and sometimes perceptive. I see that to do these courses properly it would take a year of getting them up. . . . If the students are stimulated to

read further in any author, that is what I want. I have started
on the reading course with Hopkins, then Housman, Bridges,
Hardy, Lawrence, and Yeats; next term I will go on to the
Georgians, Eliot, Pound, etc. up to 1930; and in Spring term
from our beginning to the present.

He also had the pleasure of telling some of his friends of their fate
in academia. In the spring term for instance, he was able to write
William Carlos Williams,

> You will be glad to know that you rate high among the stu-
> dents here—they like you very much. You are tops. Maybe
> only Pound is higher, as some seem to worship him. I had the
> pleasure of "teaching" you in class, something I never dreamed
> I would be doing. It came off well. I read them the whole first
> book of Pat. And they read the rest, most of them. I also put
> two of your imagist, early short poems on the exam.

Earlier he had not been sure of the value of his teaching, but by December he came to realize the degree of validity in Angleton's talk,
back in the *Furioso* days, about the university audience for poetry.
"I am teaching you on Lawrence right now," he wrote Rexroth in
December,

> and look forward to doing your poems in class in Spring
> quarter. What a sort of dubious thing it is this talking shop all
> the time—but these are the places where poetry counts.

Probably still more interesting were his classes in creative writing.
"In the writing course they have turned out a lot of work already,"
he told Roethke, "some pretty good." He had been very doubtful
about the idea of teaching people how to write creatively, but the
course

> turned out to be extremely vital. It was the surprise of the
> year, a great throwing about of youthful brains, interlockings
> of sometimes highly individualistic personalities, together with
> help for the meek!

The course was scheduled as a verse-writing class, but a good deal of fiction was handed in, and at least two of his students were sufficiently interesting for him to send their stories in for consideration by *New World Writing,* though without success.

He also made at least two public appearances while in Seattle. In December he appeared at the University for an evening of readings, doing about two-thirds of the reading himself, leaving the other third to students in the Speech Department, which sponsored the event. Then in April he appeared for a performance in the Seattle Public Library. After the teeming literary life of Cambridge, however, Seattle seemed rather slow, and Eberhart set about trying to help it along, developing a simple system that Heilman later called "the tradition so well established by Eberhart, of trying to snatch everybody within range." Richard Wilbur, for instance, was living then in New Mexico, was in fact a neighbor of Eberhart's sister. Eberhart wrote him in December, and the letter gives a good idea of how the "tradition" worked:

> Oscar Williams appeared for three days and gave himself a terrific workout with classes, readings and general holdings forth. Rexroth is coming in January. Which brings me to the point of this letter. Is there any chance of your coming here any time this year? This is not an official proffering of a check; it is a personal sounding out, with approval of the head of the department, Dr. Robert Heilman, whom we so much like. . . , who is actually entitled "Executive Director," which gives a Navy-like tone to this vast establishment. They never seem to know how much money is available, but they do seem to get people here. I derive the notion that there are various possible baskets of plums sitting under various trees. If one is sharp-eyed enough maybe a February or a May basket can be found, to the general edification of all. Or maybe not. Sometimes the storms blow over the baskets and ruin them for the time being. The point is, would you have time and inclination to come if it could be arranged? The arranging would be another matter, in the hands of Bob Heilman, and of course there might not be funds available. . . . It wd. be swell to have Charlee [Mrs. Wilbur], but I suppose it all comes down to hideous gold.

However many storms may have ruined baskets during the year, they had many visitors on the campus, "which stirs the waters and refreshes the spirit," and he wrote in March,

> Rexroth was here last term. We gave a party for him. He stood by the fireplace and talked for three hours to the students. He is in good form, has a beautiful new young wife, and an attractive daughter with big blue eyes, about three. Then Dick Wilbur came and stayed with us and we gave a party for him and had a lot of fun. He read his poetry well. This term Caroline Gordon is here, pleasing and nice as ever.

Not all the "baskets of plums" were exclusively for outsiders, however; Eberhart himself had the pleasure of seeing a production of some of his verse drama. He had been at once glad and disappointed when he first arrived to find that "There are *three* theaters here, all apparently booming, but none for original verse plays." A few months later, however, he wrote Edith Sitwell that *The Visionary Farms* "may be produced here. Glenn Hughes has three theaters going full tilt and is just now beginning to give credence to experimental, creative work." A week later he told Monroe Spears:

> The good news since my last is that Glenn Hughes is producing an evening's performance of my verse plays here. . . . This will take place early in May. Preamble I . . . will begin the show, followed by "The Apparition." After an intermission "The Visionary Farms" will be produced. I am of course delighted. I believe it is the first time they will have done original verse drama here.

In the process of rehearsal, the cast found *The Visionary Farms,* which deals with the events of 1922 in Eberhart's family, somehow incomplete, and it was then that Eberhart wrote the final scene that appears in *Collected Verse Plays,* showing Hurricane Ransome (Cy Thompson) in prison. The play was presented, under the direction of Robert O'Neil-Butler with music by John Verral, for two successive weekends in the last half of May. "My play has had two performances," he wrote,

> and has two more coming up this week, tomorrow and Saturday. They are doing it in fine formal style, only now getting the true speed of the action and bringing up the comedy. The dress rehearsal was by invitation to 200 faculty etc. At curtain call I put on Indian feathers and stalked the stage as Chief Sealth [sic], read off a long line of Indian names and gave some of his famous speech of capitulation to the white man. I ended on "When I was last here there weren't so many egg heads."

While the production was in preparation, the printers for the New American Library were rushing to get out *New World Writing 3*, which included *The Visionary Farms*, although without the final scene. They were finished in time and several hundred copies were rushed to Seattle and sold in the foyer of the theater during the play's run.

At about the same time that Hughes's production of *The Visionary Farms* went into rehearsal, Eberhart received a request from Leonard Dean, a good friend of Heilman's and then chairman of the English Department at the University of Connecticut, that he come to Storrs and teach for one semester, and his request was seconded by William Clark, a member of the department whom Eberhart had known during his weeks as a tutor at Palm Beach. Eberhart hesitated, first because it was only for half a year, and secondly because he had another possibility "which would have been professionally tops." The other prospect, however, "was contingent on somebody's getting something else which did not come through;" and Dean was able to offer him a full year as a replacement for Robert Wooster Stallman, who was going abroad on a foundation grant. So he obtained another leave of absence from the polish company and accepted.

In the spring of 1953, therefore, the Eberharts left Seattle and drove south through San Francisco and on to the home of Eberhart's sister in New Mexico; then after a visit, they turned north again, driving through Nebraska and the Midwest to Maine, where they spent the summer. About the first of September they moved into the small faculty apartment they had rented from the Stallmans, and Eberhart began his second tour of duty in the teaching profession.

His schedule was a little more strenuous than that at Washington but he found that he was quite able to handle it. He taught a graduate course for the first time, in modern poetry the first semester and modern drama the second, and a section of juniors and seniors studying Shakespeare. He also had responsibility for thirty-five freshmen and sophomores in a general "Introduction to Literature" course. "Teaching Shakespeare is a curious thing to be doing," he wrote Rexroth. "I stumble around in my vast ignorance. The other duties are more or less like last year."

So far as can be gathered from his correspondence, there was less extracurricular activity in poetry at Storrs than there had been in Seattle, but they were at least close enough to Cambridge to visit Mrs. Eberhart's family, and Eberhart was able to accept several speaking engagements in the area. He went to appear at the YM-YWHA Poetry Center with Wilbur once, for instance, and he took Mrs. Eberhart and "spent four days in riotous New York. I am glad to report that the old place is as wicked as ever." And in December 1953 he went to Chicago to read a paper on the Poets' Theatre at the convention of the Modern Language Association and to give a reading of his poetry at the University of Chicago. He also appeared during 1953–54 at the Yale Divinity School, the University of Rhode Island, the Philadelphia Art Alliance, and Harvard. In addition, he read his poems to a group of University of Connecticut alumni at Bristol, Connecticut, in May 1954.

Then in March 1954 his past began to catch up with him in a very fortunate way. When he had given the Founder's Day address at Wheaton College in 1952, he had written of the experience of appearing before 500 young women, "Whoopee! One wonders what fate has in store for them!" As it turned out, for some of them at least fate had Eberhart in store, for when Katherine Burton, the acting chairman of the English Department at Wheaton, wrote Norman Holmes Pearson that they were looking for a poet for their new visiting professorship, Pearson recommended Eberhart, who had helped them judge a poetry contest in 1953 and whom he had met again during his recent appearance at Yale. Then about the second week of March, Wheaton's president A. H. Meneely invited Eberhart to Norton for a chat and finally offered him the post. It was clearly the best opportunity he had had to that time and by March 23rd he had accepted.

The following summer he wrote MacLeish,

> they have instituted a Visiting Professorship there and asked me to be first incumbent. What does one do with 500 girls? This is a one-year post with a sky salary, but what startled us was that they threw in a 3-bedroom house rent and service free. I have to teach a year course in American Literature. My ignorance of this subject is vast and formidable. I don't mind 35 in a class but 75 have signed up—I tremble to think of it. . . .

He had only one other course, however: in modern poetry the first semester and modern prose the second. He was assigned a graduate student from nearby Brown, furthermore, to help with the grading of papers. So the teaching load was hardly oppressive and he hoped to develop some publishable criticism, but he "found out, either due to my lack of ability or to the exigencies of the teaching situation with large classes, that by December I could not follow this policy;" so from that time on he "taught in an old-fashioned, direct way, verbalizing texts and drawing on my own experience."

One of the "exigencies" which consumed much of his time was the number of poets whom he persuaded to come and read and/or talk at the college, as he had at Washington. It was somewhat different this time, however, since he could offer little or no money. Nevertheless, the campus was visited during his year there by Merrill Moore, Adrienne Rich, John Holmes, and Donald Hall; and he was also instrumental in getting Dame Edith Sitwell and her brother Osbert to come in March. The most important of such events, however, was the observance of Founder's Day in April. This was usually an assembly with an address, but in 1955, at Eberhart's suggestion, it was expanded into a two-day affair, with a presentation by the Poets' Theatre company and a discussion by a panel of poets.

The Founder's Day address was delivered by Stephen Spender. A faculty committee chose him, but it was Eberhart who contacted him (he was in India at the time) and who more than anyone else seems to have made it possible for him to come. The fee for the address and panel discussion could not of course cover Spender's transatlantic travel expenses, so Eberhart took it upon himself to secure other engagements. This was accomplished by writing a virtually interminable series of letters to various institutions, arranging schedules and cajoling fees, until the requisite funds were assured. Then he had to gather other members of the symposium, which he moderated. These were Louise Bogan, who had just won the Bollingen Prize; John Brinnin, whom he had known since Cambridge days and who had been his colleague at Storrs; Donald Hall, poet, anthologist, and critic, then a member of the Society of Fellows at Harvard and active in the Poets' Theatre; Daniel Hoffman, then at Columbia; John Holmes and Robert Lowell. (This appearance was the second at Wheaton for Hall and Holmes.) It was in all a lively weekend, certainly the most elaborate and probably the most interesting Founder's Day program that Wheaton had had in many years.

By the end of his year at Wheaton, it was clear that Eberhart found academic work congenial, and he chose for the next year one of three offers of further college teaching. The first was from Coe College in Cedar Rapids, Iowa, under terms similar to those at Wheaton with the possibility of continuing after the year of the appointment. The Eberharts were looking for something more definitely permanent, however, and Eberhart was still serving on the board of directors of the family business and wanted to continue to attend the board's meetings, so they turned it down. About a month later, he was offered a one-year post at his alma mater, Dartmouth, which had awarded him an honorary degree in 1954, to teach modern poetry and creative writing. It was an extremely attractive position, but he had already accepted another post.

On January 14th, Richard Blackmur, whom he had not seen in many years, wrote from Princeton to ask if he would be interested in a half-time, one-year appointment in creative writing. Eberhart replied:

> I was surprised and delighted to get your letter. It set off a chain of memories of the times I used to come to see you across the river. Stimulating memories!
>
> . . .
>
> It would be a pleasure to work at Princeton and a special pleasure to be associated with you. . . .
>
> This is the third year I have taken my family around the country. My wife, as most wives would, wants to settle down. Our young are at the age where moving may do them little good, whereas staying fixed would probably be most beneficial. Thus, is this job potential of further years or is it only possible for one year? It sounds just about ideal for me. . . . Could you give me more work and build it up in salary to a full professor's requirements?

Blackmur explained that the creative writing position was a matter of policy a one-year post. "This has been a matter of my own determination," he wrote, "since it seems to me very important to save the job as a kind of portable fellowship for a reasonably distinguished writer." He also saw, however, that the half-time pay was not sufficient for a family the size of Eberhart's and hoped to find a second, supplemental post. Less than a week later he could write,

> We had a meeting of the Christian Gauss Seminar Committee on Friday afternoon after I had talked to the chairman of the English department and to others concerned, and I am very happy to say that we can offer you . . . a double role of being my associate in handling the Creative Writing courses for one and for the second to conduct a single seminar of six

weeks one evening per week on a subject to be arranged between ourselves. Mr. Borgerhoff, the director of the Seminars,
will write you officially within a few days, but in the meantime
you may consider this a firm offer or invitation for the favor
of your presence.

To give Eberhart a clearer idea of the double job, he went on to say

that the Creative Writing job amounts in fact to rather less
than half time and can be conducted on three days of the week
between 11 and 5 without any extraordinary amount of advance
preparation. Furthermore, as I don't think I said previously,
there are no committees to which you will be attached and there
are neither examinations nor grades given in the course. In
short we have always regarded this job as a species of fellowship.

He also gave further details on the Gauss seminars, which

are intended to give you the liberty and opportunity to work up
a subject within your own interest and ours. Presumptively this
would either finish a small book or have you well along towards
publication in the shape of six lectures which, as you know, run
to about 50,000 words. Here again there is no committee work
of any kind, and there is in addition the expectation that you
will attend the other three seminars during the year. I may say
that the particular berth you would occupy has been held by
Robert Fitzgerald, Randall Jarrell, Jacques Maritain, Robert
Speaight, and Hannah Arendt. So you will not be in bad
company.

Eberhart was "glad to accept" and the following fall moved into a
house in Princeton next door to R. W. B. Lewis and began work. In
the creative writing courses he had a little over thirty students
whom he met individually every other week and in groups of six or
seven once or twice a week. He seems to have enjoyed the work
and the young men. "The students were enthusiastic about their
work," he wrote Carlos Baker in his report on the class at the end
of the year,

a condition which has obtained since the inception of the course and is due psychologically to the challenges offered. With the utmost of freedom and a minimum of coercion they progressed according to the laws of their personalities and produced, by and large, commendable work.

He goes on in the same report to discuss the progress of various students and to suggest that such students should not be content to publish in undergraduate magazines but should "try their wings among editors on the national scene, where possible . . . on the grounds that a final value of writing is beyond the praise or censure of their college professor." It should be added that he encouraged them in very concrete ways, sending some of their poems to Philip Booth, who was guest poetry editor of one issue of *New World Writing,* as Eberhart had been while at the University of Connecticut, and who accepted one of these submissions.

Along with these responsibilities, he also had time to help with a seminar in modern poetry at nearby Bryn Mawr, besides preparing his Gauss lectures. These he began in the summer of 1955, but he was of course already thinking about them in February:

> At one point I thought I might have become a professional critic. Was it necessities of society, or something in the genes, that made me turn more to poetry? . . . . If I were to write a critical paper it ought to be entitled "Abeyance Criticism:" bring all to view, make no dogmas. Crystallization is death; the way of life is ever in the new, the unfolding.

By the time he was scheduled to begin the lectures, a year later, he had developed a somewhat more definitive scheme, under the title, "Will and Psyche in Poetry," setting up a characteristic Eberhartian dualism between poetry of the Real and that of a quasi-Platonic Ideal and presenting the degree to which various writers fall in the one category or the other. These lectures were delivered in February and March 1956, and three of them have since been published.[1]

By the time he delivered the Gauss lectures, he had already received the most important offer in his professional career. There had apparently been some hint of it much earlier, for in September his friend Philip Booth, whom he had seen on a vacation in Maine the previous summer, wrote to express the hope that "another year may see you more settled in the good hills. Nothing, surely, could be better for Dartmouth." The following December he got a confidential note from Carlos Baker, a good friend of Arthur Jensen, the Dean of the Faculty at Dartmouth: "Have just heard by grapevine that you may expect good Big Green news circa Jan. 15," Baker told him. "Hope and pray it's to your liking. I can say no more now, but see if Betty can find her ski-boots." Less than a week later he received word from Jensen himself:

> At long last I am able to pick up again the correspondence we had last year. I have been authorized by the President to open negotiations with you with a view to asking you to join the staff at Dartmouth next September.
>
> From our previous correspondence it was clear that you did not wish a one-year appointment. What we have in mind is a three-year appointment as Professor of English. . . .

Eberhart was not worried about the outcome of the negotiations: "I am delighted to receive your letter of January 3," he replied, "and look forward to coming to Dartmouth." A few weeks later Jensen visited him at Princeton and details of salary and duties were arranged and agreed upon. Eberhart was returning to his alma mater.

So the following fall the Eberharts moved into what was to be their permanent home, on a steep slope covered with cathedral pines through which they could glimpse the Connecticut River 100 feet below, and Eberhart began his teaching duties in the English Department. He was assigned two classes per quarter, one in creative writing, primarily verse-writing, and another in some aspect of literature or composition. These classes have varied over the years but usually include one in the writing of poetry or verse drama and another in modern poetry.

Since he is a regular member of the department, and in no sense a visiting professor, he has also participated in the normal extracurricular duties of any faculty member, such as counselling students on their academic or personal problems and serving on various intra- and inter-departmental committees. In 1957, for example, he helped to draft a "Report of the Committee on Writing Courses" that went to the departmental curriculum committee. In 1958, he suggested and served on a committee for an All-Arts Festival, partly in connection with the inauguration of the new seven-million-dollar Hopkins Center for the performing arts on the Dartmouth campus, then in the planning stages. Another typical duty was his service on the committee to set up procedures for the Marcus Heiman Awards to promote work in the creative arts, in 1959.

Most important, however, has been his work in what might be called the promotion of poetry. Besides his direct contact with and encouragement of young poets and potential poets among his students, his work in this area has taken primarily two forms: the securing of poets to speak and read at the campus and the editing of little anthologies of student verse. Funds for both of these come mostly from the same source: annual grants from the Charles Butcher Foundation. The first such grant, of $500, was given in 1957 "to create interest in poetry" and has been renewed in varying amounts in succeeding years and administered by a committee made up of faculty members, of whom Eberhart is of course one, and sometimes students.

The procedure for getting poets to the campus is somewhat similar to that used by Eberhart when he was at the University of Washington and Wheaton, and its results are indicated by Eberhart's first report to the Foundation:

> Last year we had William Jay Smith and his wife Barbara Howes, of Pownall [sic], Vermont, both poets of about 40, who had recently spent a year in Italy. This was culturally valuable as it introduced excellent poets but to a small audience. They thus learned that excellence is not limited to big names.
>
> We next had I. A. Richards, "the father of modern criticism," of Harvard (once my mentor at Cambridge University) in the second public reading of his poems. A critic for 40 years, he

turns poet this year with his first book of poetry, from which he read. He projected his poems on a large screen and used a pointer, adding eye to ear. His lively mind and personality made it a fine evening.

Then John Ciardi, of the *Saturday Review,* came and drew a large crowd. He is young and successful and full of controversy. He charmed everybody.

We then had Kenneth Rexroth, because he happened to be working in New York. He was at the peak of the whole build-up of the San Francisco movement in poetry, of which he is father and king. This crowded the Tower Room [in Baker Library] to the rafters, made a great stir and commotion and caused a lot of comment in the papers.

Marianne Moore read under the Lecture Series, but we helped to entertain her at our house.

Eberhart's correspondence after about 1953 no longer contains the long, vivid descriptions of visiting luminaries that characterized his letters in the 'forties and during his tenure in Seattle, perhaps because they have become so much a commonplace of his working life, but the procedure for these visits usually follows the same pattern. Eberhart or some other college representative, often his colleague and friend from undergraduate days, Alexander Laing, acts as impresario and manages, as it were, the visit. The poet usually holds an hour of informal conversation with anyone who cares to come in the afternoon in the Poetry Room of Baker Library, under the auspices of the Thursday Poets, a loosely organized group, established by Laing, of local writers who meet informally every week to discuss and read their work. Then in the evening there is usually a small supper party at the Eberharts' or the Laings', just before the reading or lecture, which is given in the Tower Room of the library or in Sanborn House, the home of the English Department at Dartmouth. The more prominent figures, such as Edith Sitwell or Robert Lowell, both of whom have appeared under Butcher Fund auspices, sometimes appear in larger halls such as Dartmouth Hall or one of the auditoriums in the Hopkins Center. After the reading, then, the Eberharts hold an open house, with refreshments, where students or other members of the community can meet and talk with the visitor.

Although funds have been supplied to the English Department by the College to be used principally for bringing older, more prominent poets to the campus, the visiting poets program is not confined to "big names." In an effort to cut across the whole spectrum of contemporary poetry, Eberhart and his colleagues have also made a point of getting figures who have very little national reputation and those who are known but not extremely widely known. Thus besides such established figures as Edith Sitwell, Richards, and Marianne Moore, the list of poets who have appeared at Dartmouth in the last ten years includes such less known figures as W. S. Merwin, W. D. Snodgrass, Brother Antoninus, Robert Pack, Philip Booth, Donald Hall, Jean Garrigue, Bink Noll, and David Ignatow.

The other major benefit of the Butcher Foundation grants is also mentioned in Eberhart's first report to the foundation:

> The final action [in 1957–58] under the Charles Butcher Fund was to publish "Thirteen Dartmouth Poems," a beautifully made pamphlet of poems. One poem was reprinted in the *New York Times Book Review*, p. 2, in a July number. The edition is 150 copies. We have sold about 70 in the Dartmouth book store, retail $1.00, 20% discount to us, and hope to sell out the edition this Fall, which will pay the printer's bill of about $120.00 and bring back that much into the Fund for this year. . . .

Although these little anthologies have not always come so close to paying their way, Eberhart has continued to edit them, using almost exclusively poems by Dartmouth students, and has produced ten of them over the years since he came to Hanover.

In Eberhart's case, at least, it is then safe to say that his "post is right on the nubbin, to be wanted for what you are and given pretty free rein." At Dartmouth he is able to work for poetry on a full-time basis, to be what he is; and that he is wanted for what he is was finally proved when in 1958 his colleagues voted him that hallowed academic fact and symbol: tenure.

A few months before he was voted tenure, on August 5, 1958, Eberhart was offered the most substantial recognition he has received, the position of Consultant in Poetry at the Library of Congress. This appointment was the third important honor that he had received since 1952, for in 1955, he had been awarded a fellowship of $1000 by the National Institute of Arts and Letters, as well as the University of Chicago's $500 Harriet Monroe Memorial Award. The consultantship itself, furthermore, had been offered him before. The first time was when he was informed in person that the Fellows in Literature of the Library of Congress had voted him to the position; but apparently because of a misunderstanding with the incumbent, Conrad Aiken, the offer was never officially extended. Then in 1956, the Librarian of Congress, L. Quincy Mumford, wrote to sound out his interest in the position. At that time, however, he was just in the process of negotiating with Dartmouth and, more importantly, had been moving every year for the last four and hoped to settle down for the sake of his family, and he made the same decision after a similar preliminary letter in 1958, again because he felt he "owed our children continuity of education." In July 1958, finally, he was asked if he would be available for the post in the fall of 1959, and when he replied this time that he expected he would, the official offer was made. By November he had secured a leave of absence from Dartmouth and accepted the position.

With the assumption of this new role, Eberhart became a public figure, as he realized as soon as he began planning for his move to the national capital, in September 1959. The Information and Publications Office of the Library informed him that he should not delay giving a press conference, for if he waited more than a day or so reporters would be hounding him for "exclusive" interviews which, if granted, would offend those reporters who did not get them. The Press Officer went on to explain:

> Since Princess Beatrix of the Netherlands and Premier Kruschev [sic] are to arrive in Washington on September 14

and 15, respectively, we can consider the entire week beginning
September 14 a lost week so far as a well-covered press conference is concerned, and a further delay would not be feasible.
. . . Since Wednesday of any week is apt to see a Presidential
press conference (with which we do not try to compete!), the
most practical day would be Tuesday, September 8, or Thursday, September 10. . . .

He gave the conference as advised and spoke spontaneously on the
role of poetry in the modern world, and also gave at least one interview.

According to the Library's Information Bulletin's summary of his
duties, the Consultant, whose salary comes from a 1936 gift of the
late Archer M. Huntington,

> gives advice on improving the Library's collections of literature;
> recommends the purchase of new materials; assists in acquiring
> important manuscripts and books through authors and col-
> lectors; advises on bibliographical and reference work in his
> field; confers with scholars and poets using the Library's collec-
> tions and facilities; and provides editorial supervision of the
> Library's program of recording 20th century poets in the read-
> ing of their own works.

In Eberhart's case, most of these duties were performed as routinely
as his work in the Navy had been in 1945. The one that seems to
have taken a considerable amount of time was that of arranging for
the recording of contemporary poets. Already in progress when he
arrived was a special album of 46 poets edited by Oscar Williams;
he had little if anything to do with this collection, but he edited
selections of several other poets who were dead, and supervised the
production of records of several living poets, including Robert Hil-
lyer, Oscar Williams, John Hall Wheelock, John Ciardi, W. D.
Snodgrass, Ned O'Gorman, and I. A. Richards.

One program initiated at Eberhart's suggestion, apparently, was a
series of seminars held in the Library's Woodrow Wilson Room
with students and faculty of Washington area universities. These

meetings varied from about twelve to about thirty-five participants in two-hour sessions. George Washington, American, Catholic, and Howard Universities and the University of Maryland took part in the program.

He was also able to perform other services from time to time. Once, for example, he was invited to help receive the King and Queen of Nepal, because someone in the State department had found out that His Majesty was himself a poet. Eberhart was able to get only a few minutes of conversation with him, and "only ascertained that he did in fact write poetry and when asked how often or to what extent, he replied, somewhat furtively, 'Sometimes.'" Eberhart and his wife also helped to entertain the King and Queen of Thailand when they came to the Library. On another occasion his knowledge of the personnel in the Library enabled him to contribute further to international understanding:

> One of the most interesting events occurred when I was called by telephone by an official of the Treasury Department and asked whether I could write a poem on inter-allied Latin American banking amity to be read the next week at a dinner for twenty-three Latin American countries in El Salvador. Secretary Anderson and Mr. Dillon and the inquisitor were flying down and wanted a poem within twenty-four hours. I recalled that in the Hispanic Foundation we have a young poet, William Rivera, who knew Spanish; in less than the required time he wrote a fine occasional poem on the subject and it was delivered by special messenger in English and Spanish. When the party returned from El Salvador we learned that the poem added a great deal to the occasion.

He also had more direct contact with international figures, and accounts of three such meetings survive, all three with Russians. The first was with Mikhail Sholokov, author of *And Quiet Flows the Don,* who accompanied Premier Khrushchev on his 1959 visit and who met with several prominent intellectuals in Washington. An account of the meeting in the *New York Times* emphasized the novelist's characterization of Boris Pasternak as a "hermit crab," but Eberhart felt that this was a minor part of his remarks and suggested that the language barrier was an important factor in the discussions:

> Here is an example of the difficulties of such a meeting. I suggested through the interpreter that Mr. Sholokov's notion of character seemed to be not "in depth," that he described and narrated actions of a vast, panoramic scale, but that one did not discover depth-motivations because of the objectivity of the writing. . . .
>
> The answer, through the interpreter, made me think that he had not understood the term "in depth." His unexpected, pithy reply was that "I give the roast beef, not the hamburger." . . .[2]

Sholokov apparently wanted to overcome the language barrier, however, for a few days later he sent Eberhart "via an emissary from the Russian Embassy a four-volume set of a quietly flowing Don done in English in Moscow."

He had a less formal meeting with Evgeny Evtushenko, who in the course of a private tour of America visited the Eberharts' Georgetown home in May 1961 during Eberhart's second year as Consultant:

> Evtushenko was tall, handsome, open in manner and acted with a friendliness and charm. With his short-cropped blonde hair and grey flannel suit, he could have passed very easily for an Ivy League college student or graduate, except for one unmistakably Russian touch: fireman red bow tie and matching bright red socks. He professed to know no English, but appeared to understand much of what was said, judging from the quick ironic smile that often illuminated his face.

They exchanged tokens, Evtushenko receiving a copy of Eberhart's recently pressed recording for the Yale Series of Recorded Poets and inscribing a copy of his most recent book, mentioning to the astonished consultant that it had sold over a million and a half copies in the Soviet Union. Evtushenko had with him his friend the poet Vosnesenskii and both read their poems,

> with a total commitment, an exercise of the whole being, which was deeply moving. In response, I read a poem of mine, "The Horse Chestnut Tree." Somebody had given me a horse chestnut in Washington after a reading. My wife took this from a silver dish and gave it to the Russians, a shiny token of the poem. Only the memory of Dylan Thomas reading his own poems could match the Russians reading theirs, although we could not understand the words.

The third contact with the Soviet Union was less literary. Eberhart wrote Lowell about it in the fall of 1959:

> Sat. nt. B and I attended perhaps the most lavish party we have ever been to. The Dowlings were hosts at the Westchester to about 40 guests for Zuchov, No. 2 Russian who flew in from Camp David in an helicopter. He had an interpreter. This was purely a social occasion, no reporters, but Mr. Z. dandled a champagne glass for over fifteen minutes in a most warm-hearted, friendly off the cuff talk. He was impressive, big, wide-faced, with straight black hair, "cultivated," and we rose to repeated toasts to the President, the Dowlings, etc. and when we drank to "Mrs. Zuchov in Moscow" B and I felt we were in a comic opera. Over brandy the men were passed hugest cigars marked "Churchill." I thought this was laying it on with a trowel as it were. I didn't notice whether Z. took one but at any rate he did not smoke one.

Eberhart also had the good fortune, of course, to be in Washington for the inauguration of President Kennedy and the new official enthusiasm for the arts. He was invited along with other literary figures to the inauguration and wrote Eric Bentley:

> We have just lived through a cold, spectacular Inauguration week-end. The President invited a group of Artists to attend,

of whom I was gratefully one. This included the Ball which also included free Presidential champagne and kept us up most of the night. The Tates were our house guests and we took the Lowells and Katherine Ann Porter and got in toward dawn as if it were back in the old days. Auden came to supper along with Madame Perkins who originated social security. It was all quite gay.

Robert Frost was probably the most publicized beneficiary of the new dispensation. Shortly after the inauguration, Eberhart wrote Louis Untermeyer:

Last Sunday our friend Robert went to the White House to see Kennedy. In the evening, at a party at the Coxes on 35th St. near our house, I sat by him and asked him what Kennedy had to say. He turned and without hesitation said "I did most of the talking." He was in fine shape; at the Ball we encountered him talking animatedly to all comers at 2 A. M.

Frost was again in the Capital the following spring:

Last night it was Frost at the new State Dpt. auditorium with everybody in black tie, Chief Justice Warren alongside the French Ambassador and Mrs. Alphand, poets and scholars down for the occasion, and Robert in high form. The President and First Lady stayed away, the former no doubt to do his world homework while Robert philosophized. He was introduced by the new Secy of the Interior, Udall, also by Dillon in lieu of Rusk—Rusk was across the way pitching for our side in re Laos.

Eberhart himself had one official appearance as Consultant in his first year and two in his second, and he spoke for three different Voice of America broadcasts; but these were the least of his public life. Under the terms of the consultantship, the incumbent is allowed to accept speaking engagements outside of his regular duties, and the publicity that attends the office assures many invitations, with and without fees.

The problem of which and how many invitations to speak I should accept when not paid for, as against fee-paid public readings, I resolved by an enthusiastic acceptance of practically all of them although I do not know how wise this course was to follow. The public should not abuse the good-will of the Consultant, yet I confess that every one of these readings or talks to clubs or groups of all sorts in and around Washington was a pleasure.

After he left Washington, he remembered about two dozen such gratuitous appearances, but they were less than half his public life. In his two years as Consultant he was on the platform at various institutions around the country over sixty times. Many of these, especially in the first year, were in the Washington area, mostly at clubs of various kinds and at high schools. He did take time in March 1960, however, for a tour of colleges on the west coast, and some of his letters, especially from his second year as Consultant, give the impression of being always on the run:

In December I am going to the U. of Virginia for a week as poet-guest; in March for all of it I am going to Cincinnati to give their Elliston lectures on poetry. Then there are readings, and poetry seminars here in the Library, and editing lp records of poets dead and alive to keep one's time occupied.

And in the spring of 1961:

The Howard lecture last night to 600 or more (standing in the rear of their comfortable chapel) was a good experience.

Pardon the brevity of this. I go to Randolph-Macon Tuesday, Brown Thursday, and will give the Founder's Day Address at Wheaton next Saturday.

There is nothing to suggest that Eberhart was unhappy about the demands that these appearances made on his time, and a general tendency to accept as many speaking engagements as possible is evident after he left Washington in June 1961 and resumed his academic duties at Dartmouth the following fall. Part of his motive is clearly that this is one area of a poet's activity where the remuneration is in fair proportion, on the average, to the time involved. His attitude toward this compensation is suggested by this letter from 1962:

> Sometimes I read for nothing. Other times the stakes are good. It has to even out somewhere. . . . My readings usually draw, in addition to expenses, from 500 to 200. However, it was not always so and back in the early days one was lucky to get 100. Our society thinks nothing of spending millions on rockets but it still tends to think that the still, small voice of the spirit is free. Maybe it is. There are poets I could name who have suffered a lot more than I have.

He naturally tries to make the spirit pay, to suffer as little as possible. Once during his tenure at the Library of Congress, for example, he was offered a fee that would scarcely have covered his travel expenses. Confident that there were always "baskets of plums" around, he asked if it could not be raised a little. The man arranging the visit replied:

> My main support is hard work, interested poets, people and interested students. For a while I had the support of the School in payment of poets—then I could set a fee at 150.00. Now, due to an economy at the school, my fee has dropped because it is the members of the WRITER'S CLUB of the school (interested students) who are. . . . willing to foot the bill to hear and talk with you and others, which I believe to be one of the greatest things I have heard of in this area.

In this case Eberhart replied immediately that he would come.

His frequent, though by no means invariable, willingness to appear *gratis* is explained in part by the pleasure he takes in appearing before an almost infinite variety of audiences:

I enjoy reading my poetry before audiences. I have done a good deal of this in the past ten years and have learned somewhat closely, but not with finality, which poems are readable and which are not. Or, which ones are more readable than others. Certain of my poems I would not read before an audience. These would be the most complex ones, what I have called inspissated poetry. Perhaps the most perceptive audience would be a rather large one, say three hundred, made up of men and women students mostly, with maybe a fourth adults. Last Spring I made "The grand tour" of the west coast centers of Mrs. Witt-Diamant at the San Francisco State College. She turned out 600–700 and they were fine. It is no harder to read to a large audience like that than to the fifty women I read to yesterday at Lyme, New Hampshire, mostly dear old ladies up to over eighty. Last week there were about 100–150 at Radcliffe where I was entertained by *The Harvard Advocate*. That was a fine audience, mostly Harvard-Radcliffe undergraduates, with some older professors. Last fall I read at Penn State to about 300–400, an audience similar to the one at S. F. State. Up in Seattle there were several hundred, but more grownups, it seemed, than young. At Berkeley this was also the case. And so on. Last month I read at the YMHA in NY; they always have a large, appreciative audience. Last Spring (a year ago) I read at the Library of Congress, 200–300 (300–400?) I guess, who seemed to be mostly adults.

A later example tells of a still different example, which will serve as a contrast to the ladies in Lyme: ". . . at the opposite pole were 800 junior high teenagers in Wilmette, Illinois. I had the wit to begin . . . on limericks: they became roarers and all was well. I introduced my daughter Gretchen, about ten, onstage."

The largest audience he ever addressed was 10,000 at a meeting of the National Education Association in Atlantic City, New Jersey, in the hall where beauty queens are crowned. Usually, however, the audience is provided by a college or university campus, and the reading or lecture is frequently the least of the demands on his time. His visit to Oberlin College in 1961 is typical. He arrived the eve-

ning of February 8th and attended a reception given in his honor by
the English department two hours after he got off the train. Then
on the morning of the 9th he held an informal discussion with "students interested in creative writing" for forty-five minutes before
going to deliver his forty-minute reading at noon. After a lunch in
the Snack Bar, he held a press conference, at 1:30. Then at 2:30 a
professor of speech recorded his remarks on the reading of poetry
"for use in his class on interpretation." That evening he had dinner
with the President of the college (a frequent part of such visits,
sometimes in black tie), before leaving by train from Cleveland
later in the evening. It will be noticed that in the twenty-four hours
of his visit, he spent less than four hours in actual, scheduled reading or discussion of poetry. The rest of the time was used for informal contact with students and faculty.

A clearer picture of a fairly typical event emerges from a letter
from his friend Daniel Hoffman regarding Eberhart's 1958 appearance at Swarthmore:

> Swarthmore College has a great need of a fine poet, good
> speaker, and incorruptible judge. We have a student writing
> contest the final few poems of which we'd like to send you in
> advance of your visit. We have a program for the cultural
> refurbishing of Bell Telephone Co. executives who take a full
> semester of art, lit, music, history, etc., and are exposed to
> contemporary arts and artists. . . . We have a series of lectures
> for the college community, fees for which are provided by the
> Wm. J. Cooper Foundation. The committees for the Bell and
> Cooper projects have instructed me to write to you. . . .

He goes on to outline the program:

> Arrive in time for lunch on Thursday with the Bell group.
> Talk to them during the afternoon—say 30–40 minutes prepared
> speech, then talk off the cuff, on your view of the relation be-
> tween the life of business and the life of art. Or, how a poet
> and a Vice-President of a Company come to live under the

same skin and how they get along with each other. . . . Thursday evening, give a public lecture at the college. The topic the committee asked me to suggest is: Your view of the contemporary poetic situation, with readings from your own work and from other poets you care to discuss. . . . Friday morning, an informal chat with interested students; by Friday noon you'd be free to catch the ski-lift back to Hanover. If you can't stay overnight the meeting with students can be rescheduled or dropped. But Eliza and I add our hopes to those of the committee that you can come—and stay over with us. There's a great deal of faculty enthusiasm in the background of this letter, Dick. And those involved in teaching the Bell boys are beside themselves with expectation of bringing before those solid citizens a first-rate poet who sits on meetings of boards of directors.

Most of Eberhart's appearances are arranged by such correspondence. He has never relied on any agency or organization in this regard, nor has he been on any of the poetry "circuits" that have sprung up in the East in the last few years, such as the Trinity College circuit established by Holly Stevens, the daughter of Wallace Stevens; but he has twice taken advantage of similar arrangements on the west coast. In 1956 and again in 1960 he gave several readings under the auspices of the Poetry Center at San Francisco State College. Involved here was a series of appearances similar to those at Oberlin and Swarthmore. In 1956 he appeared at five campuses in about ten days and at six in 1960 over a period of about three weeks. After expenses, he made $350 on the first tour and $600 on the second. It should be noted, however, that such series would be a good deal more remunerative if they did not require paying for roundtrip plane fare across the country.

On his second trip to the west, Eberhart stayed at the University of California at Berkeley for three days. Such extended stays have not been infrequent, especially in the last five years or so, and are especially useful, since they allow students more personal contact with the poet. In 1960, for example, he spent five days at the University of Virginia, where besides delivering one public lecture-reading, he visited several classes. The chairman of the committee administering the program explained:

> In the case of each of these courses, I am sure that the instructors will not expect any kind of formal lecture from you nor, indeed, anything other than the comments you might wish to make on the material being studied from the point of view of a professional poet and teacher.

He goes on to outline a schedule that includes visits to six classes and two hours of conferences with aspiring student poets. In addition there were several social functions—cocktails, teas, dinners—which it was hoped he would attend.

Another extended stay, at John Hopkins in 1961, is also an example, of a different kind of event, one where he participates along with other poets in a broader program, the sort of thing he organized on a smaller scale when he was at Wheaton. John Holmes, Robert Lowell, May Sarton, Richard Wilbur, and Randall Jarrell were on hand, along with Eberhart, for readings, lectures, receptions, and other events.

Although none of the poets, each of whom delivered a lecture, was required to stay the whole week, Eberhart did and enjoyed it immensely. He delivered one of his Gauss lectures for the John Hopkins' Turnbull Memorial series, and gave a reading under a grant from the Bollingen Foundation. The five Turnbull lectures were later published in a book entitled *The Moment of Poetry*. Holmes, Lowell, and Eberhart made a two-hour film for the National Broadcasting Company on Saturday morning at the end of the week in the garden at the front of President Milton Eisenhower's house, directed by Stanley Schulberg, but the film was never broadcast.

The longest such term of service that Eberhart has had, however, was in 1961, when he spent a month at the University of Cincinnati under the auspices of the George Elliston Poetry Foundation. The core of his service was the delivery of a revision of his six Gauss lectures, but he also held a seminar in poetry for students interested in creative writing, several readings, including one before the University Park Women's Club. He also attended several luncheons and other quasi-social events. The most important event, finally, for Eberhart at least, was the production by a student cast of *The Visionary Farms,* which had

> a three-day run. . . . with a thoroughly sophisticated and able group which understood and conveyed the meanings and connotations of the play is a most rewarding presentation.

Such work is usually, of course, much more concretely "rewarding" (as in the case of his stay at Cincinnati) producing substantial fees. Another mode of support, magazine publication, gives less of a return on time and energy. Most of Eberhart's published poems have appeared first in various periodicals. His attitude toward these is clear in a 1962 letter to a former editor of the *New Yorker*

> Recently the Sat. Post asked for poems and will make up a page with picture in forthcoming months. This pleased me as they pay $10 a line. If you want to help poetry and poets why don't you get your Board to come into line with this kind of payment? . . . . How curious a business. I give some poems to little magazines for nothing; sometimes one gets $2 a line. Sometimes there is a jackpot check for $500. And the point is that money has nothing to do with the motivating forces of poetry.

His remark here about the gratuitous publication of poems is supported by his correspondence, which shows that he has frequently tried to help out little magazines. While he was in Washington, D. C., for instance, the editor of *Dasein,* at Howard University, wrote to thank him "for the interest you have shown in *Dasein* and for your helpful suggestions at its inception." Later the same editor sent him proof of a poem to appear in *Dasein* and added: "It is with pride that we refer to you as the godfather of Dasein." Usually, however, his contribution is limited to sending poems, as he did in response to this letter from an editor of *Lynx,* in Plainview, Texas:

We want only the best—and since we are a new magazine, paying only with a contributor's copy, many of the better poets hesitate to submit until, as they must think, we are more firmly established. Actually, without these poets we cannot become firmly established because we refuse to print inferior poetry.

It is perhaps a sign of the integrity of these little periodicals that they sometimes reject these solicited submissions, as *Compass* in St. Louis, did in 1958, with this remark from the editor:

It may seem ungrateful, disrespectful, etc, etc., but I (and the other people on the staff more or less agree with me) think this is not a poem that successfully comes up to your own standard.

Sometimes, finally, these struggling journals do not last long enough to use a poem, as was the case with *Poems in Folio:*

Unfortunately we are not publishing Poems in Folio next year and so I am returning "Prospectus" to you. Our reasons for suspending operations are purely financial. Three hundred subscribers simply couldn't foot the bills and we are not organized so as to be eligible for foundation money.

A few of the established periodicals, however, do pay something that approaches being commensurate with the labor that goes into writing a poem. To take a few representative entries from Eberhart's account book, for four poems in the fiftieth anniversary issue of *Poetry,* he received $40.50. The less well-known *Shenandoah,* published at Washington and Lee University, paid $10 for two short poems in 1963. The more prestigious reviews also pay respectable rates; *The Sewanee Review,* for instance, gave $35 for "Meditation One," and the *Kenyon Review* paid $62 for "The Parker River." Sometimes money comes across the ocean, as when *Encounter* sent $55.40 for "The World Situation," and *Botteghe Oscure* $70 for "The Verbalist of Summer" in 1950. The "slick" magazines pay especially well, such as the *New Yorker,* which remitted $47 for "The Oak" in 1958, and $72 for "Moment of Equilibrium among the Islands," in 1960; and the *Saturday Review of Literature* gave $15 for the sonnet, "Am I My Neighbor's Keeper?" in 1963. From the *Nation* and the *New Republic,* Eberhart usually gets between $10 and $15 for a poem.

These various fees add up to considerable compensation, but considering the labor involved in marketing poems, at least for Eberhart, it is doubtful that any businessman would be willing to invest the necessary time and energy for the small returns. In the first place, in looking over Eberhart's records of submissions, acceptances, and rejections, which he has kept more or less systematically since 1942, one cannot help wondering if postage alone does not eat well into the money he receives, for he has always had several rejections for every acceptance. One reason for this, of course, is that he usually sends out poems in groups, from which the editor generally selects not more than two or three because of his own limitations of space. Just as often, however, the whole group, or a single poem, will be rejected for a variety of other reasons.

Sometimes these are purely technical, as when the *American Scholar* rejected "The Incomparable Light" because there was not time to publish it before it appeared in *Collected Poems.* In 1958, the *Sewanee Review* rejected "Devils and Angels" because the editor, Monroe Spears, could "see no prospect of finding space for a piece this long in the foreseeable future. . . ." Occasionally a poem, or even the poet, does not fit a firm policy of the magazine. *New World Writing,* for example, also rejected "Devils and Angels," for the reason that

> We have something of a policy of not printing any one writer more than two or three times. This is an effort toward catholicity, and to keep us from turning into one of those mags with a predictable stable of writers.

And the *Paris Review* inaugurated around 1955 another policy that militated against Eberhart: "to stick to a generation except . . . with someone relatively unknown. I expect the policy will stay with us; gen [sic] is loosely in '20's and '30's."

Just as often, of course, perhaps more often, poems are returned because the editors do not like them. When John Crowe Ranson rejected "Devils and Angels" for the *Kenyon Review,* he wrote,

> I think the tone, the language, is fine—very modern and stylish, but whimsical, fingers crossed, theatre style. But I think it lacks body, plot. That's my Philistine reaction. It just sort of goes off when we are expecting some conclusive action. Forgive me.

Edward Weeks wrote of "Spirit," in rejecting it for the *Atlantic:*

> It is a song of exuberance, released in a moment of wonder, and which either comes very close to the listener or passes over him like the wind. The first half of the poem came close to me, but the summation did not seem to me as effective, and I can see from the other readers' reports that they too had their misgivings. I regret that we cannot send you a unanimous decision for we should like to have you in our columns again.

Although these poems are frequently, perhaps usually, accepted elsewhere, Eberhart very rarely sends them back to the same editor for reconsideration. When he did that once, however, the result was an exchange that shows a great deal about the relationship between an established poet and the editors of periodicals. The poems involved were "Father and Son" and "Father and Daughter," both of which appear in *The Quarry.* They were rejected by *Poetry,* and Eberhart wrote the editor, Henry Rago:

> I don't think I have sent poems back to an editor for revaluation but I return the Father-Daughter-Son poems if you would please read them again and give me your critical judgment. . . . I know the difficulty of everything about poetry. But these have a recent history which may interest you. They are new this Fall. . . . . I felt in the Father-Daughter-Son poems a new rhythm, a new departure, an attempt at "universal" utterance

that any reader could understand and I hope enjoy. The
rhythms, going back to early English, may be specially notice-
able in the Son poem. It was with some trepidation that I
elected to read these two poems as the last ones in my reading
at the recent Johns Hopkins Poetry festival. I did so. I also read
them to the assembled Park School in Baltimore. In both cases
the response was keen. At least ten persons, maybe more, at
Hopkins, both students and faculty and "the public" spoke to
me later of their enjoyment of those last poems. At the School
their enthusiasm was very marked and some even asked for
copies. What does this signify? Maybe nothing. You are the
first editor to see them. Maybe they come over vocally better
than as eye-poems? At least you might give them another try
and let me have any comments in the light of the above knowledge.

Rago replied that, as Eberhart had suggested, the poems did not
"have quite the same kind of life on the page that I can imagine
for them in performance." He went on to explain his attitude, as editor, toward Eberhart's work:

What I measure your poems against . . . is the best work of
yours I have seen, not just some abstractly conceived "norm"
for publication in POETRY. So THE STANDARDS and LOOKING AT
THE STARS surely stand out in any ordinary comparisons; if I
return them, it is only because I don't put them quite with the
DREAM JOURNEY OF THE HEAD AND HEART or that luminous little
thrush poem we published a few years ago—a beauty it was—
or that long poem of yours that Ransom published five or six
years ago;—and I like to feel that even if these poems came in
separate envelopes at different moments in time, it is as if they
were spread out in a broad, continuous choice: the point for
me not being to make an absolute judgment on any one of them
but to take, from so generous a range, the three or four that
suggest themselves most cogently on all my readings.

Eberhart occasionally sends the same poem to two magazines.
Usually this happens when the first magazine is slow to report, but

sometimes it is an accident or the result of a misunderstanding. In 1953, for example, Donald Hall asked Eberhart to submit some poems for the *Paris Review*. Eberhart sent five poems, from which "The Noble Man" was accepted. Then several months later Hall had to write:

> Did I ever get a shock when I picked up a copy of the summer *Kenyon Review!* I was mad at you for a while until Dick W[ilbur] pointed out that you probably had the idea that the *Paris Review* was mainly restricted to Paris. The *Paris Review* sells 3000 copies in the United States, and 1000 in Paris and 1000 in England. So I airmailed George Plimpton to pull the Noble Man out of our fall issue. Luckily, a French printer's strike or something had delayed the issue, so he was able to pull it out at the last minute, or we would have been in trouble with J. C. Ransom et al. Needless to say I am pleased to realize that the *Paris Review* and *Kenyon Review* get, and choose, the same poems! but still, we can't print the same ones.

A similar situation developed once in Eberhart's relationship with Marguerite Caetani's *Botteghe Oscure,* a fine periodical published in Rome. Eberhart's letter to Princess Caetani tells the whole story:

> Last Saturday three of us made 7000 feet of talk about poetry for educational television in St. Louis, Ciardi was flown from Rexroth from San Francisco and I from Hanover. . . .
>
> But out there I got a telegram, hence this letter. I am going to Swarthmore in March to read a lecture, read poetry and talk. . . . Dan Hoffman [at Swarthmore] wanted some mss. so I sent him recent hand manuscripts. His wife Liz, [Elizabeth McFarland] is poetry editor for the *Ladies Home Journal.* They saw Clam Diggers [and Diggers of Sea Worms] Ospreys [in Cry], 2 forthcoming in the *New Yorker* and so forth. The telegram said the Ladies H. J. loved Clams and offered $10.00 a line for it. I counted up to 46 lines, 48 with title and was staggered at the result—the most I have ever been offered for one poem. You sent me a good check once, but for several.

Therefore, (to pay this summer's rent in Maine) please withdraw Clam Diggers from those I sent you on Jan. 12. I don't suppose you would want to pay $20. a line for it. What a sociological event! I thought the New Yorker's $2 a line was good, but the Ladies make them look like pikers.

Mrs. Hoffman's letter about "Clam Diggers . . ." shows that the grapevine operates in poetry as in any other profession:

> I have been very happy about all this mail from friends of yours! Thank you for spreading the word. You ought to tell them, though, that we have bought no other poems as long as yours in the past nine years—or else this old lady's memory is beginning to curdle. Anyhow, a phone call this morning from Dan reports the reception back home of a poem three pages long from one of your Dartmouth colleagues. It is doomed. Eight-or-twelve liners are what we can use.
>
> If you want to know why Bruce Gould okayed *your* long poem, the answer is simple. It is great, I am good, you are beautiful.
>
> Please let us know as soon as the Princess [Caetani] releases THE CLAM DIGGERS. Until then, I can't do a thing, so intricate, business-like and guarded is our vasty Curtis empire. . . .

The rent was paid again by the "vasty Curtis empire" a few years later. In the summer of 1961, an editor of the *Saturday Evening Post* asked Eberhart to contribute to a new, full-page poetry feature "in the redesigned *Post*." Eberhart sent in a poem called "Lincoln's Eagles" and later the Father-Son-Daughter poems mentioned in the exchange with Henry Rago quoted above. He was told that these latter poems were too long and that the subject of "Lincoln's Eagles" "was not good for us because we are in all areas of the magazine right now avoiding new material related to the Civil War period." Eberhart did not send anything else until the following year, when the editor wrote again to tell him of the success of the poetry series to that point and to ask again for poems. On this round the new poetry editor, Stephen Berg, accepted three poems: "The

Rush," "The Gesture," and "A New England View: My Report."
Eberhart then not only had the prospect of being read by the vast
millions who see the *Post,* but also received a check for $480. Appar-
ently, however, the circulation was more important to him, judging
by the vigorous protest he made when the *Post* decided to discon-
tinue the poetry feature. "In addition to your lack of faith you are
out $480," he wrote the Associate Editor who had sent him the
news,

> and as a former business man myself I would suggest that,
> even though you have given up your estimable project for
> serious poetry in the *Post,* you should run these three short
> poems at once. . . . These poems, which I consider good ones
> of mine, were with-held from other places, notably the 50th
> anniversary number of *Poetry* (Chicago), where they might
> have appeared this Fall with a group of mine in that issue com-
> memorating the founding of the magazine by Harriet Monroe.
> Since you have paid for them I don't see why you don't use
> them. . . . You can be of service to me by reconsidering your
> position in the light of integrity and good business ethics. You
> ought to make good on your commitment. I have been publish-
> ing poems, as you know, for thirty years but your tactic is
> unique with me. . . . Is this the standard that I as a citizen
> should expect from the *Post?*

The editor replies that unfortunately the decision to eliminate the
poetry series was final:

> However "unique" this may seem to you, I may assure you that
> it is not extraordinary: not infrequently material completely
> prepared for publication, with plates made and ready to go to
> press, is replaced by something else and never sees print. I my-
> self have labored long and lovingly over words which were at
> the last moment killed. I would suspect that even the Butcher
> Polish Company has purchased material which stayed forever in
> inventory.

He went on to assure Eberhart that the *Post* had no objection to publication of the poems elsewhere, but that the Curtis company was entitled to half of all proceeds. That was the end of their correspondence until the following April, when Eberhart wrote:

> A New England View: My Report appears in the current issue of *The Kenyon Review*. My payment was $6.00. Enclosed take ironic pleasure in my check for $3.00, or 50%, which I hope will grease the wheels of your industry.

II

The scope and extent of Eberhart's contributions to magazines little and otherwise and to anthologies since 1952 defies all summary, although some idea of his relationships with these publications can be gathered from the preceding discussion and from the bibliography. More importantly, he published three books between 1952 and 1960. Less than a month after Chatto's publication of *Selected Poems,* Parsons wrote that he looked "forward to helping you make 'Poems 1946–1952' the best ever, and now have my suggestions ready." Eberhart sent additional poems, however, and Parson's preliminary selection was not ready until July, 1952. He wrote that the next book, by this time called "Poems 1946–1953,"

> should, I think, deviate towards exclusion rather than inclusion, since costs of production are so astronomic at the moment over here that a larger book inevitably means a higher price than the small public of genuine poetry readers is usually prepared to pay.

He had, however, good news with regard to sales of *Selected Poems:*

> . . . Oxford have nearly sold out their 500 copies of the "Selected," and have ordered a further 250. I am afraid we have not done quite so well here, but poetry sales have been at an

all-time low for the last two years, and the "Selected" has at any rate done as well as any other book of verse on our list.

Eberhart replied from Yaddo:

> There could be two principles for this book. One, rigid selection from about a hundred poems (I count 109 sent you) to make up a small volume supposedly of the best. I would agree to the wisdom of such a choice, but where is the Absolute Critic to say what poems merit inclusion, which precisely should be excluded?
>
> Two, following upon the rigid selection in "Selected Poems," which was one of the merits of the book and may have accounted for the good marks given it . . . the consideration of this volume as a workshop, a showroom, an exhibition of a considerable amount of work done. There is much to be said for a large net full of fish, at this mid-point (perhaps) of life and poetry. Scope has its advantage, despite the high price of paper!

He then appended a list of poems with comments. Beside "On Shooting Particles beyond the World," for instance he wrote:

> considered good (voluntarily even here, by a wonderful painter Miss Sparhawk-Jones, in her sixties, a friend of Edwin Arlington Robinson the last 14 years of his life, who was present at his death bed in 1936). Printed by Oscar Williams in his Scribner Little Treasury. . . .

No immediate reply from Parsons was forthcoming, and in November, Eberhart forwarded a new suggestion for a title, which was finally adopted:

> UNDERCLIFF. How about that? It is the name of the place we go to in Maine [every summer] . . . . would not this word, for heavy labors in mid-career, give the idea of aspiration? Wearing the whole weight of English poetry on one's back?

By this time, however, Parsons was "engulfed in the usual wave of autumn publishing" and did not answer until January of 1953, when he came to terms with Eberhart's comments, omitting some poems and including others at Eberhart's suggestion. Of "On Shooting Particles . . ." he wrote, "I bow to Oscar Williams and the terrifying Miss Sparhawk-Jones. Included." Then, however, the usual delays ensued and the publication date seemed to recede as the months passed. The making of the book was finally completed, however; Oxford again imported five hundred copies, and the book appeared in England and America almost simultaneously in November 1953.

Less than a month later Eberhart wrote Parsons, "It is time . . . to initiate the next book . . ." and suggested inclusion this time of some of his verse drama. Parsons, however, wrote again of the slow market in poetry and on that basis rejected the idea of doing plays. About the poems he said, "I should prefer to wait six months and then put in hand a new book of verse to appear in Spring '55." Eberhart dutifully waited until the following July, then sent a manuscript (from Yaddo again) and reiterated his desire to print the verse plays. He had still heard nothing from London in October, when he wrote again:

> Poetry is going concern or it is nothing. All statements about it are relative. That sentence, for instance. One might wait for 10 years before publishing another book and produce one's best work then. Who knows? In that case it would not be "going" in my intentions. I feel that you should not wait, even though UNDERCLIFF did well (over here at least), but put another on the market as soon as possible.

Parsons replied in March with apologies for the delay and reiterated the importance of economic considerations, "and a book of yours every two years is about all we can manage without being unfair to the other poets whom we publish." He did have ready, however, a preliminary list of inclusions. The idea of including verse plays or publishing them separately he ignored entirely. Then almost another year rolled over them before he had a final list. Then still further delays, generally unexplained, complicated the matter further, for just as Chatto's was ready to go to press, Eberhart sent additional poems and produced still further delay, for Parsons replied by wire:

> Your letters with still further suggestions for additions and alterations to book reduced me to despair from which I am not yet recovered stop hope to surface and sort out tangle this weekend.

They finally got rolling in January and Eberhart returned corrected proofs in February; Chatto's might have then published in March or April, but shipping delays held them back, since they wanted to publish simultaneously with Oxford, which they finally did in June. The title, suggested by Leonard Dean from a poem in *Undercliff,* was *Great Praises.*

Before the publication of *Great Praises,* Eberhart was of course already thinking about "a next book of mine," and although work did not begin on it until 1959, the publication of *Collected Poems* went considerably more smoothly than that of the two preceding books. In January 1959 Eberhart wrote Parsons:

> What I would like to do today is to ask you pointblank if you can publish this book one year from now, that is, early in 1960? I have a certain reason why this would be a strategic time for its appearance. This is still a matter of confidence, so I enjoin you to keep it so, but I am to be the next Consultant in Poetry at the Library of Congress. . . .

He points out that the production of *Great Praises* took "abysmally long" and goes on:

> Oxford New York wants a 250-page book, thereabouts. We talked of all possibilities, as you and I have heretofore. We finally decided the best presentation would be to have about 200 pp. of old poems from all previous books and I agreed to a run-on set-up, although I would like it better one poem to a

page. Then that last 50 p. or so would be a really strong showing of new poems, about 50 of them. This would leave out (reluctantly) again the verse plays; Oxford says a whole book of these alone would be better sometime later. Since only Great Praises and Undercliff are in stock, the *Early Collected* is in order for readers to get the whole works, so to speak, to date.

They almost immediately proceeded to the processes of selection and production, all of which went unusually quickly (possibly because of the promise of sales in the Library of Congress position), although proofs were not returned until June 1960. From that time on production proceeded rapidly, except that Oxford, which imported 1000 copies this time, out of an edition of 1750, did not like the English dust jacket and produced one of its own, and *Collected Poems* 1930–1960 appeared in both countries in the fall of 1960, in plenty of time to capitalize on Eberhart's position as Consultant.

Critical response to Eberhart's books in the 'fifties continued to be respectful but mixed. There is a general consensus that he is an uneven poet, but opinions vary as to the proportion of good poems to less good ones. Most critics agree, however, that the general level of his achievement is an adequate reward for the risks imposed by his individualism, and some make perceptive efforts to go further toward a definition, in both the contemporary and the etymological sense of the word, of that achievement.

There are of course extreme views on either side. The negative report on *Undercliff* of one Byron Vasakas, published by *Poetry* along with a more respectful review by Reuel Denney, discussed below, seems to find nothing to admire in Eberhart's work. In a stinging polemic Vasakas asserts that Eberhart "has achieved, after many years, the status of an authentic North American primitive, a paesan [sic] of poetry." The only kind words in the review are in the suggestion that *Undercliff* is disappointing, "coming so soon after the many virtues of his Selected poems." He characterizes the poems as "echolalia," which, he tells us, is the psychoanalytic term for "the rhythmic and verbal repetitions and babblings of primitives, children, psychotics, and poets." Vasakas's basic objection is to Eberhart's lack of discipline, a failure, as he sees it, to impose "a discipline of the imagination" upon emotional material:

> Such disembodiment, such dissociation from the responsibilities of content and form suggests a reversal to primitive mumbojumbo, or the inspirations of a gaseous oracle less in the Greek than in the Victorian "tradition," . . . As such, sincerity pervades his work. The pity and the paradox is that he tries to juggle too many contradictions.[3]

The reference to sincerity is the only mitigation of the review's attack, and although some of its points would be conceded by more sympathetic critics, that attack is extraordinarily hostile in both tone and content.

At the other extreme is Kenneth Rexroth, who in what purports to be a review of *Great Praises* in the *Saturday Review* found an opportunity to celebrate his long-standing admiration for his friend's work. He concentrates primarily on Eberhart's independence. He suggests that "The years in which Richard Eberhart came to maturity as a poet were not good ones for American literature." The theory was, he says, that out of depression, social upheaval and war a great new age of poetry would dawn.

> The terrible tragedy, considering all the expense of spirit is that almost nothing came, almost nothing at all. Muriel Rukeyser, Kenneth Patchen, Kenneth Fearing, Louis Zukofsky, the degree of their survival is the measure of their independence.
>
> Richard Eberhart, in some mysterious way, remained close to totally independent, and survives intact.

Rexroth goes on to attempt to relate Eberhart to the various episodes in the history of twentieth-century American poetry.

> In the days when art was a weapon and poetry purveyed spurious salvations, Eberhart ran the changes on "Go Lovely Rose," beauty perishes, value wastes away in the world of fact.

How silly that all seemed in the days when all MacDougall Alley spoke up with one voice for the proletariat.

And he finds Eberhart equally unmoved by

the time of the Reactionary Generation, of Seven Types of Ambiguity in every cornbelt English seminar . . . the days when Paul Valery's instrumentalism was quoted to justify good advertising copy on Madison Avenue and bad sonnets in Ashtabula. None of this seemed to touch Eberhart. . . . (I will never forget a famous poetry festival at Bard College when everybody was so embarrassed by a long poem Dick read about the experiences of a prisoner of war [Brotherhood of Men]. As a leading writress said, "After all the subject is a bit obvious.") He escaped from the workers and peasants of the Village cafeterias; how did he escape from the aristocrats of ambiguity?

Rexroth's flashing polemicism takes this as an opportunity to have his say on the entire generation of the New Criticism:

While Mr. Eliot and Mr. Empson were holding up as models the cloying hysteria of Richard Crashaw and the crossword puzzles in Saintsbury's "Minor Caroline Poets," Dick, with cool effrontery, turned away to the simplest voices in the language. People who are anxious to put up a good appearance at cocktail parties in outland English departments simply do not do things like that.

At the end of this lengthy admixture of diatribe and adulation, he finally has a few vague words to say about *Great Praises* and concludes: "Time brings fruition and magnanimity, but, alas, not to all. It has brought it abundantly to Richard Eberhart, now in his fifty-third year." [4]

In terms of evaluation, these two reviews can stand as a frame within which the other reviews of *Undercliff, Great Praises* and *Collected Poems* fall into place. It is also important to notice, however, that descriptively both reviews say, to a large degree, the same things. Rexroth attributes to Eberhart "Innocence. Wisdom. A pure heart. He was foolish enough to concern himself primarily with the only subjects of poetry, the great platitudes, the facts of life." To all of this Vasakas's review, though written earlier, can be considered a representative response, calling innocence primitivism and suggesting that "Naiveté, like innocence, can be carried too far." That his work is marked by these qualities, however, is not in dispute. The idea of discipline, furthermore, of finding precisely the *mot juste* and the well-wrought phrase, appeals most intensely to those most in sympathy with the fashionable critical dicta of Eliot and Empson, those of whom Rexroth relishes the characterization, "aristocrats of ambiguity." In short, it is easy and to a degree just to miss in Eberhart's poetry the crystalline precision and elegance of Wallace Stevens, but it is also easy and also just to object that such an approach is an indefensible demand that a contemporary poet must continually rewrite "Sunday Morning." Between these two poles the critical response to Eberhart's later work is perpetually suspended.

This suspension cannot be illustrated, however, by setting up one reviewer or group of reviewers against another, for on the whole it exists within each individually. The result is the consensus that Eberhart's work is "uneven." The *Times Literary Supplement* reviewer calls him "one of those copious, uneven poets," and Donald Hall says in a parenthesis, "I suppose that no good poet since Wordsworth has written so many bad poems." [5] This point of view is especially pronounced in the reputable academic reviews, which consistently give Eberhart brief notice along with several other volumes. Joseph Bennet in the *Hudson Review* makes one of the strongest statements: "A handful of poems show that Eberhart is capable of first-rate work; that he has the potentiality of greatness. What then makes him so frequently irresponsible and childish?" [6] James Dickey, writing of *Great Praises* in the *Sewanee Review,* puts a similar judgment into the form of a left-handed compliment, averring that Eberhart

has all but perfected a number of devices that he employs, cleverly and with increasing skill, to hide the fact that he is one of the most authentically gifted and instinctively poetic minds of our time.[7]

Louis Simpson, writing about the same book in the *Hudson Review*, gives small comfort to Eberhart and Parsons for all their labors in selecting poems for inclusion: "It seems that Richard Eberhart is unable to criticize his own writing, and apparently there has been no editor to do it for him." [8] It is the *Nation*'s reviewer of *Undercliff*, however, who gives the clearest and most concise summation of the consensus on Eberhart's "unevenness," saying

> that Eberhart is not only one of the best of the poets now writing but certainly one of the most outrageous at times, an innocence that really makes new where it succeeds, and a mannerism that shatters completely where it fails.[9]

It should be noticed that some reviewers think that a bridle on Eberhart's inspiration would necessarily include blinders, that if he adopted the discipline that some have said would place him among the very best, he would cease to be one of the most exciting. Dickey is "willing" to accept this viewpoint, and G. P. Meyer, in the *Saturday Review*, while conceding that Eberhart is uneven, goes on to declare, "but how unexciting an even poet can be," and favors Eberhart's individualism "naked and unashamed." [10] M. L. Rosenthal, writing of *Great Praises* in the *Nation*, states the point more elaborately:

> But though we should not quite forgive him his failures of self-criticism, it is quite likely that Eberhart needs to work as he does; that if he allowed himself certain kinds of "doubts," the greater successes, those poems in which we sense the god's presence at every moment, would be impossible.[11]

G. S. Fraser makes a similar point, and also shows the kind of frustration that can be felt by a strict critic looking for a final judgment. He thinks that "The Horse Chestnut Tree" has only a good beginning and that "Beaudelaire" has only an effective ending, "but if one is beginning to feel superior about this, one suddenly discovers that he can do a Blake, and not look silly." He goes on to comment on what might be called Eberhart's lack of style:

> Perhaps a "style" is sometimes the mere crystallising of stereotyped responses. Though the unevenness and imperfection of much of his work is a heavy price to pay for this, Mr. Eberhart has a quality which is very rare indeed in contemporary poets.[12]

If there is wide agreement with Vasakas's strictures on Eberhart's tendency to lose control of his material, there is just as much agreement with Rexroth's praise of his independence of contemporary fashions. The *Times Literary Supplement* reviewer of *Undercliff,* for instance, praises his "fearless tackling" of crucial problems of form and content. Making a point of Eberhart's identity as an American poet, this reviewer asserts:

> After the genteel amateurism of contemporary English poetry, it is salutary to come upon a real, professional poet. . . . Another mark of Mr. Eberhart's independence and professional pride is his refusal to be scared away from traditional "romantic" ideas and images.[13]

Even Geoffrey Moore's review of *Collected Poems* in the *New York Times,* which concentrates a good deal on Eberhart's weaknesses, nevertheless finds him "an attractively individual poet."[14] And Hayden Carruth's review of the same book, though it too marvels at Eberhart's lapses, also finds that while his "style is really the central or common poetic style of the twentieth century," it is marked by a characteristic individualism and he goes on to describe that individualism as "a quality of feeling, an appealing awkwardness of metaphor, a brilliant erratic play with common rhyme and meter." The most telling index to Carruth's affinity with Rexroth's point of view, however, is his concern that Eberhart's "recent poems have often been stony and too technical," suggesting that his sympathy with

Eberhart is closely related to an antipathy, like Rexroth's, for the icyness of much contemporary verse.[15]

Several critics have found that Eberhart is peculiarly American as well as peculiarly himself. The London *Times* review quoted above, for example, asserts that a book like *Undercliff* "does more to anatomize the essentials of American life during the dramatic, contradictory post-war years than . . . speeches or . . . memoirs." It goes on to say that the poems,

> in their eagerness, their curiosity, their lust to explore any subject that might prove a source of interesting speculation, and in their great strength and vitality, . . . must stand as a document of the American mind at a key passage of its history.

Hayden Carruth again, writing of *Great Praises* in *Poetry,* finds much of Emerson and Emily Dickinson in Eberhart, who, he says, "writes in a good grainy language that puts him squarely in the most attractive tradition of American verse. . . ." [16] Selden Rodman, whose review of *Undercliff* is considerably more attractive than that of *Burr Oaks* had been, finds in this "Americanism" part of the source of Eberhart's independence of currently fashionably intellectual pretensions:

> For all his intellectual preoccupation with death, there is a sunny disposition, an even temper, a healthy optimism, a muscular goodwill in Eberhart that stamps his writing as peculiarly American. It was, in fact, the conflict of this inherited Americanism with an acquired Anglican accent that gave his early poems their special savor.[17]

More importantly, this approach is also taken by A. Alvarez in his book, *The Shaping Spirit.* In his final chapter, "Art and Isolation," Alvarez attempts to demonstrate that "The specifically American difficulty comes from the poet's inability to rely on any steadying [moral or intellectual] framework outside himself." He then uses Eberhart as an example, in one of the earliest serious critical discussions of his work. He sees in Eberhart "a great lust for system," a straining to invent some metaphysic that will systematize his inner feelings in the absence of any traditional system of feeling and thought. He concludes with remarks on the much-noticed roughness of Eberhart's work:

> That awkwardness, which is typical of his best verse, does not come because Eberhart cannot manage anything more polished. Rather, it is a way of emphasizing the isolation of his statements: they presume on no prior means and no accepted manners. The awkwardness is a product of the man himself, as though his sharply original intuition came almost against his will, accompanied by the enthusiastic embarrassment of the conventional American in him. . . .
>
> Richard Eberhart and Robert Lowell are the two most impressive American poets since the generation which flourished in the twenties.[18]

There are several commentators, finally, who treat Eberhart as an established figure, without devoting much space to whether he is "good," "bad," or "uneven." These reviews attempt to discover the poems' salient characteristics and accomplishments much as Rosenthal's earlier reviews of *Burr Oaks* and *Selected Poems* had done, although Rosenthal's own review of *Great Praises* is not remarkable in this regard, except perhaps for its discerning critique of "The Roc," a poem which other critics have ignored. Reuel Denney, in a combined review of *Selected Poems* and *Undercliff,* attempts to trace in Eberhart's work a development "from an early concern with mortality, through an intermediate concern with the problem of human knowledge into a later concern with God and nature." Denney is more interested, however, in the development of Eberhart's style, specifically of the dramatic element. The early poetry, he says, combined "quasi-dramatic brusqueness" with the metaphysical tradition, then developed

> from the sharply lyrical toward more free-handed narrative and satiric forms and from them, by a leap, into verse dialogue

and drama. . . In a discriminating way, he has dissociated from each other some of the plural voices that were present, unnamed, in his lyrics, and he has displayed them as *personae* of drama, each one with a diction of his own.[19]

Another review of *Undercliff,* Gerald Weales's in *Commonweal,* though it does not attempt to trace any development through time, also tries with an unusual degree of success to examine essential aspects of the poetry. Weales defines Eberhart's central vision as one "of man that emphasizes his mortality without losing a note of affirmation," which comes primarily from a faith in the power of the imagination, "the often ephemeral realization of the combining nature of man and the aspiration of that combination," which works with the old essential duality between reason and passion, emotion and intellect, with the emphasis on emotion. He quotes "Phoenixes Again," and avers:

> Here there is not so much a disclaimer of man's intellectuality as a reduction of its size, an insistence that it should share the stage of man with the passions. The ordering principles of reason are forsaken for something greater that breaks too careful definition.

He also points out that this dualism

> is apparent in the poet's continual return to the idea of "forked" or "cleft" being; it is present in the images of sea and sky in "Seals, Terns, Time," and of sea and mountain in "Chiliasm." [20]

There seems to have been no such thorough and perceptive discussion of *Great Praises,* but Donald Hall's review of *Collected Poems* takes up, as it were, where Weales's leaves off, seeing also the dualism in Eberhart and pointing to poems which lean to the intellect and others which lean to emotion; he goes beyond Weales, however, by finding this dichotomy more integral to the language. To the "polarity"

A counterpart, though not precisely a parallel, occurs in the language of the poems. Eberhart is able to move from the most artificial and rhapsodic language to the utterly prosaic.

Louis Martz, finally, rounds out this approach to the poetry when he points to the same polarity and says,

> But when these two tendencies blend, each controlling the other, as they do in most of the poems here [in *Collected Poems*], we have the essential achievement of Eberhart, some of the finest poems of the twentieth century, where we find, as Tate would say, "knowledge carried to the heart." [21]

These reviews, especially those of Denney, Weales, and Hall, are notable because they are satisfied neither with the polemics of Vasakas and Rexroth, nor with the cryptic assessments of most reviews of any book. They attempt instead to develop generalizations with which the reader can profitably approach the poet's work as a whole. Three full-length articles which take a similar approach were also published between 1952 and 1960. James Hall's article in *Western Review* in 1954 attempts a critical introduction to Eberhart's work through an analysis of individual poems and a general discussion of his major themes, defining his characteristic structures and approaches to experience. [22] Selden Rodman's article the following year in *Perspective USA* is not as helpful in terms of technique as Hall's but attempts to trace the development of Eberhart's relationship with reality from book to book.[23] Peter Thorslev's article in Northwestern University's *Tri-Quarterly* also takes a historical approach, which is given further coherence by its emphasis on Eberhart's affinities with the early Romantics.[24]

Most critics have emphasized Eberhart's attempt at an almost transcendental resolution of what Rosenthal calls "the old war in Eberhart's verse between the ecstatic, instinct-ridden subjective man and his other, scientific-intellectual self," a war which at its best results in "driving conceptions . . . emotionally ignited by a visionary intensity." Some critics, moreover, consider this conjunction of reason, emotion, and perception a deliberate approach to reality, an approach which is essentially mystical; in Carruth's words:

> a species of poetic mystic centered upon such concepts as the efficacy of the creative imagination, the motivational force and value of love, the favor bestowed upon substance by the unknown, etc.

Elizabeth Jennings is more explicit, saying that "the vast majority of his poems are attempts to ensnare, to hold down, a transcendent experience of . . . in traditional Christian terms, a personal awareness of God." [25]

The critical consensus, then, seems to be that Eberhart is, in the words of Daniel Hoffman,

> a stubborn individualist who has been true to his own gifts regardless of what contemporaries were writing or what others thought the times demanded. . . . [and] early found a vein of ecstatic revelation whose felicities none other has approached.[26]

III

The social and economic success of Richard Eberhart reflects more than his own effort and achievement, but only so much more. That he has benefitted from the widely discussed "culture explosion" that has occurred in the United States since World War II is obvious, but it is not equally clear that either Eberhart's career or that explosion reflects a massive interest in serious poetry on the part of the American people, however generous its institutions. That generosity expresses itself in the very unpoetic form of money, which has at least the merit of being more measurable than the equally important acceptance and status that it accompanies. The institutions which have exercised this generosity are primarily those of higher education, which provide the funds for public appearances, periodicals, sometimes even publication, and especially academic salaries, even for young poets with no more reputation than Eberhart had after the publication of his first book.

The sales of Eberhart's books suggest, as might be expected, that this institutional support is provided not because of but in lieu of any widespread consumer interest. The figures for the early volumes verge on the ridiculous, except for the inexpensive and vigorously promoted *Poems, New and Selected,* in 1944, which sold 1300 copies. Fewer than 500 copies of the earlier books were sold by both Chatto and Oxford. The American sales of *Burr Oaks* were about the same, and Eberhart bought out Chatto's remaining 300 copies and gave them away at his final reading as Consultant. American sales have continued to increase, of course, but the returns remain negligible in terms of supporting a family. *Collected Poems* sold about 2000 copies in its first year, for example, which means a return for the poet of only $1200.

His income from other extracurricular sources, public appearances, phonograph records, book reviewing, etc., does not affect the picture appreciably. The total of all this income very rarely approaches a living wage. Only in 1961, when royalties from *Collected Poems* began to come in and when his position as Consultant brought an unusual number of speaking engagements, did he make as much from poetry as a young instructor in a good college—a little over $8000. Since 1961, he has earned outside of his Dartmouth salary an amount equivalent to that of a teacher in one of our less affluent public school systems, less than $5000. Before 1950 he never earned more than $700 (the total was $140 in 1947, for instance, when he was just learning the polish business), and the total figure did not reach $2000 until 1956. His winning of the Pulitzer Prize and the availability of his work in paperback may help matters considerably, but to the extent that these figures are typical, it is nonetheless clear that a poet depends heavily on institutional recognition and support. Eberhart is among the most widely known and widely read serious poets writing today, and yet but for his position at Dartmouth, which amounts to that of poet in residence, he would have very little professional identity in relation to society as a whole. The point of the present study, however, is perhaps that he does hold that position and thus is able to maintain that identity. In short, conditions have come a long way since he worked in a slaughterhouse, and as he and other poets continue to be an influence in colleges and universities, the audience for serious poetry will presumably increase; and younger men will find it less difficult than he did to be a poet in America.

AFTERWORD

It is safe to say that when Eberhart was appointed Consultant in Poetry to the Library of Congress, he had reached the end of the long road from obscurity to recognition. It should not be inferred, however, that the course of his career since his return to Dartmouth in the spring of 1961 has been downhill or even that it has leveled off. He has scarcely gone into retirement or ceased creative work. He continues to be active at Dartmouth (where he was appointed to the Class of 1925 Professorship in 1968), and to read his poems publically wherever he can, from California to Morocco, where he gave a reading at Rabat in 1965. He also returned to the University of Washington to teach for a term "out of love for Bob Heilman who . . . first set me on my second course as teacher." His personal travels during these years include trips to Mexico, Switzerland, the British Isles, North Africa and Kenya. Also during this period, honors have continued to accumulate. Besides the Bollingen Prize in 1962 and the Pulitzer Prize in 1966, he has received honorary doctorates from Skidmore and Wooster Colleges, in addition to Dartmouth, honorary membership in Phi Beta Kappa in 1967 (at Harvard, where he delivered the annual Phi Beta Kappa poem), and he was invited to read a poem at the inauguration of the President of Brandeis University in 1968. He also won the 1969 Fellowship of the Academy of American Poets with an award of $5000.

Such a brief sketch only gives some idea of the scope of Eberhart's activities during these years. The critical attention and recognition that he has received in the same period deserves more thorough examination, since it has itself been more careful, detailed, informative, and accurate in its evaluation than most of the criticism discussed in the main body of the present study. There have been innumerable reviews of the books published during these years, of course, and Eberhart's work generates its quota of items in such publications as *Explicator* and *English Journal,* and anthologies such as Anthony Ostroff's *The Contemporary Poet as Artist and Critic,* where Eberhart's "Am I My Neighbor's Keeper?" receives commentary by Louise Bogan, Philip Booth, and William Stafford, as well as a response by the poet himself. Essays have also begun to appear on limited aspects of the poet's work, such as Richard J. Fein's "The Cultivation of Paradox: The War Poetry of Richard Eberhart," in the *Ball State University Forum,* and Donna Gerstenberger's study of his drama, along with MacLeish's and Barnes's, in William E. Taylor's *Modern American Drama: Essays in Criticism.* The only previous full-scale study of Eberhart's verse drama is in Denis Donogue's *The Third Voice.* Bernard Engel, finally, has written a useful critical introduction in his *The Achievement of Richard Eberhart,* a selection in the Scott Foresman Modern Poets Series. Engel has also written the Twayne United States Authors Series volume on Eberhart (currently in press), which will be the first full-length critical study.

The most useful and representative works published since 1962, however, are review articles by Philip Booth and Daniel Hoffman, and Ralph Mills's Minnesota pamphlet, an expansion of an essay in his *Contemporary American Poetry.* It is probably Booth who strikes the keynote of this recent criticism when he writes, "Whenever it might have been when critics could tell Eberhart how to write somebody else's poems, that time has long since passed." It is also Booth who points out that reviewers' complaints have been as much a function of critical fashion as of Eberhart's allegedly uneven talent, and he insists that the poet be taken seriously on his own terms. This is the most salient characteristic of recent Eberhart criticism: that the value of his poetry is largely taken for granted, so that the critic can get on with the work of understanding. Once that work (which was begun to be sure, by earlier critics such as Blackmur, Rosenthal, and others) is under way, central emphases begin to emerge.

Most critics have taken careful note of Eberhart's inspirational method of composition. Most of his poems come upon him, he insists, in a state of heightened awareness and are composed almost spontaneously, requiring little or no revision. There are exceptions of course; "New York, 1929," for example was written first in prose, and many others result in whole or in part from conscious intellectual effort. Indeed, poems which are *completely* the result of the sort of divine possession which Eberhart sees as the core of his method are rare. But that core remains, not a sudden awareness of exact words, necessarily, but moments of extreme sensitivity, alertness, perception of the connection of a particular experience with a world, a vision, which the poet does not hesitate to call spiritual. Hoffman, for example, calls attention to this conviction, and Mills uses it as the central referent of his pamphlet, suggesting that "A sense of the processes of [Eberhart's] art is indispensable for a full understanding and appreciation of what it attempts."

These processes remain at all levels, of course, extremely mysterious. To take only the most intriguing example, we have already seen something of the genesis of "The Groundhog" in the letter quoted in Chapter Four. We can also learn, from a loose sheet in Eberhart's handwriting in his files, that he saw another dead groundhog near the same spot on the Foster farm two years later, "already partly disembowelled . . . ," a vulture circling above it, and that he returned later that same evening, "stopped and contemplated it, eaten all but bones and some entrails. . . ." The whole story takes on added interest, furthermore, when one knows that this last extant reference to a dead groundhog in the real world was written on June 18, 1932, the day of the marriage of Louise Hawkes, the Maia irrepressible in his consciousness until overshadowed by his wife and the war almost a decade later. We still do not know the precise

circumstances under which the poem itself was written, except that
it must have been composed at St. Mark's in 1933 or 1934; and although the wealth of information (in the Richard Eberhart Collection) on a large number of poems will probably keep future scholars
busy for many hours, no more satisfactory explanation of the creative process is likely to emerge than Eberhart's own conviction of
the power of "the spirit" in resolving the disharmonies of "objective"
reality.

Virtually all of Eberhart's critics, however, have seen that that
reality is as central to Eberhart as the spirit which provides its metamorphosis into art. Mills points out that one notices primarily in the
poems not only spontaneity, but also "the immediate presence of, involvement with, a particular experience." And Philip Booth, the
critic perhaps best attuned to Eberhart's sensibility, says of "Am I
My Neighbor's Keeper?", "it's important to this poem's success that
Eberhart finally grounds it in place and event." Bernard Engel also
recognizes this quality as characteristic, for "When he attains a vision, he comes to it at least partly through an experience or object
accessible to his senses," and Engel would agree with Hoffman who
sees that the poet "rejects Spirit without reality." But the Spirit remains; and Hoffman also sees that "his gritty acknowledgements of
physical reality are joined with an insistence upon the reality of
spirit, and it is this which few of his contemporaries can so directly
experience or make us believe."

This observation brings us finally to the most frequently noticed,
and by this time surely obvious, quality in Eberhart's work, his "Romanticism." His reliance upon inspiration, his insistence upon the
primacy of intuition over intellect, and his clearly expressed assumption of the existence of a noumenal world—these all point in this
direction, as all of his critics have perceived. Complicated, frequently strained discussions of his "Romanticism" are sufficiently
abundant, and it is not necessary to belabor the point here. They are
so abundant that it may be well to conclude this discussion in simplicity, with the perception of Philip Booth, who is "sure beyond
doubt that he is fundamentally a religious poet, and that at his best

his religion and poetry are one." For Eberhart does not, perhaps cannot, indulge in the tortuous philosophy of a Coleridge, nor is he the elegant theoretician that Eliot was. He does not attempt to reassemble the sensibility shattered in the seventeenth century; at the deepest level of awareness, he simply takes it for granted.

Thus it is not surprising to find that the most fashionable thing to say about Richard Eberhart is that he is unfashionable. Coming to maturity during a period that stressed discipline and craft, he relies unblushingly on inspiration. In the age of the Absurd, his poetry is at heart religious. For Eberhart never made the transition, described by Joseph N. Riddel in comparing Walt Whitman and Wallace Stevens, from cosmic consciousness to existentialist consciousness. The latter assumes, with Henry Adams, that Chaos is the law of Nature; Order is the dream of Man. That is: evil, chaos, disorder are real; and the "spirit" of which Eberhart says so much, as well as the order and value that dwell in the spirit, are merely imaginative fictions, myths to give us an isle of solace in an infinite sea of despair. From this conviction, many modern poets and most modern critics have turned to the power of the ordering imagination for a kind of salvation. The goal is no longer to find order and value and to actualize it in the total life of the individual or the society, but to create it in the forms of art.

The conflict between the good of which the poet can conceive and the evil which he experiences is, to be sure, central to much of this poetry. For Eberhart, however, this conflict is not between ideal conception and real experience. For him the spirit is real too; he sees himself not as a maker but as a seer, and his poems function as reflections, actualizations of that assumption, not highly polished, skillfully worked out wish-fulfillments. He rejects the one-dimensional reality demanded by post-Descartes rationalism and post-Enlightenment scientism and insists upon the existence of another dimension, a moral dimension, a dimension which turns out to be central to the purposes of this essay.

"Turns out to be," because the course of recent events has thrown this study of a poet's relationship with his society into a perspective different from that with which it was begun, five years ago, amidst the same kind of academic tranquility in which Eberhart himself has functioned since 1952, perhaps since 1947. While Eberhart was Consultant in Poetry, forces were already at work, on buses and campuses, in lunch counters and swimming pools in the South, that would finally pose a serious threat to that tranquility. For the students who form the greatest proportion of poetry's audience were learning to deal directly with social realities, learning lessons they were soon to apply in a movement to end the longest American war since the one for national independence. It now seems to have been inevitable that the activists would finally take the movement into their own immediate community, the campus, first in peace protests, then for their own involvement in decision-making, and finally against the involvement of their educational institutions in what they see as the machinery of oppression, from admissions policies to military training and research.

Eberhart's own involvement in these events has of course been minimal, and it is safe to say that he is far from sympathetic toward not only the obstructive, disruptive tactics and but even many of the goals of the New Left. For those tactics and goals flow out of a loss of faith in American social, political, and economic institutions, a loss of faith that Eberhart is unlikely ever to share. And the young people, in turn, are equally skeptical of anything as mystical as Eberhart's poetry.

I want to suggest, however, that this movement, perhaps even in its least attractive forms, springs from basic attitudes toward reality that are not entirely dissimilar from his. For Eberhart and those who threaten the stability of the institutions that make his work possible have in common a fundamental rejection of the necessity of evil, a rejection which has become for these young people a conviction that neither one's personal life nor the order of society must necessarily be characterized by oppression and exploitation, brutality and waste. They see the phenomena that their professors call "problems," to be analyzed "objectively," as crimes to be eliminated immediately and systematically. In short they have reached intuitively the same conclusion reached by the intellection and experience of such diverse personalities as Herbert Marcuse and Eldridge Cleaver: that social, political, and economic relationships have moral content. Like Camus, they would like to be able to love their country and still love justice.

The connection between these convictions and the vision of Richard Eberhart exists, to be sure, only (but most importantly) at a very basic level. Indeed, the radical young would attack his work because it involves no real social analysis. Works such as "The Visionary Farms," which caricatures the acquisitive ethic, or poems like "New York, 1929," which dramatizes the infernal brutality of modern life, are rare, and like his war poetry they are put into a cosmic rather than a political frame of reference. The radical would argue that the poet is supported by the Establishment precisely because he encourages an apolitical emphasis and acts therefore as a safety valve for discontent. A poetry which begins from an instinctive faith in the existence of value, however, rather than from the existential despair so fashionable in modern literature, a poetry that implicitly demands order in the world rather than fabricating the sterile felicities of pure form, is profoundly radical. It is no accident that the same qualities—innocence, naïveté, etc.—are frequently ascribed (often with the same sneer) both to the poetry and to the most active members of the generation that reads it. For at the deepest level of awareness Eberhart rejects the assumption that reality is inherently evil, rejects a world in which "nothing is possible but necessity," and the most significant aspect of the story of his life is that social institutions have allowed such a poet the freedom to develop. It is not clear whether this situation will continue. One suspects that the financial demands of war and poverty will be made first on those widely considered marginal in their usefulness, such as poets. Many of those most in favor of radical social change, furthermore, see academic and artistic freedom as limited to a very few at the expense of great masses of people. So it remains to be seen whether American institutions, or those which develop out of present conflicts, will allow a poet to live so completely as a free man. Meanwhile, I shall be content to suggest, borrowing a favorite term from our students, that Richard Eberhart may turn out to be the most relevant poet of his time.

Madison, Wisconsin
October 1, 1969

NOTES

CHAPTER THREE

[1] This account of his trip is taken from a 158-page typescript in the Richard Eberhart Collection, apparently constructed from diaries and letters.

[2] For more on the Irish trip see Richard Eberhart, "Memory of Meeting Yeats, Æ, Gogarty, James Stephens," *Literary Review,* I (Autumn 1957), 51–56.

[3] "Empson's Poetry," *Accent Anthology,* eds. Kerker Quinn and Charles Shattuck (Harcourt, Brace: New York, 1946), pp. 571–88.

[4] The primary source for this discussion of Eberhart's relationship with Richards is I. A. Richards in conversation with the author on February 26, 1966. Unless otherwise indicated, quoted words and phrases are Mr. Richards's.

[5] "Under the Hill," "Looking Down," "The Village Daily," "Schopenhauer," "Windy," "Twenty-two," "Search," and "Song" ("Cover me over, clover"), under the general title "Things Known," *Poetry,* XXXI (November 1927), 80–85.

[6] Under the general title, "The Slope Sun—1927," *Poetry,* XXXV (December 1929), 122–27. "Sumatra Shore Leave" is in *Collected Poems* (pp. 2–3) as "The Bells of a Chinese Temple" with the two lines restored.

[7] Eds. Christopher Saltemarshe, John Davenport, and Basil Wright (London, 1929), pp. 28–32.

[8] *The Cambridge Review,* L, 317.

[9] *A Bravery of Earth* (London, 1930), p. 128. Cited in text hereafter.

[10] James Thornton, "Poetry and Experience," *Nation and Athenaem,* XLVII (April 26, 1930), 117.

[11] Anonymous, "Books in Brief," *The Nation,* CXXXI (July 16, 1930), 75–76.

[12] William Rose Benét, "Round about Parnassus," *Saturday Review of Literature*, VII (July 26, 1930), 9.

[13] Edith H. Walton, "A Bravery of Earth," *The New Republic*, LXIII (July 9, 1930), 214.

[14] Eda Lou Walton, "Young Poets," *New York Herald Tribune Books*, VII (June 22, 1930), 17.

[15] *Poetry*, XXXVI (September 1930), 343–44.

[16] Richard Church, "Still the Brave Poets," *Spectator*, CXLIV (April 12, 1930), sup. 623.

[17] *Thirty One Sonnets* (Eakins Press: New York), 1967.

CHAPTER FOUR

[1] His father had remarried in 1924.

[2] "Necessity," "Fragments," "Cellar," "Request for Offering," "Cynic Song," *New Signatures: Poems by Several Hands* (Hogarth: London, 1932), 58–65.

[3] Anonymous, "The New Poetry," *Times Literary Supplement*, March 17, 1932, 197.

CHAPTER FIVE

[1] *Time*, XXVIII (July 13, 1936), 56.

[2] Charles Powell, "Recent Verse," *The Manchester Guardian*, December 11, 1937.

[3] C. Day Lewis, "Autumn Verse," *Life and Letters*, Winter 1937, 39–40.

[4] Rex Hunter, "Four Books," *Poet Lore*, XLIV (Spring 1938), 53–55.

[5] Anonymous, "Old Age and Youth, a Contrast," *Poetry Review*, XXVIII (February 1937), 77.

[6] John Peale Bishop, "A Little Legacy," *Poetry*, L (June 1937), 164–66.

[7] Clifford Dyment, "New Poetry," *Time and Tide*, January 9, 1937.

[8] Janet Adam Smith, "Books of the Quarter," *The Criterion*, XVI (January 1937), 332–333.

[9] F. R. Leavis, "Reading the Spirit," *Scrutiny*, V (December 1936), 333–34.

[10] Anonymous, "Two Dynamic Poets of Today," *Times Literary Supplement*, May 29, 1937, 408.

[11] Philip Horton, "Reading the Spirit," *The New Republic*, XCV (June 29, 1938), 226–27.

[12] R. P. Blackmur, "Reading the Spirit," *Partisan Review*, IV (February 1938), 52–56.

CHAPTER SIX

[1] "In a Gunner's Eye," *Common Sense*, XII (March 1943), 88–89, published anonymously.

[2] The reference to kites has to do with the enormous target kites that Eberhart learned to fly while a gunnery instructor and later flew as a hobby.

[3] "You Would Think the Fury" (sic), "Dam Neck, Va.," "Speech from a Play," *The Kenyon Review*, VI, 189–92.

[4] "But to reach the archimedean point," *Partisan Review*, VII (Sept.-Oct. 1940), 357–58.

[5] "To a Poet" ("Go to the shine that's on the tree"), *New Yorker*, XV (September 9, 1939), 52.

[6] "Rumination," *The Atlantic Monthly*, CLXVII (May 1942), 603.

[7] *The Harvard Advocate*, CXXVII (November 1940), 10.

[8] "Poem in Construction," from "The Human Being," *Furioso*, I (Summer 1939), 15–16.

[9] "A Meditation," *Furioso*, I (Spring 1940), 7–10; "Letters anent the *Meditation*," 42, 43.

[10] "The Groundhog," "The Soul Longs to Return Whence It Came," "A Meditation," *New Poems: 1940* (New York, 1941), pp. 91–100.

[11] More than 200 copies of *Reading the Spirit* were also "blitzed" in a London warehouse.

[12] The selection was now to become a "Poet of the Year" pamphlet, since the Book of the Month Club had claimed copyright on "of the Month."

[13] Conrad Aiken, "Themes with Variations," *The New Republic*, CXII (April 2, 1945), 451–53.

[14] J. M. Brinnin, "Stigmata of Rapture," *Poetry*, LXI (December 1942), 508–11.

[15] John Crowe Ransom, "Lyrics Important, Sometimes Rude," *Furioso*, I (Summer 1941), 68–70.

[16] Kerker Quinn, "Forty Poems," *New York Herald Tribune Books*, XIX (November 29, 1942), 28.

[17] W. H. Mellers, "Cats in Air-Pumps," *Scrutiny*, IX (December 1940), 293–97.

[18] David Daiches, "Towards the Proper Spirit," *Poetry*, LXVI (May 1945), 92–95.

CHAPTER SEVEN

[1] *Collected Verse Plays*, pp. viii–ix (Chapel Hill: University of North Carolina Press), 1962.

[2] According to a program in a scrapbook in Eberhart's personal library, his statement in *Collected Verse Plays* (p. ix) that the first production was in January 1951 is clearly in error.

[3] The Poet's Theatre did, however, produce his *Devils and Angels* in January 1956, according to Eberhart, *Collected Verse Plays*, p. xi.

[4] *Poetry*, LXVIII (July 1946), 202–7.

[5] John Holmes, "Compassion and Wisdom," *New York Times Book Review*, C (August 19, 1951), 5.

[6] *War and the Poet*, eds. Richard Eberhart and Selden Rodman (Devin-Adair: New York), 1945.

[7] Selden Rodman, "Heady Grope for a New World, upon an Old's Effacement," *New York Times Book Review*, XCVII (December 21, 1947), 8.

[8] Howard Nemerov, "The Careful Poets and the Reckless Ones," *Sewanee Review*, LX (1952), 328–29.

[9] Arthur Mizener, "The Earnest Victorian," *Poetry* LXXIII (January 1949), 226–28.

[10] Babette Deutsch, "Poems of Lively Complexity," *New York Herald Tribune Weekly Book Review*, XXVII (July 8, 1951), 3.

[11] G. P. Meyer, "Ecstasy and Awareness," *Saturday Review of Literature*, XXXI (April 10, 1948), 18.

[12] William Arrowsmith, "Five Poets," *Hudson Review*, IV (Winter 1952), 623–24.

[13] M. L. Rosenthal, "The Mysterious Art of Singing Words," *New York Herald Tribune Weekly Book Review*, XXIV (July 4, 1948), 6; "Three Poets in Focus," *The New Republic*, CXXV (December 10, 1951), 27–28.

[14] *Collected Verse Plays*, p. ix.

CHAPTER EIGHT

[1] "Will and Psyche in Poetry," *The Moment of Poetry*, ed. Don Cameron Allen (Johns Hopkins Press: Baltimore), 1962, pp. 48–72; "Tragedy as Con-

trol and Resolution," *Tulane Drama Review,* VI (June 1962), 3–15; "Emerson and Wallace Stevens," *Literary Review,* VII (Autumn 1963), 51–71.

2 *Liberation,* IV (November 1959), 9.

3 Byron Vasakas, "Eberhart: A Negative Report," *Poetry,* LXXXV (November 1954), 106–8.

4 Kenneth Rexroth, "The Finest of the Lost," *Saturday Review of Literature,* XL (December 28, 1957), 15–16.

5 Anonymous, "A Poetry of Celebration," *Times Literary Supplement,* 398. Donald Hall, "Polarity and Its Counterpoint," *Saturday Review of Literature,* XLIV (February 11, 1961), 65–66.

6 Joseph Bennet, "Recent Verse," *Hudson Review,* VII (Summer 1954), 305–6.

7 James Dickey, "In the Presence of Anthologies," *Sewanee Review,* LXVI (1958), 309–10.

8 Louis Simpson, "Poets in Isolation," *Hudson Review,* X (Autumn 1957), 458–59.

9 Anonymous, "But Always a Poet," *Nation,* CLXXVIII (March 20, 1954), 246.

10 G. P. Meyer, "Death and Rhyme," *Saturday Review of Literature,* XXXVII (May 22, 1954), 22.

11 M. L. Rosenthal, "Leaper into Vision," *Nation,* CLXXV (December 21, 1957), 480–81.

12 G. S. Fraser, "Poetic Intelligence," *New Statesman and Nation,* n.s. XLVI (1953), 646–47.

13 Anonymous, "Inventive Surprise," *Times Literary Supplement,* December 25, 1953, 834.

14 Geoffrey Moore, "Some Credits and Debits," *New York Times Book Review,* CX (January 8, 1961), 52.

15 Hayden Carruth, "The Errors of Excellence," *Nation,* CXCII (January 1, 1961), 63.

16 Hayden Carruth, "Maturity and Responsibility," *Poetry,* XCI (October 1957), 53–56.

17 Selden Rodman, "Two Poetic Voices of Our Time," *New York Times Book Review,* CIII (November 22, 1953), 5.

18 A. Alvarez, *The Shaping Spirit* (Chatto & Windus: London, 1958), pp. 184–85; published in the United States (Charles Scribner's Sons: New York, 1958), as *Stewards of Excellence.*

19 Reuel Denney, "The Idiomatic Kingdom," *Poetry,* LXXXV (November 1954), 102–5.

20 Gerald Weales, "Furtive Marks on Paper," *Commonweal,* LIX (1953–54), 408–10.

[21] Louis L. Martz, "The Virtues of Collection," *Yale Review*, L (March 1961), 443–45.

[22] James Hall, "Richard Eberhart: The Sociable Naturalist," *Western Review*, XVIII (Summer 1954), 315–21.

[23] Selden Rodman, "The Poetry of Richard Eberhart," *Perspective USA*, No. 10 (Winter 1955), 42–52.

[24] Peter Thorslev, "The Poetry of Richard Eberhart," *Northwestern Tri-Quarterly*, II (Winter 1960), 26–32. Reprinted in *Poets in Progress*, ed. Edward Hungerford (pub: Chicago, 1962), pp. 72–91.

[25] Elizabeth Jennings, "Searching with Words," *New Statesman*, LX (October 15, 1960), 576.

[26] Daniel Hoffman, "Hunting a Master Image; The Poetry of Richard Eberhart," *The Hollins Critic*, I (October 1964), 1–12.

SELECTED BIBLIOGRAPHY

To list all the letters and other primary material used in this study would be as useless as it would be tedious. Instead, the following is a list of works by and about Richard Eberhart; it is selected in the sense that it is no more complete than the author could make it. From references in the correspondence and other of Eberhart's personal records, it is certain that there are omissions, because the author was not always able to search out the material referred to. This is especially true of the years since 1962, which is the end of the period covered in the main body of the study. Limitations of time and resources have prevented the author from doing anything approaching justice to the volume and variety of Mr. Eberhart's publications during these years. Inclusions of his work in anthologies and textbooks, finally, have been generally omitted for this period. In earlier years, such inclusions were indicative of his growing reputation; now, however, they merely add to the distinction of the books themselves. The core of the following list was provided by a substantial bibliography in Baker Library at Dartmouth College, which has been to a large extent verified and supplemented by standard bibliographical sources and procedures.

Poetry and Prose by Richard Eberhart

1921

"The Shell Vase," *The Austinian* (Austin High School: Austin, Minn., 1921), p. 16.

1924

"Beneath Rich Stars," *The Bema*, XIII (December, 1924), 23.
"Go Your Own Way," *The Tower*, I (October 17, 1924), 4.
"Impressions," *The Tower*, I (November 6, 1924), 9.
"The Inevitable," *The Tower*, I (October 17, 1924), 8.
"Searchers," "Barriers," *The Tower*, I (December 15, 1924), 8.

1925

"Altars," *The Tower*, I (June 1, 1925), 9.
"Bruges," *The Tower*, II (October 9, 1925), 15.
"Circe," *The Tower*, II (October 9, 1925), 15.
"Despair," *The Tower*, II (September 25, 1925), 3.
"Ghost—Chaste and White," "Homo Sapiens Aetat 21," *The Tower*, I (June 1, 1925), 10.
"Hyacinthus and the Jonquil," *The Tower*, I (April 24, 1925), 9.
"The Lady Styx," *The Tower*, I (February 7, 1925), 8.
"M. D.," *The Tower*, II (November 19, 1925), 12 (under the pseudonym "R. E. Ghormley").
"Nirvana" ("Cover me over clover"), *The Tower*, II (November 6, 1925), 6.
"Recognition," *The Tower*, II (September 25, 1925), 15.
"Renunciation," "Sculptor," *The Tower*, 10 ("Sculptor" is printed under the pseudonym "R. E. Ghormley").

"Revolt on Seeing the Cimitro Monumentale di Milano," *The Tower*, II (November 19, 1925), 14.

"Searcher," "The Village Daily," "Moosilauke Phantasy," *The Arts Anthology: Dartmouth Verse, 1925* (The Arts: Portland, Me., 1925), pp. 8–10.

"Silver," *The Tower*, I (March 23, 1925), 12.

"To a Proud Lady," *The Bema*, XIII (March, 1925), 26.

"Truth," *The Bema*, XIII (April, 1925), 8.

"The Ultimate," *The Bema*, XIII (June, 1925), 41.

"Veil," *The Tower*, I (April 15, 1925), 7.

"Wonder and Shadow," *The Bema*, XIII (June, 1925), 37.

"Worshiper," *The Tower*, I (May 8, 1925), 7.

1926

"Day Song," *The Tower*, II (June 14, 1926), 15.

"For Rupert Brooke," *The Tower*, II (February 6, 1926), 11.

"Hierarchy," *The Tower*, II (March 1, 1926), 8.

"Illaria del Caretto," *The Tower*, II (May 15, 1926), 13.

"Life-Necessity," *The Tower*, II (June 14, 1926), 22.

"Poem," *The Tower*, II (March 19, 1926), 16.

"Schopenhauer," "Search," *The Tower*, II (April 22, 1926), 16.

1927

"Things Known:" "Looking Down," "The Village Daily," "Schopenhauer," "Windy," "Twenty-Two," "Search," "Song" ("Cover me over clover"), *Poetry*, XXXI (November, 1927), 80–85.

1929

"Boulder," "Hill Climber," *London Mercury*, XX (July, 1929), 238–39.

"For a Lamb," *Experiment*, No. 4 (November, 1929), 19.

"Fragments," *Experiment*, No. 3 (May, 1929), 6.

"Maze," "Nannette," "Caravan of Silence," *Cambridge Poetry,* eds. Christopher Saltemarshe, John Davenport, and Basil Wright (Hogarth: London, 1929), pp. 28-32.

"Request for Offering," *Experiment,* No. 2 (February, 1929), 23.

"The Slope Sun:" "Wentworth Place," "L'après-midi d'un faune," "The Kiss of Stillness," "Nightwatch on the Pacific," "Sumatra Shore Leave," *Poetry,* XXXV (December, 1929), 122–127.

"This Is," *Experiment,* No. 3 (May, 1929), 44.

"To Maia," *Experiment,* No. 3 (May, 1929), 48.

1930

A Bravery of Earth (Jonathan Cape: London, 1930; Jonathan Cape and Harrison Smith: New York, 1930).

"Necessity," *Experiment,* No. 5 (February, 1930), 4.

"Notes on Novels: *Sincerity,* by John Erskine," *New Republic,* LXI (January 8, 1930), 204. (Review)

"Prose and Music: *Indian Earth,* by Witter Bynner," *New Republic,* LXII (March 26, 1930), 166. (Review)

"Quern," *Experiment,* No. 6 (October, 1930), 39.

"Request for Offering," *Transition,* Nos. 19–20 (June, 1930), 127.

1932

"Necessity," "Fragments," "Cellar," "Request for Offering," "Cynic Song," *New Signatures: Poems by Several Hands,* coll. by Michael Roberts (Hogarth: London, 1932), pp. 58–65.

1934

"The Groundhog," *The Listener* (August 22, 1934), 651.

"1934," *The Listener* (December 27, 1934), 1087.

"The Return of Odysseus," *Scrutiny,* III (June, 1934), 64.

1935

"The Groundhog," "Dissertation by Waxlight," "1934," *Poems of Tomorrow: An Anthology of Contemporary Verse Chosen from The Listener,* ed. Janet Adam Smith (Chatto and Windus: London, 1935), 38–43.

1936

"Alphabet Book," "Mais l'Amour infini me montera dans l'Ame," *Transition,* No. 24 (June, 1936), 11–15.
"Meditation Two," *Audience,* VIII (1936), 7–9.
Reading the Spirit (Chatto and Windus: London, 1936).

1937

"My Desire to Write Poetry," "Grave Piece," "Song," *New Directions in Poetry and Prose: 1937* (New Directions: Norfolk, Conn., 1937), no page numbers.
Reading the Spirit (Oxford University Press: New York, 1937).

1938

"Four Poems:" "To come closer unto thee," "Anglo-Saxon Song," "Poems" ["If I Could Only Live at the Pitch That Is Near Madness"], "Song for the Death of My Uncle in Illinois," *Poetry,* LI (January, 1938), 190–193.
"Homage to T. S. Eliot: A Symposium," *Harvard Advocate,* CXXV (December, 1938), Eberhart's contribution, 18–19.

1939

"Foundation," *New Directions in Poetry and Prose: 1939* (New Directions: Norfolk, Conn., 1939), pp. 239–242.

From "The Human Being," *Vindex* (St. Mark's School), LXIII (June, 1939), 176.

From "The Human Being," *Furioso,* I (Summer, 1939), 16.

"A New Word-Sculpture," *New York Herald Tribune Books,* XV (April 30, 1939), 20. (Review: Dudley Fitts and Robert Fitzgerald, trans., *The Antigone of Sophocles.*)

"Notion of Hell," *Poetry,* LV (November, 1939), 101–103. (Review: Ronald Bottrall, *The Turning Path.*)

"Poem," *Hika* (Kenyon College), VI (June, 1939), 12.

"Poem in Construction," *Furioso,* I (Summer, 1939), 15.

"Rumination," *Seven,* No. 4 (Summer, 1939), 32.

"To Critics," *New Republic,* C (October 18, 1939), 314.

"To a Poet" ("Go to the shine that's on the tree"), *New Yorker,* XV (September 9, 1939), 54.

"To a Poet," *In-between Times* (October 27, 1939), 2.

"Two Poems," *Harvard Advocate,* CXXXV (June, 1939), 10.

"Warmth and Ease and Charm and Aptitude," *Poetry,* LIV (June, 1939), 160-163. (Review: Merrill Moore, *M: 1000 Autobiographical Sonnets.*)

"When I Think of Her," *Kansas City Journal* (February 22, 1939), 22.

1940

"But to reach the archimedean point," *Partisan Review,* VII (September–October, 1940), 357–358.

"Early Poems:" "Beyond Cambridge," "I Seek Tall Trees for Melodies," "Twelve," *Hika,* VI (May, 1940), 14.

"For John Brooks Wheelwright," *The Modern Quarterly,* XI (Summer, 1940), 110.

"The Groundhog," *A Book of Modern Verse* (Chatto and Windus: London, 1940), pp. 60–61.

"A Meditation," *Furioso,* I (Spring, 1940), 7–10.

"A Mixed Bag," *Poetry,* LVI (August, 1940), 274–277. (Review:

Glyn Jones, *Poems:* Roy Fuller, *Poems;* Henry Treece, *38 Poems*.)

"Metamorphosis," *Harvard Adovocate,* CXXVI (April, 1940), 16.

"The Needle of the Eye," *Common Sense,* IX (December, 1940), 25.

"Poem in Construction," *Poetry,* LVI (June, 1940), 140–143.

"Q's Revisions," *Kenyon Review,* II (Autumn, 1940), 496–499. (Review: Arthur Quiller-Couch, ed., *New Oxford Book of English Verse, 1200–1918*.)

"Recollection of Childhood," *Four Dartmouth Poems, 1940* (Baker Library Press: Hanover, N. H., 1940).

"The Scarf of June," *Furioso,* I (January 1, 1940), 11.

Song and Idea (Chatto and Windus: London, 1940).

"Those Who Love Struggle," *Vice Versa,* I (November–December, 1940), 20.

"To a Girl Suffering from a Leg Injury for Three Years," *Hika,* VI (May, 1940), 14.

"Two Loves," *New Republic,* CIII (September 2, 1940), 300.

1941

"Angelic Perspectives," *Poetry,* LVII (January, 1941), 276-278. (Review: Eugene Jolas, *Planets and Angels*.)

"Burden," *New Republic,* CIV (January 13, 1941), 46.

"Ce pays nous ennuie, O mort! appareillons!," From "Poem in Construction," *Decision,* I (January, 1941), 22–23.

"The Expense of Critical Reason," *Accent,* II (Autumn, 1941), 51–55. (Review: R. P. Blackmur, *The Expense of Greatness;* John Crowe Ransom, *The New Criticism;* Allen Tate, *Reason in Madness*.)

"A Human Good," *Poetry,* LVIII (June, 1941), 146–148. (Review: W. de la Mare, *Collected Poems*.)

"The Groundhog," "The Soul Longs to Return Whence it Came," "A Meditation," *New Poems: 1940,* ed. Oscar Williams (Yardstick Press: New York, 1941), pp. 91–100.

"Poem," *Diogenes,* I (Autumn, 1941), 108.

"Poem in Construction," I (January–February, 1941), 1–3.

"The Recapitulation," *Vertical* (Gotham Book Mart: New York, 1941), ed. Eugene Jolas, pp. 33–35.

"The World View," *The Tuftonian,* I (May, 1941), 16–17.

1942

"Band of Usable Monuments," *American Prefaces,* VIII (Autumn, 1942), 51.

"Big Top," *Poetry,* LX (June, 1942), 165–168. (Review: *New Directions in Poetry and Prose: 1941.*)

"The Blindness of Poets," "The Dream," "Dublin Afternoon," "New Hampshire, February," "Of Truth: The Protagonist Speaking," "To H. E. B.," "To Evade The Whirlwind," *Poetry,* LX (April, 1942), 1–8.

"From Poem in Construction," *Vice Versa,* I (January, 1942), 33-36.

"In the Night When Destruction Shall Shake the World," "I Walked Out to the Graveyard to See the Dead," "The Extreme Water," *Southern Review,* VII (Spring, 1942), 861–862.

"Kafka's America," "The Dream," "Hand-View," "The Largess," *New Poems, 1942,* ed. Oscar Williams (Peter Pauper Press: Mt. Vernon, N. Y., 1942).

"Poems in Construction," "The Perturbation," "The Inspissation," "Ingathering," "A World-View," *New Directions Number Seven: 1942* (New Directions: Norfolk, Conn., 1942), pp. 47–72.

"Rumination," *Atlantic,* CLXIX (May, 1942), 603.

Song and Idea (Oxford University Press: New York, 1942).

"Song from 'Poem in Construction,'" *Life and Letters Today,* XXXV (November, 1942), 90.

"Three Poems," *Harvard Advocate,* CXXVIII (April, 1942), 31.

1943

"Beginning of a Beginning," *New Republic*, CVIII (June 14, 1943), 803. (Review: Delmore Schwartz, *Genesis*.)

"The Game," *The Chimera*, I (Winter, 1943), 44.

"Heavenly-Mindedness," *Poetry*, LXII (September, 1943), 347–350. (Review: John Pick, *Gerard Manley Hopkins: Priest and Poet*.)

"Letter to the Editor," *Nation*, CLVI (May 8, 1943), 681.

"The Preacher Sought to Find Acceptable Words," *Nation*, CLVII (August 21, 1943), 214.

"Song," *Furioso*, II (1943), 7.

"Speech From a Play," "Of Truth: The Protagonist Speaking," *New Poems: 1943*, ed. Oscar Williams (Howell, Soskin: New York, 1943), pp. 80–84.

"Triptych," *The Chimera*, II (Autumn, 1943), 15–25.

"Ur-Review," *Accent*, III (Winter, 1943), 121–122. (Review: Wallace Stevens, *Notes Toward a Supreme Fiction*.)

1944

"Dam Neck, Virginia," "The Fury of Aerial Bombardment," *New Poems: 1944*, ed. Oscar Williams (Howell, Soskin: New York, 1944), pp. 219–220.

"Empson's Poetry," *Accent*, IV (Summer, 1944), 195–207. (Article)

"The Groundhog," *An Anthology of Famous English and American Poetry*, eds. W. R. Benét and Conrad Aiken (Modern Library: New York, 1944), pp. 911–912.

"The Largess," "Experience Evoked," "The Groundhog," "1934," *Twentieth Century American Poetry*, ed. Conrad Aiken (Modern Library: New York, 1944).

"Verse More or Less Topical:" "Dam Neck, Virginia," "You Would Think the Fury," "Speech from a Play," *Kenyon Review*, IV (Spring, 1944), 189–191.

"White Lily and Hail," *The Chimera,* II (Winter-Spring, 1944), 33–34.

"Poem," ("Sometimes the longing for death"), "The Vision of the Swans," "The Drunkard," *Accent,* V (Spring, 1945), 179–180.

Poems, New and Selected (New Directions: Norfolk, Conn., 1945). This is the actual year of publication, although the book was officially listed as of 1944.

War and the Poet, ed. with Selden Rodman (Devin-Adair: New York, 1945).

1946

"An Airman Considers His Power," *Furioso,* II (Fall, 1946), 53.

"Empson's Poetry," *Accent Anthology,* eds. Kerker Quinn and Charles Shattuck (New York, 1946), pp. 571-588.

"Nonino Dialectic," "An Allowance," "Leave Me My Golden Horn of Hours," *Sewanee Review,* LIV (1946), 275-280.

"On Seeing an Egyptian Mummy in Berlin, 1932," "Ode to a Chinese Paper Snake," *Quarterly Review of Literature,* III (1946), 29–32.

"Search for Perfection," *Poetry,* LXVII (January, 1946), 212–215. (Review: John Crowe Ransom, *Selected Poems.*)

"At the End of War," *The Ark* (Spring, 1947), 16–18.

Burr Oaks (Oxford University Press: New York, 1947; Chatto and Windus: London, 1947).

"A Ceremony by the Sea," *Virginia Quarterly Review,* XXIII (Spring, 1947), 232-234.

"Death Then the Last, Then the Depth," "Pink Elf, O Master Child," "God to Man," *Contemporary Poetry,* VII (Autumn, 1947), 4–5.

"Four Poets," *Sewanee Review,* LV (Spring, 1947), 324–336. (Review: Pablo Neruda, *Residence on Earth and Other Poems;* Robert Lowell, *Lord Weary's Castle;* Thomas Merton, *A Man in the Divided Sea;* Reed Whittemore, *Heroes and Heroines.*)

"Notes to a Class in Adult Education," *Accent,* VII (Summer,

1947), 251–253. (Review: Wallace Stevens, *Transport to Summer.*)

Poetry Lecture, Mills College, April 1946, *Pacific* (Mills College), II (April, 1947), 18–26.

"Pound's New Cantos," *Quarterly Review of Literature,* V (1947), 174–191. (Article)

"A Word for Modern Poetry," *The English Leaflet,* XLVI (December, 1947), 142–143. (Lecture?—Article)

1948

"Art and Zeitgeist," *Poetry,* LXXIII (December, 1948), 173–176. (Review: Muriel Rukeyser, *The Green Wave.*)

"At the End of War," *Now,* VIII (May–June, 1947–48), 28–30.

"Burned Alive," *The Poetry Chapbook,* VII (Fall, 1948), 20.

"Chant of the Forked Lightning," *The Tiger's Eye,* No. 6 (December, 1948), 68.

"From Letter I," *Poetry,* LXXII (April, 1948), 14–16.

"Grave Piece," *Explicator,* VI (February, 1948), It. 23 (with Eberhart's own explication).

"Sestina," "Helldiver Gunner," *New Directions in Poetry and Prose: 10* (New Directions: New York, 1948), pp. 42–45.

"Song of the Nerves," *Poetry,* LXIII (October, 1948), 43–45. (Review: John Berryman, *The Dispossessed.*)

"*The Young Hunter,*" *Explicator,* VI (February, 1948), It. 24 (with Eberhart's own explication).

1949

"Bright Hour of Europe," "Seascape with Parable," *Botteghe Oscure,* II (1949), 282–284.

Brotherhood of Men (Banyan Press: Pawlet, Vt., 1949).

"8:29," *Glass Hill 2* (December, 1949), 7.

"For Goethe in His Youth," *Glass Hill 2* (December, 1949), 1.

"A Legend of Viable Women," *Poetry-Ireland,* No. 7 (October, 1949), 10–13.

"A Legend of Viable Women," *Kenyon Review,* XI (Winter, 1949), 83–86.

"Muse with Yankee Accent," *Saturday Review of Literature,* XXXII (March 19, 1949), 8–9, 36. (Article on recent verse by New England writers.)

"Poem" [The truth hurt worse than a thought bullet"], *The Wind and the Rain,* V (Winter, 1948–49), 164.

"The Poet as Tightrope Walker," *Saturday Review of Literature,* XXXII (March 19, 1949), 30.

"Reality, Reality! What Is It?" "Nefretiti," "The Visionary Eye," "A Love Poem," *Wake,* No. 8 (Autumn, 1949), 5–8.

"The Rock," "God and Man," *Virginia Quarterly Review,* XXV (Spring, 1949), 226–228.

"Seascape with Parable," *Hudson Review,* II (Spring, 1949), 54–55.

"Select Seventy," *Saturday Review of Literature,* XXXII (June 4, 1949), 20. (Review: Kenneth Rexroth, ed., *The New British Poets.*)

"Subdued Poetic Fire," *New York Times Book Review,* XCIX (December 11, 1949), 5. (Review: Osbert Sitwell, *England Reclaimed.*)

"The Tobaccaconist of Eighth Street," *American Letters,* I (February, 1949), 9.

"The Tobacconist of Eighth Street," *Poetry-Ireland,* No. 7 (October, 1949), 13.

"West Coast Verse," *New York Times Book Review,* XCVIII (July 10, 1949), 10. (Review: Ivor Winters, ed., *Poets of the Pacific: 2nd Series.*)

"What if Remembrance?" *Glass Hill* 2 (December, 1949), 33.

1950

"Baudelaire," *Nine*, II (May, 1950), 110.

"The Defense of Poetry," *Poetry*, LXXVII (November, 1950), 89–97. (Account of the Harvard Poetry Conference, August, 1950.)

"A Gauze," "The Roc," *Wake*, No. 9 (Autumn, 1950), 40–42.

An Herb Basket (Cummington Press: Cummington, Mass., 1950).

"The Image of Ourselves," *New York Times Book Review*, XCIX (February 12, 1950), 5. (Review: Vivienne Koch, *William Carlos Williams;* William Carlos Williams, *Paterson III.*)

"Indian Summer," "Order and Disorder," "Politics," "Talk at Dawn," "The Forum," "Forms of the Human," *Poetry*, LXXVI (April, 1950), 10–15.

"Letter I," "A Legend of Viable Women," *New Directions in Poetry and Prose: 12* (New Directions: New York, 1950), pp. 105–117.

"Letter I," *Quarterly Review of Literature*, V (1950), 243–254.

"Major Poet and Literary Innovator," *New York Times Book Review*, C (December 17, 1950), 1. (Review: W. C. Williams, *The Collected Later Poems.*)

"The Middle Way," *Poetry*, LXXV (January, 1950), 239–242. (Review: Edwin Muir, *The Labyrinth.*)

"Oedipus," *Inventario*, III (Autumn, 1950), 68–69.

"Speech from a Play," *Saturday Review of Literature*, XXXIII (July 1, 1950), 28.

"Theme from Haydn," *Furioso*, V (Fall, 1950), 68–69.

"The Verbalist of Summer," *Botteghe Oscure*, V (1950), 367–371.

"War and Poetry," "That Final Meeting," *The Beloit Poetry Journal*, I (Fall, 1950), 6–7.

1951

"The Apparition," *Poetry*, LXXVII (March, 1951), 311–312.

"At Night," *University of Kansas City Review*, XVII (Spring, 1951), 204.

"Baudelaire," *Sewanee Review,* LIX (Spring, 1951), 293.

"Deep, Lyrical Feelings," *New York Times Book Review,* CI (December 16, 1951), 4. (Review: Theodore Roethke, *Praise to the End.*)

"An Excellent Redaction," *Poetry,* LXXVIII (April, 1951), 49–53. (Review: Theodore Morrison, *The Dream of Alcestis.*)

"The Look," *The Wind and the Rain,* VII (1951), 123.

"The Mischief," *Beloit Poetry Journal,* I (Summer, 1951), 16.

"Oddments of History," *Origin,* I (Spring, 1951), 60.

"The Poet-Weathervane," "To Bill Williams," "The Horse Chestnut Tree," "To My Son Aged Four," "The Look," "Indian Pipe," "To One Who, Dead, Sees His Poems in Print One Hundred Years Later," "On the Fragility of the Mind," *Wake,* No. 10 (1951), 13–18.

Selected Poems (Oxford University Press: New York, 1951; Chatto and Windus: London, 1951).

"The Verbalist of Summer," *Kenyon Review,* XIII (Summer, 1951), 381–384.

"A Vision Welded to the World," *New York Times Book Review,* C (June 17, 1951), 5. (Review: W. C. Williams, *Paterson IV.*)

"War and Poetry," "Phoenixes Again," *Botteghe Oscure,* VII (1951), 336–339.

"What the World Is," "The Power of Art," *Poetry-New York,* No. 4 (1951), 16–17.

1952

"Book of Nature," *Virginia Quarterly Review,* XXVIII (Summer 1952), 369–370.

"Five Poets," *Kenyon Review,* XIV (Winter, 1952), 168–176. (Review: *Selected Poems of Horace Gregory;* Randall Jarrell, *The Seven League Crutches;* Robert Lowell, *The Mills of the Cavanaughs;* Howard Nemerov, *Guide to the Ruins;* Radcliffe Squires, *Where the Compass Spins.*)

"The Great Stone Face," *Dartmouth Alumni Magazine,* XLIV (June, 1952), 25.

"Lines to an Old Man," *Voices,* No. 149 (September–December, 1952), 12–13.

"The Pattern of MacLeish's Poetry," *New York Times Book Review,* CII (November 23, 1952), 5. (Review: Archibald MacLeish, *Collected Poems: 1917–1952.*)

"Pleasures of the Morning," "Society of Friends," *New World Writing, Second Mentor Selection* (1952), 211–213.

"Poem," "Motion as Grace," *Beloit Poetry Journal,* II (Spring, 1952), 16–17.

"The Skier and the Mountain," *Poetry,* LXXXI (October, 1952), 33–34.

1953

"Book About Modern Poetry," *Poetry,* LXXXII (August, 1953), 282–287. (Review: Babette Deutsch, *Poetry in Our Time.*)

"Creators," *Paris Review,* I (Summer, 1953), 50.

"Easter Absolutes," "Blessed Are the Angels in Heaven," "Grape Vine Shoots," "The Voyage," "Order Again," "The Lost Poem," *Poetry,* LXXXI (March, 1953), 357–362.

"The Noble Man," "Resources of the World," *Kenyon Review,* XV (Summer, 1953), 411–413.

"On the Fragility of the Mind," "Jealousy," "Seeing Is Deceiving," *Poetry,* LXXXII (August, 1953), 261–263.

"To Evan," "The Human Being Is a Lonely Creature," "The Dry Rot," *Hudson Review,* VI (Summer, 1953), 206–208.

Undercliff: Poems 1946–1953 (Oxford University Press: New York; Chatto and Windus: London, 1953).

"The Visionary Farms," *New World Writing: 3rd Mentor Selection* (1953), 63–97.

1954

"Analogue of Unity in Multiety," "The Hand and the Shadow," *Contemporary Poetry,* XIV (1954), 11–13.

"Closing off the View," "The Meaning of Indian Summer," *Trinity Review,* VIII (May, 1954), 24.

"The Giantess," "World's Havoc," "The Project," *Poetry* LXXXV (November, 1954), 94-97.

" 'The More I Have Travelled,' " *New York Times Book Review,* CIV (October 10, 1954), 14. (Review: *Songs for Eve.*)

"Prose, Poetry, and the Love of Life," *Saturday Review of Literature,* XXXVII (November 20, 1954), 20. (Review: *Selected Essays of William Carlos Williams.*)

"Saucy Love of Life," *New York Times Book Review,* CIII (May 9, 1954), 5. (Review: Dylan Thomas, *Under Milkwood.*)

"Some Men Have It Early," "Yonder," *Chicago Review,* VIII (Spring–Summer, 1954), 52-53.

1955

"Centennial for Whitman," *The London Magazine,* II (October, 1955), 37-40.

"The Forgotten Rock," *The London Magazine,* II (April, 1955), 48-49.

"Silver and Gold," *Poetry,* LXXXVII (October, 1955), 48-50. (Review: Edith Sitwell, *Collected Poems.*)

"Soul," "The Day-Bed," *Botteghe Oscure,* XV (1955), 203-208.

"Sunday in October," "A Young Greek, Killed in the Wars," *Poetry,* LXXXVI (February, 1955), 273-274.

"To the Heart's Depths," *New York Times Book Review,* CV (December 18, 1955), 4. (Review: Ruthven Todd, *A Mantelpiece of Shells;* Ben Belitt, *Wilderness Stair.*)

"Using the Meditative Means," *Kenyon Review,* XVII (Summer, 1955), 447-448.

"The Wisdom of Insecurity," "The Forgotten Rock," "Cousin Florence," *Hudson Review,* VIII (Spring, 1955), 82-85.

"With Images of Actuality," *New York Times Book Review,* CIV (July 17, 1955), 4. (Review: Elizabeth Bishop, *Poems.*)

"Words," *Encounter,* IV (February, 1955), 20.

1956

"American Passion," *Saturday Review of Literature,* XXXIX (February 18, 1956), 49. (Review: W. C. Williams, *Journey of Love.*)

"Anima," *New Republic,* CXXXIV (April 30, 1956), 17.

"Attitudes," "Only in a Dream," "Thrush Song at Dawn," *Poetry,* LXXXVIII (August, 1956), 318–320.

"By the Stream," *The Colorado Review,* I (Winter, 1956–57), 31.

"The Fig that Floats," *Poetry, London-New York,* I (Winter, 1956), 29–31.

"Futures," *Nation,* CLXXXII (April 12, 1956), 343.

"Gusto, Verve and Flair," *New York Times Book Review,* CV (October 21, 1956), 59. (Review: Roy Campbell, *Talking Bronco.*)

"The Kite," *Hudson Review,* IX (Summer, 1956), 165–177.

"Lines to the Dead in an Old New Hampshire Graveyard," *Dartmouth Alumni Magazine,* XLVIII (November, 1956), 20.

"Love Among the Ruins," *Nation,* CLXXXIII (October 13, 1956), 310.

"The Mother Part," *Sewanee Review,* LXIV (1956), 600–602.

"The Other Side of the Mind," *Nation,* CLXXXII (April 4, 1956), 309. (Review: Aldous Huxley, *Heaven and Hell.*)

"The Poet as Teacher," *Dartmouth Alumni Magazine,* XLVIII (November, 1956), 20–23.

"Sea Ruck," *Poetry, London-New York,* I (March–April, 1956), 10.

"Song of Remembrance," *New Republic,* CXXXV (November, 1956), 19.

"Sportive Accolade," *Nation,* CLXXXIII (September 8, 1956), 206.

"Strong, Sensitive, and Balanced," *New York Times Book Review,* CV (June 24, 1956), 5. (Review: Richard Wilbur, *Things of This World.*)

"Summer Landscape," *Folder 4* (1956)

"The Supreme Authority of the Imagination," "The Record," *Prairie Schooner,* XXX (Winter, 1956), 352.

"To Helen, with a Playbill," *Nation,* CLXXXII (April 7, 1956), 283.

"Vast Light," *Nation,* CLXXXIII (August 4, 1956), 104.

"West Coast Rhythms," *New York Times Book Review,* CV (September 2, 1956), 7. (Article involving several poets, mostly "beatnik.")

1957

"Clocks," "Snow," *Ark II, Moby I* (1957), 40.

"Fables of the Moon," "The Return," *Encounter,* VIII (April, 1957), 53.

"The Form is New," *New York Times Book Review,* CVI (February 24, 1957), 37. (Review: Irving Layton, *The Improved Binoculars.*)

Great Praises (Oxford University Press: New York, 1957; Chatto and Windus: London, 1957).

"Hoot Owls," *Nation,* CLXXV (December 7, 1957), 437.

"Like a Broad River Flowing," *New York Times Book Review,* CVI (January 13, 1957), 6. (Review: W. S. Merwin, *Green with Beasts.*)

"Memory of Meeting Yeats, AE, Gogarty, James Stephens," *Literary Review,* I (Autumn, 1957), 51–56. (Prose)

"Protagonists," *Audience,* V (May, 1957), 54.

"The Spell of Time," *Voices* (January-April, 1957), 18.

"To Auden on His Fiftieth," *Times Literary Supplement* (March 15, 1957), 162.

"True North," *Nation,* CLXXIV (March 16, 1957), 238.

"Villanelle," *Spectrum,* I (Winter, 1957), 37.

"Willkie's Life and His World in This Many-Sided Medley," *New York Herald Tribune Book Review,* XXXIII (April 28, 1957), 4. (Review: Muriel Rukeyser, *One Life.*)

1958

"At the Canoe Club," "The Visitor," "Tonal Depth," *Mutiny,* I (Winter–Spring, 1958), 93–94.

"Central Violence," *Saturday Review of Literature,* XLI (July 12, 1958), 30–32. (Review: Kenneth Patchen, *Selected Poems.*)

"Clam Diggers," *Ladies Home Journal,* LXXV (July, 1958), 126.

"Creative Splendor," *New York Times Book Review,* CVIII (November 9, 1958), 34. (Review: Theodore Roethke, *Words for the Wind.*)

"Escape to Discovery," *New York Times Book Review,* CVIII (September 28, 1958), 26. (Review: Harry Roskolenko, *Poet on a Scooter.*)

"Fortune's Mist," *Nation, CLXXXVI* (June 7, 1958), 518.

"The Garden God," *Nation,* CLXXXVI (February 22, 1958), 160

"Half-Bent Man," *New Yorker,* XXXIV (June 7, 1958), 38.

"Holderlin, Leopardi, and H. D.," *Poetry, XCI* (January, 1958), 260–265. (Review: *Selected Poems of Holderlin; Poems from Giacomo Leopardi; H. D., Selected Poems.*)

"In After Time," *Nation,* CLXXXVII (December 27, 1958), 500.

"The Oak," *New Yorker,* XXXIV (November 29, 1958), 47.

"The Parker River," *Kenyon Review,* XX (Winter, 1958), 20–22.

"A Ship Burning and a Comet All in One Day," *New Yorker, XXXIV* (August 23, 1958), 77.

"A Soldier Rejects His Times Addressing His Contemporaries," *Nation,* CLXXVII (November 1, 1958), 315.

"Some from the Top of the Head, Others from the Heart," *New York Times Book Review,* CVII (June 22, 1958), 4. (Review: R. G. Everson, *Three Dozen Poems;* Denise Levertov, *Overland to the Islands;* Kenneth Patchen, *Poemscapes.*)

"The Tears of the Ancients," "Request," "Ospreys in Cry," *Botteghe Oscure,* XXII (1958), 255–257.

"To Bill Williams," *Nation,* CLXXVI (May 31, 1958), 501.

"Tree Swallows," *The London Magazine*, V (June, 1958), 15–17.

"Ur Burial," *Explicator*, XVI (May, 1958), It. 48 (with Eberhart's own explication).

"A Vision of Life and Man that Drives the Poet on," *New York Times Book Review*, CVII (September 14, 1958), 4. (Review: W. C. Williams, *Paterson V*.)

1959

"Birth and Death," *Times Literary Supplement* (November 6, 1959), xxxii.

"Equivalence of Gnats and Mice," *Times Literary Supplement* (November 6, 1959), xxiv.

"The Hard Structure of the World," *Nation*, CLXXXVIII (April 25, 1959), 368.

Liberation, IV (November, 1959), 9. (No title; an account of Eberhart's meeting with Sholokov.)

"Light from Above," "Blue Grains," "The Spider," "Testament," "Late Summer," "Riches," *Poetry*, XCV (October, 1959), 1–7.

"A Poet's People," *New York Times Book Review*, CVIII (May 3, 1959), 4. (Review: Robert Lowell, *Life Studies*.)

"The Still Spirit," *Ladies Home Journal*, LXXVI (November, 1959), 152.

Collected Poems: 1930–1960 (Oxford University Press: New York, 1960; Chatto and Windus: London, 1960).

"Divarication," "Ernest Chenaur, 1937–1958," *The Northwestern Tri-Quarterly*, II (Winter, 1960), 25.

"The Gods of Washington, D. C.," "A New England Bachelor," *The Transatlantic Review*, No. 4 (Summer, 1960), 92–93.

"Incomparable Light," *Nation*, CXCI (October 15, 1960), 250.

"Ives," *Chelsea*, VII (May, 1960), 75.

"Loss: (to V. R. Lang), "*The Massachusetts Review*, I (February, 1960), 297.

"Moment of Equilibrium among the Islands," *New Yorker*, XXXVI (July 16, 1960), 64.

"Their Craft the Lyric Line," *Saturday Review of Literature,* XLXII (July 2, 1960), 23, 32. (Review: Hayden Carruth, *The Crow and the Heart;* David Galler, *Walls and Distances;* Ramon Guthrie, *Graffiti;* Reed Whittemore, *The Self-Made Man.*)

"Why I Say It in Verse," *Writing Poetry,* ed. John Holmes (The Writer: Boston, 1960).

1961

"Divorce," *Shenandoah,* XII (Spring, 1961), 43.

"Elegance of Stately Measures," *New Yorker,* XXXVI (February 4, 1961), 34.

"Encounter and Letters" (with Wallace Stevens), *Dartmouth College Library Bulletin,* IV (December, 1961), 57.

"Extremity," *Voices,* No. 176 (September–December, 1961), 16.

"The Inward Rock," *Nation,* CXCIII (October 7, 1961), 232.

"Mirror of MacLeish," *Nation,* CXCII (April 8, 1961), 308–309. (Review)

"Rationalists and Naturalists," *Poetry Dial,* I (Winter, 1961), 11.

"Spirit," *Prairie Schooner,* XXXV (Spring, 1961), 60–61.

1962

"Celebrations for Mankind," *New York Times Book Review* (September 9, 1962), 4. (Review: Muriel Rukeyser, *Waterlilly Fire.*)

Collected Verse Plays (University of North Carolina Press: Chapel Hill, 1962).

"Devils and Angels," *Tulane Drama Review,* VI (June, 1962), 15–32.

"Lament of a New England Mother," *Quarterly Review of Literature,* XII (1962), 3–5.

"A New England View: My Report," *Greensleeves* (Dartmouth), IV (February, 1962), 22.

"Sea Burial from the Cruiser 'Reve,'" *New Yorker,* XXXVIII (August 25, 1962), 107.

"The Struggle," "Dream Journey of Head and Heart," "Hark Back," "Winter Kill," *Poetry,* CI (November, 1962), 34–37.

"Tragedy as Control and Resolution," *Tulane Drama Review,* VI (June, 1962), 3–15. (Essay)

"Will and Psyche in Poetry," *The Moment of Poetry,* ed. Don Cameron Allen (Johns Hopkins: Baltimore, 1962), pp. 48–72. (Essay)

1963

"Am I My Neighbor's Keeper?" *Saturday Review of Literature,* XLVI (February 2, 1963), 37.

"Death by Drowning," "The Gesture," "Hardening into Print," "Kaire," *Greensleeves* (Dartmouth), VI (Fall, 1963), 16–20.

"Emerson and Wallace Stevens," *Literary Review,* VII (Autumn, 1963), 51–71. (Essay)

"Evtushenko in Washington," *Massachusetts Review,* IV (Summer, 1963), 785–789. (Memoir)

"Flux," *New York Review of Books,* I (October 31, 163), 21. (Badly misprinted; cf. text in *The Quarry,* p. 68.)

"Introduction," *Progressions and other Poems,* by Albert Cook (University of Arizona Press: Tucson, 1963), pp. x–xi.

"Meditation One," *Sewanee Review,* LXXI (Winter, 1963), 82–83.

"Meditation Two," *Dartmouth Alumni Magazine,* XLIX (March, 1963), 9–12.

"The Music of Values," *New York Times Book Review* (May 5, 1963), 4. (Review: Conrad Aiken, *The Morning Song of Lord Zero.*)

"A New England View: My Report," *Kenyon Review,* XXV (April, 1963), 294.

"Poetry at Dartmouth," *Dartmouth Alumni Magazine,* LV (March, 1963), 25–32, 92. (Article)

"Ruby Daggett," *Greensleeves* (Dartmouth), VI (Fall, 1963), 16.

"The Seal," *The Green World,* I (Spring, 1963), 21.

"To a Poet Who Has Had a Heart Attack," "Later or Sooner," *Shenandoah,* XIV (Spring, 1963), 15.

"Ultimate Song," *The New England Galaxy,* IV (Winter, 1963), 46–47.

"Vision," *New Yorker,* XXIX (October 5, 1963), 54.

"The World Situation," *Encounter,* XX (April, 1963), 16.

1964

"Again," *Poetry Review* (Tampa), II (February, 1964), no page numbers.

"The Ascent," *Sewanee Review,* LXXII (Fall, 1964), 620–623.

"Cold White Death," *Atlantic,* CCIV (September, 1964), 73.

"Death By Drowning," *Saturday Review of Literature,* XLVII (February 8, 1964), 35.

"Desire," *New York Times Book Review,* LXIX (February 23, 1964), 2.

"Gestures Rich in Purpose," *Shenandoah,* XV (Summer, 1964), 5.

"An Interview with Richard Eberhart," *The William and Mary Review,* II (Winter, 1964), 1–12

"May Evening," *The Kenyon Collegian Supplement: John Crowe Ransome, a Tribute,* XC (1964), 19.

"Memory, Desire, Confrontation," (Phi Beta Kappa) *Key Reporter,* XXIX (Winter, 1963–64), 1.

"Off Pemaquid," *Times Literary Supplement* (January 16, 1964), 51.

"On Richard Wilbur's 'Love Calls Us to Things of This World,'" *The Contemporary Poet as Artist and Critic,* ed. Anthony Ostroff (Little, Brown: Boston and Toronto, 1964), pp. 4–5.

"Ordeal," *The Hollins Critic,* I (October, 1964), 9.

The Quarry: New Poems (Oxford University Press: New York, 1964; Chatto and Windus: London, 1964).

"Ruby Daggett," *Nation,* CXCVIII (April 20, 1964), 398.

1965

"Birth of the Spirit," "Robert's Rules of Order," "Eclipse," *Harvard Advocate,* XCIX (April, 1965), 10.

"Echoes of Keats and Shakespeare," *New York Times Book Review* (July 18, 1965), 4. (Review: John Masefield, *Old Raiger and Other Verse.*)

"The Echoing Rocks," "Tones of Evening," *Greensleeves* (Dartmouth), VIII (Spring, 1965), 32–33.

"Hill Dream of Youth, Thirty Years Later," *Atlantic,* CCXVI (July, 1965), 63. (According to Eberhart, several thousand copies of this issue of *Atlantic* went out with serious misprints before the error was caught and repaired for the rest of the printing.)

"The Immortal Type," "The Eclipse," *The Southern Review,* I, n.s. (Spring, 1965), 428–429.

"The Matin Pandemoniums," *New Yorker,* XLI (April 10, 1965), 42.

"On Theodore Roethke's Poetry," *The Southern Review,* I, n.s. (Summer, 1965), 612–620.

"A Quiet Tone from a Rich Interior," *The New York Times Book Review* (June 20, 1965), 5. (Review: *The Complete Poems of Frederick Goddard Tuckerman.*)

Richard Eberhart: Selected Poems, 1930–1965 (New Directions: New York), 1965.

"Tones of Evening," "Fishing for Snakes," *Encounter,* XXIV (March, 1965), 41.

1966

"How I Write Poetry," *Poets on Poetry,* ed. Howard Nemerov (Basic Books: New York, London, 1966), pp. 17–39.

"Looking Head On," *Harvard Advocate,* CL (December, 1966), 19.

"New Love," *Saturday Evening Post,* CCXXXIX (December 31, 1966), 43.

"McSorley's Bar," "Action and Poetry," "The Illusion of Eternity," *East Side Review,* I (January, 1966), 54–55.

"Speaking Plain and Fancy," *New York Times Book Review* (January 23, 1966), 35. (Review: *The Selected Poems of John Holmes;* Louis Zukofsky, *All.*)

"The Vastness and Indifference of the World," *Saturday Review of Literature,* XLIX (February 12, 1966), 46.

"Vicente Huidobro (1893–1948)," *East Side Review,* I (January, 1966), 66–71.

1967

"Enigma," *New Yorker,* XLIII (November 18, 1967), 64.

"Haystack," *Nation,* CCIV (March 13, 1967), 346.

Letter on Wallace Stevens, *Shenandoah,* XIX (Autumn, 1967), 68–69.

"Lions Copulating," *Nation,* CCIV (April 24, 1967), 520.

"Mexico Phantasmagoria," *Poetry,* CX (September, 1967), 400–405.

"Music over Words," *Nation,* CCIV (June 19, 1967), 791.

"Old Question," *Poem* (Huntsville, Alabama), I (November, 1967), 3.

Thirty-One Sonnets (Eakins Press: New York, 1967).

"Winds," *Nation,* CCIV (February 13, 1967), 218.

1968

The Achievement of Richard Eberhart, sel. with an introduction by Bernard Engel (Scott, Foresman: New York, 1968).

"Cutting Back," "Half Way Measure," *Mundus Artium,* II (Winter, 1968), 88.

"Personal Statement," *New York Times Book Review* (June 23, 1968), 24–25. (Review: Murial Rukeyser, *The Speed of Darkness.*)

"Poems of a Japanese Sojourn," *Nation,* CCVI (April 22, 1968),

548–549. (Review: Kenneth Rexroth, *The Heart's Garden/The Garden's Heart.*)

Shifts of Being (Oxford University Press: New York, 1968; Chatto and Windus: London, 1968).

"Swiss New Year," *Saturday Review of Literature,* LI (February 10, 1968), 46.

"Thumbsucking," *Nation,* CCVI (April 1, 1968), 453–454. (Review: Conrad Aiken, *THEE.*)

1969

"Track," *New Yorker,* XLV (September 13, 1969), 105.

Introduction to Milton, *Paradise Lost, Paradise Regained, and Samson Agonistes* (Doubleday: Garden City, 1969), pp. 1–13.

"Poetry," an essay in *Quality: Its Image in the Arts* (Atheneum: New York, 1969), pp. 327–334.

1970

"Despair," *New Yorker,* XLV (February 14, 1970), 35.

"Suicide Note," *New Yorker,* XLV (March 28, 1970), 36.

"Will," *Saturday Review of Literature,* LIII (March 28, 1970), 73.

"Stealth and Subtleties of Growth," "Emily Dickinson," "Man's Fate," "Fracture Within," "Hardy Perennial," "Here and Now," *The Southern Review,* VI, No. 1 (Winter, 1970), 155–162.

"Vision," "To Kenya Tribesmen," *The Virginia Quarterly Review,* 45th Anniversary number (Spring, 1970).

CRITICAL COMMENT ON RICHARD EBERHART

Aiken, Conrad. "Themes with Variations," *New Republic,* CXII (April 2, 1945), 451–453.

Alvarez, A. *The Stewards of Excellence* (Scribner: New York,

1958), published in England (Chatto and Windus) as *The Shaping Spirit*, pp. 182–185.

Anonymous. "Books in Brief," *Nation*, CXXXI (July 16, 1930), 75–76.

———. "But Always a Poet," *Nation*, CLXXVIII (1954), 246.

———. "Inventive Surprise," *Times Literary Supplement* (December 25, 1953), 834.

———. "The New Poetry," *Times Literary Supplement* (March 17, 1932), 197.

———. "Old Age and Youth, a Contrast," *Poetry Review* (February, 1937), 77.

———. "A Poetry of Celebration," *Times Literary Supplement* (June 28, 1957), 398.

———. "Two Dynamic Poets of Today," *Times Literary Supplement* (May 29, 1937).

———. " 'Zululand,' " *Time*, XXVIII (July 13, 1936), 56.

Arnold, Aerol. "The Groundhog," *Explicator*, XV (October, 1956), It. 3.

Arrowsmith, William. "Five Poets," *Hudson Review*, IV (Winter, 1953), 623–624.

Baurle, Richard F. "Eberhart's 'Throwing the Apple,' " *Explicator*, XXVII (November, 1968), It. 21.

———. "Ur Burial," *Explicator*, XVI (April, 1958), It. 38.

Benedikt, M. "Choices and Risks," *Poetry*, CV (February, 1965), 334–336.

Benét, William Rose. "Round About Parnassus," *Saturday Review of Literature*, VII (July 26, 1930), 214.

Bennet, Joseph. "Recent Verse," *Hudson Review*, VII (Summer, 1954), 305–306.

Bishop, John Peale. "A Little Legacy," *Poetry*, L (June, 1937), 164–166.

Blackmur, R. P. "Reading the Spirit," *Partisan Review*, V (February, 1938), 52–56.

Bogan, Louise. "On Richard Eberhart's 'Am I My Neighbor's Keeper?' " *The Contemporary Poet as Artist and Critic*, ed. Anthony Ostroff (Little, Brown: Boston and Toronto, 1964), pp. 143–147.

Booth, Philip. "An Individual Diction," *Christian Science Monitor* (December 22, 1960), 5.

———. "On Richard Eberhart's 'Am I My Neighbor's Keeper?'" *The Contemporary Poet as Artist and Critic* (Little, Brown: Boston and Toronto, 1964), pp. 147–152.

———. "The Varieties of Poetic Experience," *Shenandoah*, XV (Summer, 1964), 62–69.

Bradham, Jo Allen. "Eberhart's 'The Fury of Aerial Bombardment,'" *Explicator*, XXII (May, 1964), It. 71.

Brinnin, John M. "Stigmata of Rapture," *Poetry*, LXI (December, 1942), 508–511.

Carruth, Hayden. "Errors of Excellence," *Nation*, CXCII (January 21, 1961), 63–64.

———. "Maturity and Responsibility," *Poetry*, XCI (October, 1957), 53–56.

Church, Richard. "Still the Brave Poets," *Spectator*, CXLIV (April 12, 1930), sup. 623.

Ciardi, John. *How Does a Poem Mean?* (Houghton-Mifflin: Boston, 1954), pp. 998–1003 (on "The Fury of Aerial Bombardment").

Coleman, Alice C. "Amid the Golden Fields," *English Journal*, LII (April, 1963), 300–302.

Daiches, David. "Towards the Proper Spirit," *Poetry*, LXVI (May, 1945), 92–95.

Denney, Reuel. "The Idiomatic Kingdom," *Poetry*, LXXXV (November, 1954), 102–105.

Deutsch, Babette. "Poems of Lively Complexity," *New York Herald Tribune Weekly Book Review*, XVII (July 8, 1951), 3.

Dickey, James. "In the Presence of Anthologies," *Sewanee Review*, LXVI (1958), 302–310.

———. "Richard Eberhart," *The Suspect in Poetry* (The Sixties Press: Madison, Minn., 1964), pp. 95–96.

Donoghue, Denis. "An Interview with Richard Eberhart," *Shenandoah*, XV (Summer, 1964), 7–29.

———. *The Third Voice* (Princeton University Press: Princeton, 1964), pp. 194–195, 223–235.

Dyment, Clifford. "New Poetry," *Time and Tide* (January 9, 1937).

Engel, Bernard. "Richard Eberhart—Reader of the Spirit," *The Achievement of Richard Eberhart* (Scott, Foresman: New York, 1968), pp. 1–21.

Fisk, Winifred. "Among the Younger Poets," *Saturday Review of Literature,* XXV (April 11, 1942), 34.

Fowlie, Wallace. "Package of Poetry," *New Republic,* CXXIX (December 14, 1953), 19.

Fraser, G. S. "Poetic Intelligence," *New Statesman and Nation,* n.s., XLVI (1953), 646–647.

Hall, Donald. "Method in Poetic Composition," *Paris Review,* I (Autumn, 1953), 113–119.

———. "Polarity and Its Counterpart," *Saturday Review of Literature,* XLIV (February 11, 1961), 65–66.

Hall, James. "Richard Eberhart, the Sociable Naturalist," *Western Review,* XVIII (Summer, 1954), 315–321.

Hardy, John E. "Five Poets," *Sewanee Review,* LVI (1948), 307–308.

Hoffman, Daniel. "Hunting a Master Image, the Poetry of Richard Eberhart," *The Hollins Critic,* I (October, 1964), 1–12.

Holmes, John. "Compassion and Wisdom," *New York Times Book Review,* C (August 19, 1951), 5.

Horton, Philip. "Reading the Spirit," *New Republic,* XCV (June 29, 1938), 226–227.

Humphries, Rolfe. "Verse Chronicle," *Nation,* CLXVIII (April 2, 1949), 396–397.

Hunter, Rex. "Four Books," *Poet Lore* (Spring, 1938), 53–55.

Jennings, Elizabeth. "Searching with Words," *New Statesman,* LX (October 15, 1960), 576.

Leavis, F. R. "Cambridge Poetry," *The Cambridge Review,* L, 317

———. "Reading the Spirit," *Scrutiny,* V (December, 1936), 333–334.

Lewis, C. Day. "Autumn Verse," *Life and Letters Today* (Winter, 1937), 39–40.

Martz, Louis L. "The Virtues of Collection," *Yale Review*, L (March, 1961), 443–445.

Mellers, W. H. "Cats in Air Pumps," *Scrutiny*, IX (December, 1940), 293–297.

Mendel, Sydney. "The Groundhog," *Explicator*, XVII (June, 1959), It. 38.

Meyer, G. P. "Death and Rhyme," *Saturday Review of Literature*, XXXVII (May 22, 1954), 22.

———. "Ecstacy and Awareness," *Saturday Review of Literature*, XXXI (April 10, 1948), 18.

Mills, Ralph J., Jr. "Richard Eberhart," *Contemporary American Poetry* (Random House: New York, 1965), pp. 9–31.

———. *Richard Eberhart* (University of Minnesota Press: Minneapolis, 1966).

Mizener, Arthur. "The Earnest Victorian," *Poetry*, LXXIII (January, 1949), 226–228.

Monroe, Harriet. "Brave Youth," *Poetry*, XXVI (September, 1930), 343–344.

Moore, Geoffrey. "Some Credits and Debits," *New York Times Book Review* (January 8, 1961), 52.

Nemerov, Howard. "The Careful Poets and the Reckless Ones," *Sewanee Review*, LX (1952), 328–329.

Powell, Charles. "Recent Verse," *Manchester Guardian* (December 11, 1937).

Quinn, Kerker. "Forty Poems," *New York Herald Tribune Books*, XIX (November 20, 1942), 28.

Ransom, John Crowe. "Lyrics Important, Sometimes Rude," *Furioso*, I (Summer, 1941), 68–70.

Rexroth, Kenneth. "The Finest of the Lost," *Saturday Review of Literature*, XL (December 28, 1957), 15–16.

Rodman, Selden. "Heady Grope for a New World, Upon an Old's Effacement," *New York Times Book Review*, CXXVII (December 21, 1947), 8.

———. "The Poetry of Richard Eberhart," *Perspectives USA*, No. 10 (Winter, 1955), 32–42.

————. "Two Poetic Voices of Our Time," *New York Times Book Review*, CIII (November 22, 1953), 5.

Rosenthal, M. L. "Leaper into Vision," *Nation*, CLXXV (December 21, 1957), 480–481.

————. *The Modern Poets* (Oxford University Press: New York, 1960), pp. 246–248.

————. "The Mysterious Art of Singing Words," *New York Herald Tribune Weekly Book Review*, XXIV (July 4, 1948), 6.

————. "Three Poets in Focus," *New Republic*, CXXV (December 10, 1951), 27–28.

Rukeyser, Muriel. "Straight Through to Life," *New York Herald Tribune Books*, XIV (February 27, 1938), 17.

Simpson, Louis. "Poets in Isolation," *Hudson Review*, X (Autumn, 1957), 458–459.

Smith, Janet Adam. "Books of the Quarter," *The Criterion* (January, 1937), 332–333.

Stafford, William. "No Answer to This Day: On Richard Eberhart's 'Am I My Neighbor's Keeper?'" *The Contemporary Poet as Artist and Critic*, ed. Anthony Ostroff (Little, Brown: Boston and Toronto, 1964), pp. 153–157.

————. "Touching Sacred Objects," *Poetry*, CII (May, 1963), 116–117.

Thornton, James. "Poetry and Experience," *Nation and Athenaem*, XLVII (April 26, 1930), 117

Thorslev, Peter. "The Poetry of Richard Eberhart," *Northwestern Tri-Quarterly*, II (Winter, 1960), 26–32. Revised and reprinted in *Poets in Progress*, ed. Edward Hungerford (Chicago, 1962), pp. 73–91.

Vasakas, Byron. "Eberhart: A Negative Report," *Poetry*, LXXXV (November, 1954), 106–108.

Walton, Eda Lou. "Young Poets," *New York Herald Tribune Books* (June 22, 1930), 17.

Walton, Edith H. "A Bravery of Earth," *New Republic*, LXIII (July 9, 1930), 214.

Weales, Gerald. "Fugitive Marks on Paper," *Commonweal*, LIX (1953–1954), 408–410.

INDEX